AIRCRAFT

VERSUS

SUBMARINE

In Two World Wars

Other books by Dr Alfred Price

Instruments of Darkness
Battle of Britain: the Hardest Day
The Spitfire Story
Sky Warriors
Sky Battles
Skies of Fire
The Last Year of the Luftwaffe
War in the Fourth Dimension
Spitfire at War
Battle of Britain Day
The History of US Electronic Warfare (3 volumes)
Blitz on on Britain
Battle over the Reich
Air Battle Central Europe

Books co-authored with the late Jeff Ethell
World War II Fighting Jets
Air War South Atlantic
Target Berlin

AIRCRAFT

VERSUS

SUBMARINE

In Two World Wars

by

DR ALFRED PRICE

Pen & Sword
AVIATION

This 3rd edition first published in Great Britain in 2004 by
Pen & Sword Aviation
an imprint of
Pen & Sword Books Ltd
47 Church Street
Barnsley
South Yorkshire
S70 2AS

ISBN 1 84415 091 7

First published by William Kimber Ltd 1973
Second edition published by Jane's Publishing Company 1980

A CIP catalogue record for this book is
available from the British Library

Typeset in 11/13 Sabon by
Phoenix Typesetting, Auldgirth, Dumfriesshire

Printed and bound in England by
CPI UK

Pen & Sword Books Ltd incorporates the imprints of Pen & Sword Aviation,
Pen & Sword Maritime, Pen & Sword Military, Wharncliffe Local History, Pen
& Sword Select, Pen & Sword Military Classics and Leo Cooper.

For a complete list of Pen & Sword titles please contact
PEN & SWORD BOOKS LIMITED
47 Church Street, Barnsley, South Yorkshire, S70 2AS, England
E-mail: enquiries@pen-and-sword.co.uk
Website: www.pen-and-sword.co.uk

Contents

FOR CLARE

Acknowledgements

In writing this book my aim has been to tell the story of the evolution of the aircraft as an anti-submarine weapon, from 1912 to 1945. During this period more than four hundred submarines were destroyed from the air, and many hundreds more suffered varying degrees of damage; to attempt to describe every single action would have resulted in an account both lengthy and repetitious. Instead, I have concentrated on the pattern of evolution of the aircraft in this role, illustrated with those actions I regarded as technical or tactical milestones or otherwise of interest.

I have been greatly helped and encouraged by the many historians and retired officers who patiently led me round, over and – on occasions – out of the traps awaiting the chronicler of this complex subject: in Britain, Marshal of the Royal Air Force Sir John Slessor, Air Chief Marshal Sir Edward Chilton, Air Vice-Marshal Sir Geoffrey Bromet, Air Commodore Greswell, Group Captain Richardson, Wing Commander de Verde Leigh and Squadron Leader Bulloch; in Germany *Grossadmiral* Karl Dönitz, *Kapitän zur See* Hans Meckel, *Kapitän zur See* Helmuth Giessler, Dr Jurgen Rohwer at the *Bibliothek fur Zeitgeschichte*, Herr Franz Selinger and Herr Fritz Trenkle; in the USA Captain E. Wagner and Captain W. Howell; and in Japan Yasuho Izawa. For access to official records I am indebted to Mr L.A. Jackets and Group Captain T. Haslam and the staff of the Air Historical Branch, and Rear Admiral P. Buckley and the staff of the Naval Historical Branch in London, and also the staff of the US Naval Historical Branch in Washington. Scores of others helped in lesser ways. To all of them, I tender my sincere thanks. My friend David Irving gave much sound advice on the difficult task of fashioning the mass of material into a coherent narrative, and Bob Scott drew most of the diagrams. While those listed provided much valuable advice, I must stress that I alone am responsible for the opinions expressed.

Finally I should like to thank my wife Jane for her unflagging support. Utterly indifferent to aviation matters, she was usually the first to wade through the initial drafts of the more difficult technical passages. If these are now comprehensible to the layman, it is due in great measure to her wifely candour.

Alfred Price

Foreword

MARSHAL OF THE ROYAL AIR FORCE
SIR JOHN SLESSOR, GCB, DSO, MC
C-in-C RAF Coastal Command,
February 1943 to January 1944

The author of that excellent book *Instruments of Darkness* has now done, for the battles of the aircraft against the U-boats, what he did so well for those of the bombers against Germany in Hitler's war. Like his earlier book it is practical, thorough and based on careful research on both the Allied and the German sides. Both the campaign against the U-boats, and the bomber offensive, were profoundly influenced by the science of electronics. Both were ding-dong battles fought not only between the airmen and their enemies, but also between the opposing scientists who struggled to get and keep that one jump ahead.

The German Admiral Dönitz once said, 'The aeroplane can no more eliminate the submarine than the crow can fight a mole.' During the Atlantic battle the crow ultimately pecked the life out of the mole, though no one, least of all the airmen, would claim that they did it or could have done it alone, without the stubborn bravery and the skill of the sailors in the surface escorts and the hard-pressed merchant ships. Also, in passing, it would be ungenerous to withhold a tribute to the bravery of the U-boat crews, who continued to fight on in the face of terrible losses.

This is a book about the technique and tactics of the air anti-submarine action, the second being decisively influenced by the first – though a factor that should not be overlooked is the profound influence of training. The Atlantic battle was fortunately not so bitterly costly in aircrew casualties as the bomber offensive; one of the main enemies was boredom, the endless monotony of patrolling apparently empty wastes without ever sighting a U-boat or getting the chance of a kill. That in itself contains a lesson that Alfred Price rightly emphasises, that kills were not the only yardstick for success in anti-submarine warfare: the object of the exercise was to prevent our own ships from being sunk, to ensure the 'safe and timely arrival' of the convoys. The mere presence of aircraft, circling the convoys and patrolling the U-boat transit routes, saved an uncountable number of Allied ships. In the last resort, however good the aeroplane or its weapons or its radar, it was (as is usually the case in war) the human factor of training that counted – the ability to turn a sighting into not just some splashes in the water, but into a certain kill. Today, is this all just a matter of history? It is difficult to resist the conclusion that the nuclear submarine has rendered out of date much, perhaps almost all, of the techniques and tactics developed at such a cost in blood, toil, sweat and tears between 1939 and 1945. The fact is that, as Price reminds us, in that war what we were up against was not the true submarine but the submersible, which had to come to the surface frequently to recharge its batteries. At the end of the war the anti-submarine aircraft was – for want of an adequate method of long-range detection of submerged boats – almost back where it started as the ineffective weapon of 1939. What had made the change was the development, by the Germans late in the war, of the fast *Schnorkel* submarine. Moreover: 'The scale of production planned for the Type XXI boat was such that had it been realised on time, and the U-boat been deployed in large numbers, they could well have over-run the Allied convoy escorts and massacred the merchant ships.' This is indeed a sobering thought – but true. At sea Hitler's war ended, for us, in the nick of time. And it is small consolation – even to those of us who have consistently supported the bomber offensive – that the fact that the Type XXI U-boat never launched a torpedo in anger was due largely to the efforts of the Allied strategic bomber forces. I still have a vivid recollection of flying over Germany soon after VE-Day and seeing a lot of orange-coloured objects lying along the bed of the drained Dortmund–Ems Canal; coming lower to take a closer look, I found that they were the rusted sections of these prefabricated U-boats.

I am too old to pretend to foresee clearly the pattern of a future all-out war between major powers using nuclear weapons – if indeed such a thing is conceivable. It is not for one who dates back to the time when an airman went to war carrying a carbine, flying in a tiny stick-and-string aeroplane, even to hazard a guess. Perhaps the most important thing one can learn for the future, from reading about the Second World War, is the need to get one's priorities right – and get them right before the crunch, since it will be too late afterwards.

This is not always easy. Last time, for instance, were we right in the early stages not to reduce Bomber Command by more than the seventeen squadrons we did divert to maritime work – even though the aircraft lacked the adequate range or the equipment for hunting U-boats? Were we right to take a year or more to modify the American-built escort carriers to bring them up to British standards? It meant that (apart from poor old *Audacity*, which had a brief moment of glory on the Gibraltar route in 1941) we did not have a single carrier with the North Atlantic escort groups until the spring of 1943 – by which time the 'Atlantic Gap' had been virtually closed by the very-long-range aircraft operating from land bases. Should we not have given a higher priority to the bombing of the U-boat pens before they had been completed, instead of waiting until the concrete had set and it was too late? It is easy to be clever after the event, and all of these things are now 'water over the dam'; but they are examples from which we might still draw profitable lessons.

One can always learn from history; and this is a valuable and very interesting book.

Author's Note. Sir John Slessor died in 1979. He wrote his foreword for the first edition of the book. This abridged version is relevant to this edition.

Prologue

Aircraft to hunt and destroy submarines: the notion was originally conceived long before World War I. At that time of accelerating technological development, however, it was just one of an avalanche of ideas on the pattern a future war might take. As yet the need for such an innovation was far from clear: few people with the power to influence events believed that either the aircraft or the submarine could play a significant part in any impending conflict. But when war came the importance of both the two new systems soon became evident beyond doubt.

Within weeks of its outbreak the submarine had given spectacular proof of its ability to redress the previous balance of naval power. The aircraft's debut as a counter-force was less pretentious. Yet from the beginning airships and aeroplanes engaged on oversea reconnaissance demonstrated a useful – if infrequent – capability to find submarines and thus make their operations more hazardous and also less fruitful. Later, carrying small bombs for the purpose, aircraft were able to attack the submarines they found and sometimes they even caused damage. Yet it was not until halfway through the war that aircraft, unaided, succeeded in inflicting a lethal wound on a submarine moving in open water. That first 'kill' was a milestone in the evolution of the anti-submarine aircraft, and deserves detailed consideration.

On the morning of 15 September 1916, a pilot of the Imperial Austro-Hungarian Naval Air Arm returning after a bombing attack sighted an unidentified submarine on the surface near the Austrian naval base at Cattaro (now Kotor in Montenegro) in the Adriatic. He reported what he had seen, and since no friendly craft were known to be in that position, a full-scale hunt for the marauder began. A pair of Lohner flying-boats flew to the area of the sighting but their crews saw nothing: obviously the boat had submerged. Undaunted, the aviators began systematically combing the area from 2,000 feet. Forty minutes later their persistence brought its reward: *Fregatten-Leutnant* Baron von Klimburg, observer in one of the aircraft, nudged his pilot and pointed to the cigar-outline of a submarine beneath the glass-clear waters. *Fregatten-Leutnant* Zeiezny throttled back and pulled the flying boat into a diving turn. *Linienschiffsleutnant* Konjovic, piloting the other Lohner, saw what was happening and followed Zeiezny down. The flying boats levelled off at 600 feet, and as it crossed the dark shape each plane released two bombs.

The submarine they had attacked was the French boat *Foucault*. One bomb failed to detonate, but the other three inflicted serious damage. The blast from the explosions damaged the boat's batteries, and they ceased to supply current. The submarine's electric motors ground to a halt, and, leaking and out of trim, she sank deeper. To the surprised and shaken sailors it seemed that *Foucault* had struck a mine. What else could have caused such an explosion without giving any previous hint of danger? The crew struggled to blow the ballast tanks to prevent their craft sinking further, and half an hour later she regained the surface. The boat's commander opened the hatch and clambered out, only to face the horrifying spectacle of the two flying-boats swooping to attack. Four more bombs burst uncomfortably close to the submarine, whose diesel motors now refused all efforts to get them to start. His boat leaking, lacking any form of motive power and under attack from the enemy, the French commander saw his position to be hopeless. He ordered his men to abandon, then scuttled the craft.

Seeing the boat go down and her crew bobbing on the surface, the jubilant Austrians jettisoned their remaining bombs well clear, then set down their flying-boats and taxied over to the paddling Frenchmen. In a conflict that had witnessed carnage on an unprecedented scale, there was still room for mercy. The sailors were allowed to cling to the hulls and floats of the aircraft, until an Austrian torpedo-boat arrived on the scene to pick them up. In this historic action, not a single life had been lost.

The rescue completed, Zeiezny and Konjovic took off for home. Each aircraft carried one of the submarine's officers as a 'trophy'. For the first time ever, attacking aircraft had inflicted lethal damage on a submarine in open water. From now on the notion of an aircraft to hunt and destroy submarines was no longer confined to the realms of theoretical possibility: it was an accomplished fact.

CHAPTER 1

Beginnings

1912 to 1918

To the infant invention of aviation, the War proved to be a forcing-house of tropical intensity. Fertilised by a stintless outpouring of life, of treasure, and of technical research in every belligerent country, it progressed more rapidly in the four years of war than might have been done in a score of years in peace.

War Memoirs of David Lloyd George

During the twentieth century, maritime warfare underwent a revolution, a revolution brought about in part by two methods of transportation: the submarine and the aircraft. Great are the differences between them: the submarine, slow, silent, stealthy, stalking its prey, waiting for the moment to strike at its victim before slipping back into the depths; the aircraft, fast, noisy, brash, all-seeing and open for all to see, at the same time both fragile and vicious.

It was at the turn of the century that man's knowledge reached the point where he could move freely through the air and also under the seas. For all the differences between them, however, the paths of evolution of the submarine and the aircraft did have points in common. Both had been talked about for hundreds of years before technology caught up with vision and they became a practical engineering possibility. By the beginning of World War I, both were being built in small numbers as weapons. Both cut across orthodox lines of military and naval thought, and both were thought of by many as interesting but rather worthless toys – though with some reason, for until then both had been ill armed, of short range, and frequently the subject of accidents that proved fatal to those who 'defied nature' and dabbled with them.

The greatest advantage the submarine possesses is its invisibility, the ability to approach and attack its prey unseen. And, until the advent of the nuclear submarine, the greatest weakness of the craft was the need to come to the surface from time to time and expose all or part of its structure above the surface in order to recharge the batteries and ventilate the boat. By its very nature, the flying machine is an oversea reconnaissance vehicle par excellence: anything on the surface of the sea is potentially visible to its crew. In retrospect it is, therefore, inevitable that the aircraft should have come to be used to seek out and kill the submarine.

We shall probably never know who first conceived the notion that an aircraft could be used to hunt submarines. But certainly such ideas were a matter of open discussion as early as 1911. In October of that year the Journal of the Royal United Services Institution carried a report that stated:

> Some very interesting experiments have just been carried out in Cherbourg to test the capabilities of an Aeroplane in detecting and locating Submarine craft. The Aviator who flew the machine in these tests was Aubrun, the well-known champion who volunteered to give his services . . . The machine used was a Deperdussin . . . All the trials took place on one day with a light wind and a calm sea . . . Aubrun had no difficulty whatever in locating the first Submarine, which was partly out of water. On the approach of the Aeroplane it plunged and disappeared. The Aviator then went in search of the second Submarine, and located it under water at a distance of about two miles from the first. [Although the report does not say so, it is almost certain that the boat was exposing its periscope at the time.] During these trials, which took place about three miles out to sea, Aubrun rose first to 500 feet and then flew at between 1,000 and 1,200 feet.

At this time the unreliability of the internal combustion engine meant that any but the shortest oversea reconnaissance was a matter of some risk. Just two years earlier Louis Blériot's twenty-five-mile flight across the English Channel had been considered worthy of a £4,000 cash prize.

Even as Aubrun was conducting his trials, a young Royal Navy officer was learning to fly at the Bristol Aviation Company at Larkhill, during his free time and at his own expense: Lieutenant Hugh Williamson, the commander of the British submarine *B-3*. In November 1911, Williamson received his pilot's brevet, the 160th man in the British Empire to do so.

Early in 1912 the British Admiralty, disturbed at the reports of expanding submarine fleets in other navies, appointed a committee to investigate means of defence against this new menace. The committee requested ideas from, among others, British submarine officers: one of those who replied was Hugh Williamson.

At the time Williamson's knowledge of both submarine operations and flying was such that he was almost uniquely fitted for the role of poacher turned gamekeeper: only one other submarine officer in the Royal Navy had qualified as a pilot, and there can have been few in other navies with both of these still-unusual skills. As Williamson later recalled, 'At that time the idea of using aircraft against submarines was not entirely new, but it had not been discussed in anything save the most general terms.'

In March 1912, Williamson submitted his paper, 'The Aeroplane in use against Submarines'. Since it was probably the first tactical treatise ever written on this subject, it is worth looking at in some detail. The paper began with a description of the type of aeroplane needed for anti-submarine work. Williamson talked of a monoplane with a wing span of about 40 ft, able to carry a pilot and a 'passenger' – the term 'observer' had not yet come into common use – as well as fuel for five hours and a 300 pound war load. If the plan was for a search of several hours over the sea, the machine would need a reliable engine:

> Still the present engines are not good enough. However, improvements are being made and much attention is being given to the matter by engine constructors and we should soon get something more reliable. The ultimate solution will probably lie in a 16-cylinder or 8-cylinder double-acting engine with the fuel supply and ignition separate to the different groups of cylinders. A choked petrol pipe or faulty ignition are the most common causes of failure today. . .

The paper also emphasised the need for good visibility from the crewman's position: he could do little good if he sat 'cooped up' between the upper and lower wings of a biplane. Williamson then went on to outline the tactics he envisaged for his aerial submarine hunter. They were to patrol at about 4,000 ft, where:

> . . . their useful range of vision in which they would pick up a boat would be a circle of about 10 miles radius, and in a short time they would effectively search the whole area in which Submarines might be expected. At such an altitude an

Aeroplane . . . is a mere speck to an observer on the earth, and is difficult to make out. On the other hand a Submarine [on the surface] will present a clearly defined object to the Aviator. Let us suppose however that the Submarine boat or boats see the Aeroplane as soon as or even before they themselves are observed. What can they do? Dive ? Yes, but they do not even know what the Aeroplane is out for, and if they do dive, for how long are they to stay down expending battery power? Then how shall they decide when to come up? An Aeroplane is very difficult to pick up in a periscope and in any case is quite invisible through one if its altitude is greater than 1,500 feet. [Submarines later carried a specially designed periscope to enable their crew to search above the horizon for aircraft, but this was not the case in 1912.] If the depth of water is moderate, say 10 Fathoms, and the boat sits on the bottom, she is not carrying out her duties as a blockade vessel.

In this section Williamson put his finger on precisely the manner in which the aircraft was to exert its greatest pressure on the submarine during the two world wars that were to follow: by forcing a boat to submerge, in other words by denying it free use of the surface, the submarine could temporarily be neutralised. Williamson wrote his paper round the idea of a parent ship that could launch and recover its planes from a specially constructed platform on the rear – much like the helicopter deck on many present-day warships. During the actual hunt, the ship was to co-operate with her charges:

Let us consider now what would happen on a submarine being sighted. Suppose one of the high flying machines sights a boat on the surface . . . If the boat stays on the surface they keep out of range of any guns she may carry, and fly round till the ship comes up. If the boat still stays on the surface the ship sinks her by gun fire. Should she trim and dive, the Aeroplanes at once take the offensive. They no longer have anything to fear from gun fire, and come down close over the water flying round the spot where the boat is diving . . . Compared with this 40 miles per hour [speed of the aeroplane], a boat is well-nigh a stationary object, and passing over her only a few feet above the surface they could drop special bombs to explode under water and against the hull of the boat . . .

Williamson said that there was a widely held belief that it was very difficult to drop bombs with accuracy from aeroplanes, and agreed that it was so for 'Army Aviators' who had to fly at 'something over 2,000 feet for fear of gun fire.' But from an aeroplane flying at only a few feet above the water it was, he contended, quite a different matter. Each of the aircraft he proposed should carry three or four specially designed anti-submarine bombs:

> For detonation the bomb should have a double acting fuse, and while in the aircraft should be perfectly safe. On striking the water, first impact, it should become dangerous and set a time fuse mechanism to work that will detonate it when it has sunk to twenty feet.

Like so much in the paper, this represented a remarkable piece of forward thinking: it must be remembered that, in 1912, even the simplest ideas in aerial bomb arming and fusing were new and untried.

Williamson's paper was well received, and the following month he received a letter from the Lords Commissioners of the Admiralty signifying 'an expression of their appreciation'. Also, as a special case, Williamson was permitted to qualify in both the submarine and the aviation branches of the Royal Navy.

In June 1912 the Royal Navy ran a series of trials of its own, to see whether a submerged boat could in fact be detected from the air. The aerial spotters noted that the shallow tidal waters round England's east coast were 'very opaque', and boats completely submerged were invisible. But, given clear weather and a calm sea, the wake from a periscope could be seen at a considerable distance. If visibility was poor and a submarine was surprised on the surface, it was thought that there was a 'good chance' of making a bombing run before the boat could submerge.

At this time similar trials were made in Germany, where they were coupled with experiments aimed at finding a colour scheme for submarines that would make them less easily detectable from the air. Yet the latter produced little of value.

During the summer of 1914 the war clouds began to gather over Europe. Up to that time only the British and the German Navies had devoted any serious effort to forming a naval air service to provide reconnaissance for their fleets. The Royal Navy had fifty-two seaplanes, and seven non-rigid airships, of which three were capable of oversea patrols. The Imperial German Navy had thirty-six seaplanes, and one rigid airship. Both services used seaplanes for oversea reconnaissance work, for the frequent engine failures at that time often forced machines to alight, in which case a landplane was lost but a seaplane crew could usually effect running repairs on the water or else solicit a tow from a passing ship. The German Naval Air Service had only one airship in service at the beginning of the war, but there were three civilian airships available for immediate requisition and a further three naval airships were on order. In addition the German Army had eight airships of its own, which were available for oversea reconnaissance if the Navy requested this. It should be noted that while all of the British airships were of the non-rigid type, all except one of the German ones were of rigid construction. The rigid airship had a metal framework and an outer covering of fabric; the lifting hydrogen was contained in several (typically twelve) separate gas bags inside the structure. The smaller, non-rigid airships, on the other hand, had no metal framework and relied on the pressure of the gas inside the main envelope to maintain the shape of the airship. The 'Rigids' were capable of lifting far heavier loads over much greater distances. In contrast to the small heavier-than-air machines at this time – which could carry only sufficient fuel for a three-hour patrol out to seventy-five miles from base and no worthwhile bomb load – the large German rigid airships had already demonstrated that they could fly patrols of up to twenty-four hours' duration, while carrying a bomb load of several hundreds of pounds.

By the summer of 1914 the submarine was firmly established in the navies of all the major powers that were soon to find themselves at war. Britain had seventy-five, Germany thirty, France sixty-seven, Russia thirty-six, Austria-Hungary eleven and Italy fourteen.

Representative of the characteristics of the modern submarine of 1914 were those of the *U-23* Class, the most important type of ocean-going submarine in service and building for the Imperial German Navy. These boats had a surface displacement of 675 tons, were 212 feet long and carried a crew of thirty-nine. The main armament comprised two bow and two stern torpedo tubes, which fired torpedoes of 450 mm calibre; the latter carried a warhead weighing 220 pounds, and ran at 35 knots for a distance of little over 1,000 yards. Additionally, these boats carried one or two deck-mounted 88 mm or 105 mm guns. On the surface the boat ran on her diesel motors, and the 56 tons of fuel oil carried gave her a range of 3,000 miles at 12 knots; the maximum speed on the surface was 16 knots. This class of boat, designed two years before the war and without the threat of air attack in mind, took a minimum of two and a half minutes to submerge. The maximum safe diving depth was 160 feet. Underwater top speed was nearly 10 knots, but this would have drained the batteries within an hour; the underwater cruising speed was 4 knots, and at this speed a range of about sixty miles was possible before flat batteries forced her to the surface to recharge them from the diesel engines. Quite apart from the low underwater speed and endurance, the poor search range from the periscope forced submarine crews to spend most of their time on the surface. Indeed, they would dive only when they were going to attack, or were themselves under attack or likely to be seen by the enemy. Thus the word 'submarine' was at this time something of a misnomer, for these craft did not spend anything like the whole of their time submerged; 'submersible boat' is perhaps more accurate, and all the time they were on the surface, of course, the submarines were liable to sudden attack and destruction from the air.

Great Britain declared war on Germany on 4 August 1914, and it took less than two months for the submarine to prove that it did indeed pose a serious threat to surface vessels. On 5 September *Korvettenkapitän* Hersing in *U-21* sank the light cruiser HMS *Pathfinder* off St Abb's Head; it was the first time a submarine had sunk a ship in action since the American Civil War, and the first time ever that one had sunk a ship under way. Two weeks later, on the 22nd, *Leutnant* Weddigen in the elderly *U-9* scored a remarkable triple success when, in a space of just under an hour, he sank the British cruisers *Aboukir*, *Cressy* and *Hogue* off the Dutch coast. On New Year's Day 1915 *U-24* (Schneider) sank the old battleship *Formidable* in the English Channel. In the meantime British submarines had sunk the German cruiser *Hela*, the destroyer *S-116*, and the Turkish battleship *Messoudieh*.

It was not long before the submarines found themselves under attack from the air. From the beginning of the war the German Navy had used its rapidly expanding fleet of Zeppelin rigid airships to patrol the North Sea. On Christmas Day 1914 the Zeppelin *L-5* was airborne off the island of Norderney when she came upon the British submarine *E-11* (Nasmith). The boat dived before the attack could develop, and the airship's two bombs exploded harmlessly on the surface. It was the first recorded attack by an aircraft on a submarine.

On 15 May 1915 *Kapitänleutnant* Heinrich Mathy, in *L-9*, attacked three British submarines within a space of three hours. The first and the third boats made good their escapes, but the German crew came upon the second submarine as she was in the act of surfacing. Mathy later reported:

> *L-9* thereupon turned under full rudder and attacked the boat, as she was rising to the surface, with five bombs with instantaneous fuses. The submarine was undoubtedly hit and she vanished from sight immediately, without leaving a trace.

Mathy claimed the destruction of the submarine. In fact she was the British *D-4* (Moncrieffe), which escaped with a severe shaking and the loosening of some rivets in her conning tower casing. It was the first occasion, and certainly not the last, when an attacker from the air overestimated the effect of his weapons. If a submarine has been attacked and is seen to sink, is it sunk or is it submerged?

One imaginative method of using an aircraft to counter troublesome British submarines was tried out by the German Navy in 1915. The idea was for a seaplane to alight on the water as though it was suffering from engine trouble, in an area where enemy submarines were believed to be lurking. When the enemy submarine surfaced to administer a *coup de grâce* on the seemingly helpless seaplane, a friendly submarine positioned nearby and watching the whole thing at periscope depth would torpedo the attacker. These 'live worm' tactics were tried out off Broom on 25 June, and a British submarine, once again the *D-4*, dutifully took the bait. As she approached the seaplane, submerged, there was a lively discussion inside the British boat as to whether to run in at maximum speed, submerged, surface at the last moment and ram the seaplane (an even more imaginative way of using a submarine to destroy an aircraft!). The crew rejected this idea, however, because of the danger that bombs aboard the seaplane might detonate on impact.

So, as the German plan had required, Moncrieffe brought his submarine to the surface and his gunners opened fire with the deck gun. The bait had lured the mouse out of its hole, but unfortunately for the airmen the cat – the U-boat waiting in ambush – had been delayed and was some distance away. Under uncomfortably accurate shell fire, the seaplane crew restarted their engine and managed to take off. The German Navy did not repeat the tactic.

*   *   *

Against a warship, a surprise attack by a submerged submarine was a legitimate act of war. Against a merchant ship, however, the international maritime laws of 1907 decreed otherwise. Drafted many years before the appearance of the submarine as a serious weapon of war, the rules greatly limited its effectiveness as a commerce raider. Naturally, Britain and the other maritime nations were happy that this should be the case. Under the law a submarine commander was not allowed to sink a merchant ship unless he had first sent a boarding party to check that the cargo was a prohibited one destined for the enemy. Even when this had been done, the submarine commander was still responsible for the safety of the ship's sailors.

As might be expected, the German Navy saw these rules in a different light. The British Navy mounted a powerful surface blockade to strangle German trade, imposing severe shortages of food and raw materials. Yet a 'rigged' set of rules prevented the German Navy from retaliating in the only way open to it. In February 1915 the Kaiser reacted to strong popular pressure and issued a proclamation allowing his U-boat commanders to sink on sight any ship encountered in the war zone round the British Isles. The new 'all-out' submarine campaign was slow in getting into its stride, but from May 1915 the Allies were regularly losing more than one hundred thousand tons of merchant shipping per month. Unless something was done and done soon to reduce these losses, Great Britain might be starved into submission.

By this time the Royal Navy recognised the value of aerial patrols as an anti-submarine measure: if the aircraft could keep U-boats submerged, the latter's effectiveness would be much reduced. It sounded good in theory, but there was one important deficiency: hardly any aircraft were suitable for anti-submarine patrol work. Early in 1915 the Royal Navy had only three airships suitable for this work; the seaplanes it had were all small, under-powered and unreliable.

The German Zeppelin airship had already proved its value as an oversea reconnaissance vehicle. In the Royal Navy the First Sea Lord, Lord Fisher, outlined an urgent requirement for some small, non-rigid airships to harass the U-boats. The airship needed to have a maximum speed of about 50 mph and an endurance of about eight hours; it would have to carry a crew of two, a wireless transmitter and receiver, and a bomb load of 160 pounds. The Royal Navy is at its best when called upon to meet such a challenge, and within the remarkably short space of three weeks the first prototype was being 'walked out' of a naval hangar, in March 1915. A 60,000 cubic foot capacity gas bag from an obsolescent airship provided the lift, the car was a modified BE 2 aeroplane fuselage, and a 70-horsepower Renault motor provided the power. So the first purpose-built anti-submarine aircraft was born.

The improvised airship met Admiral Fisher's requirement. Designated the SS – standing for 'Submarine Scout' – it went into production immediately. A raincoat manufacturer produced the envelopes, and a furniture company built the cars. In the summer of 1915 the Royal Navy set up five bases to operate the new craft: at Folkestone, Polegate in Sussex, at Anglesey, at Luce Bay and at Marquise near Calais. The SS airship received the nickname 'Blimp', and that term came to be used to describe all non-rigid airships. The word is said to have originated from the 'blimp' sound made when a finger was flicked against the taut envelope. By the end of 1915 a total of twenty-nine SS blimps were in service, providing air cover for ships passing through the waters around Britain.

In the meantime, however, the German Navy had been forced to cease its surprise attacks on merchant shipping. The Kaiser had not allowed for the strength of neutral opinion against his 'sink on sight' policy. By September 1915 the outcry reached a point where he felt it necessary to cease such attacks. For the Allies it was a welcome reprieve: during the eight-month campaign U-boats had sunk nearly three-quarters of a million tons of merchant shipping. That result is all the more remarkable when one considers that rarely were more than twenty submarines committed to the blockade, and on average only four were in the operational area to the south and west of England. Clearly the German Navy had opened the campaign prematurely and in insufficient strength, and there could be no doubting the effect on Britain's commerce had a greater number of boats been available. Next time, if there was a next time, the British might not be so fortunate.

During the first year of the war even the lightly armed aeroplanes then in use proved that they could execute surprise attacks that were potentially dangerous to submarines, though none had yet proved fatal.

On 26 August 1915, for example, Squadron Commander A. Bigsworth was on his way to bomb Zeebrugge in a Henri Farman biplane when he came upon a U-boat on the surface, some six miles from Ostend. Bigsworth curved in to the attack, released his bombs and observed what appeared to be two direct hits with 65-pounders. The blast from the explosions caused him temporarily to lose control of the aircraft, and when he had righted it he saw the boat going down stern first. From German records we know the boat was not lost, however.

During the weeks that followed there were several attacks by aeroplanes on German submarines operating out of the Belgian bases. Like Mathy, the British aviators claimed boats destroyed, but in each case examination of German records failed to provide confirmation. Some of the U-boats were damaged, however, and as the Historian of the German Submarine Service noted:

At the end of September in Flanders, air attacks of greater severity were begun on incoming and outgoing boats; *UB 6* and *UC 1* suffered damage as a result.

By now the nature of submarine hunting by aircraft had become established. The searchers from the air had only their own eyes, aided by binoculars, with which to find their prey. As one of the early participants put it, submarine hunting from the air was 'a serious sport, in which the fish are not at all keen to rise to the fly'.

A statistical pattern began to emerge: four-fifths of submarines seen were on the surface at the time of the sighting, the remaining fifth being at periscope depth. Three-quarters of the submarines seen had submerged completely before the aircraft reached an attacking position. The average sighting range on a surfaced submarine was about five miles; but an alert submarine lookout, under reasonable conditions of visibility, usually saw an aeroplane silhouetted against the horizon at slightly more than this. Airships were usually seen when about ten miles away.

The early German ocean-going submarines took more than two minutes to submerge; but the improved U-boats entering service in 1915 reduced that time by half. The smaller coastal boats could submerge in less than 25 seconds. An aeroplane running in at 60 mph covered two miles in two minutes; during the same time an airship at 45 mph covered one-and-a-half miles. Thus, unless the submarine lookouts were careless, or the aircraft was lucky enough to stumble upon a submarine when the visibility was below three miles, the odds were overwhelmingly in favour of the submarine having submerged before it could be attacked from the air.

Once the submarine was below the surface the water might be clear enough, as was sometimes the case in the Mediterranean and in the Baltic, for it to be seen from the air at depths down to eighty feet. Yet such conditions were rare in the waters surrounding Britain.

If the submarine was caught on the surface and the attack was pressed home, what were the chances of a 'kill'? At this time the pressure hulls of German submarines consisted of steel plates between 11 mm and 16 mm thick, riveted or welded to steel stringers and bulkheads. With the small bombs in use in 1915, only a direct metal-to-metal explosion stood any chance of causing a split in the hull.

Other types of damage could cause the loss of a submarine, however. For the safe control of a submerged boat, the pressure gauges, the hydroplanes and the high-pressure air system had all to be in proper working order. Once a boat dived beyond periscope depth, her crew had only the pressure gauges to indicate their depth. A nearby explosion might easily damage these gauges.

A boat diving fast with her gauges out of action might well go down beyond the limits of her pressure hull, or suffer damage hitting the bottom. Explosions nearby could also jam the hydroplanes; if that happened the submarine was likely to go out of control, and might dive to a dangerous depth.

When a submerged boat needed to surface, it relied on high-pressure air to blow the ballast tanks. Thick pipes distributed this air through the boat, but a severe shock could fracture the pipes and release the high-pressure air into the boat. Quite apart from causing severe discomfort to the crew, this could in an extreme case prevent the boat from surfacing. In addition to these dangers, there was the ever-present one of sea water leaking into the boat and getting into the batteries. If that happened the salt in the water reacted with the dilute sulphuric acid in the cells, to release poisonous chlorine gas into the boat.

Submarine commanders were fully aware of the possibility of an air attack causing damage that could prove lethal, and were wary of attacking ships when aircraft were about. The success of the early anti-submarine air patrols should be measured in the number of friendly ships saved, rather than the number of enemy submarines they destroyed.

During 1915 and 1916 the science of aviation advanced rapidly. The large, long-ranging oversea reconnaissance aeroplane, able to carry an effective bomb load, was gradually becoming a feasible engineering possibility. In 1914 the American Curtiss Company built a twin-engined flying-boat, the *America*, originally designed to make the first transatlantic flight. The war intervened before this took place, however, and the Royal Navy bought both the *America* and her sister craft. The type entered service early in 1915 as the Curtiss H-4, though it was usually referred to as the America. Powered by two motors, each developing only 90 horsepower, the flying-boat was grossly underpowered. Moreover, its general handling characteristics left much to be desired. One pilot who flew them noted they were 'comic machines, weighing well under two tons; with two comic engines giving, when they functioned, 180 horsepower; and comic control, being nose-heavy with the engines on and tail-heavy in a glide'. It was, perhaps, as well that this aircraft never attempted the hazardous transatlantic flight. But for its time the H-4 was the best large flying-boat available, and the Royal Navy ordered twelve more – some to be built in Britain under licence.

Later some of the H-4s were re-engined with two 100-horsepower motors, and their performance improved slightly. With a fully loaded weight of just under 5,000 pounds, they reached 75 mph and carried a small bomb load and two machine-guns. In service the H-4 showed that the large flying-boat was potentially a useful weapon, even though its own reliability and sea-keeping qualities fell short of what was needed.

Using experience gained with the H-4, the Curtiss Company built the H-8 Large America, which had a greater range and load-carrying ability. With an all-up weight of over 10,000 pounds, it was twice as heavy as the earlier type. Two 160-horsepower engines gave it a top speed of 85 mph. Impressed with the specification, the Royal Navy placed an order for fifty Large Americas. However, when the first Large America flying-boats arrived at the Felixstowe air station in July 1916, it became clear that this type was nearly as under-powered as its predecessor. To overcome that problem Wing Commander John Porte, the station commander, had one of the flying-boats re-engined with two of the new 250-horsepower Rolls-Royce Eagle motors – giving an increase in power of more than fifty per cent. That cured the trouble, and the type was accepted for service as the H-12 Large America. The all-important Rolls-Royce motors were in short supply, however, and some time would elapse before the H-12 was available in the required numbers. In the meantime the Short 184 seaplane, smaller and shorter-ranging, bore the brunt of the Royal Navy's heavier-than-air reconnaissance effort.

*   *   *

As the only major nation seriously threatened by submarines, Great Britain devoted the greatest effort to countering it. But that is not to say that others were not also active in this field. The Germans employed their Zeppelins and small Friedrichshafen seaplanes against the Allied submarines. The Austrians used the small Lohner flying-boat, a two-seat biplane able to carry 330 pounds of bombs.

The honour of being the first to sink a submarine from the air fell to the Austrian Naval Air Service. On 16 August 1916 the British boat *B-10* was at her moorings in the harbour of Venice when Austrian aircraft raided the port. One of their bombs scored a direct hit on *B-10* and she sank. A submarine sitting on the surface at her moorings can hardly be thought of in the same terms as the elusive craft she is when in open water. As the Austrians were to prove some five weeks later, however, they would sink a submarine there as well.

On 15 September 1916, as recounted in the Prologue, Austrian Lohner flying-boats located and sank the French submarine *Foucault* in the Adriatic. At last, the aircraft had demonstrated that it could find, and inflict fatal damage on, a submarine in open water.

In March 1916 the respite enjoyed by merchant ships steaming in the waters round the British Isles had come to an end. That month the German Navy stepped up its U-boat offensive against Allied trade, though the submarine commanders were not permitted to attack unarmed merchant ships without prior warning. Now there were about fifty U-boats available for operations, and during the summer of 1916 they were sinking an average of 130,000 tons of merchant shipping per month.

During the second half of 1916 the German submarine fleet expanded rapidly, and by the end of the year there were more than a hundred U-boats in action. Now, it seemed to many German leaders, the time was ripe to slip the leash of restrictions on the submarine crews. Used to maximum effect, such a force of U-boats could sweep the seas clear of Allied merchant ships. The opportunity seemed too good to miss, and from 1 February 1917 the U-boat crews were once again permitted to sink on sight any merchant ship found in the war zone. During February, the first month of the new campaign, submarines sank more than 450,000 tons. In the following month sinkings topped the 500,000-ton mark, and in April merchant ship losses were nearly 850,000 tons.

In April 1917 the United States entered the war against Germany, but still the Germans had little reason to doubt that their U-boat blockade would starve the British out of the war before the new ally could do anything in Europe: during April a quarter of all the merchant ships that set out from Britain were sunk before they had completed their return voyage. If things continued at this rate, some Royal Navy officers calculated, the Allies would be forced to sue for peace before the following November.

In May 1917, in its desperation to try anything that seemed likely to reduce the swingeing losses in merchant shipping, the Royal Navy introduced a measure that would have a profound effect on submarine operations thereafter: it began sending the merchant ships in escorted convoys rather than singly. The idea of sending ships in convoy was by no means a new one. During the years immediately following Columbus's discovery of America, the Spanish ships plying to and from the Indies suffered heavily from marauding French pirates. In 1543 the Spaniards took to sailing their ships in escorted convoys, and for the next sixty years they operated without loss from enemy action.

The first of the new convoys, comprising sixteen merchantmen and five escorts, set sail from Gibraltar on 10 May 1917. Eight days later the ships arrived, without loss, off the south coast of Ireland. There six more destroyers met the convoy, and with a Large America patrolling the waters ahead, the ships passed unharmed through the most dangerous waters of all. Off the south-western tip of Wales the ships dispersed and made for their destinations individually.

The first effect of the convoy system, so far as the U-boat crews were concerned, was that the once-busy sea lanes suddenly seemed devoid of shipping. The reason for this was that, mathematically, the chances of a convoy being sighted from a submarine were only slightly greater than those for a single independently routed ship. Given reasonable visibility, a ship was likely to be seen from a surfaced submarine at a range of about ten miles. A convoy consisting of about twenty ships, on the other hand, was about two miles wide and, visibility and other factors being equal, it was likely to be seen from a submarine at a range of about eleven miles from its centre. Thus ten separate convoys, each consisting of twenty ships, were only marginally more likely to be seen than were ten independently routed ships. But if one considers the alternative, the chances of the U-boat crew sighting a much larger proportion of the two hundred independently routed ships, the advantage of the convoy system becomes clear. Furthermore, the limited number of anti-submarine ships and aircraft could be employed much more efficiently in the vicinity of convoys, rather than in attempts to cover entire shipping lanes.

Ships sailing independently had presented U-boats with a succession of targets. There was plenty of time to take aim at a ship, and between attacks there was time to reload the torpedo tubes if necessary. Since there was usually no risk of retaliation, the U-boats would sometimes surface and sink their prey economically using their deck guns. Against a convoy, it was a different matter. On the rare occasions when a convoy came within torpedo range there was a sudden abundance of targets, but rarely was there time to attack more than a couple of ships. And even a weak escorting force would rule out a gun attack on the surface.

During the months that followed, a steadily rising proportion of Allied merchant ships sailed in convoy. In the process, the losses to U-boat attack fell dramatically. From a peak of 834,000 tons in April, losses averaged 590,000 tons in May and June and 430,000 tons in July, August and September. Those losses were still serious, but the Allies were over the worst.

Among its measures to counter the U-boat menace, the Royal Navy had greatly expanded its air arm. On the lighter-than-air side, airships of the larger 'Coastal' Class supplemented the earlier Submarine Scouts in production. By the end of 1917 the service had more than a hundred blimps in commission. Also in 1917, the Large America flying-boats became available in reasonable numbers. During their patrols the airships and aeroplanes now usually carried impact-fused 100 or 520 pound bombs; or, for use against submerged targets, there was the 230-pounder with a two-second delay fuse that detonated the weapon at a depth of about seventy feet.

The mere sight of a blimp hovering over a convoy was usually sufficient to make U-boats keep clear. Thus airship crews rarely saw any tangible result for their long patrols. One of them later recalled:

Patrols were always dull; we had given up any hope of being able to see and attack an enemy submarine. And if one should by luck spot one surfaced on a foggy day, the speed of approach of the airship was so slow that the enemy had heaps of time to dive. I never saw one in my hundreds of hours on patrol.

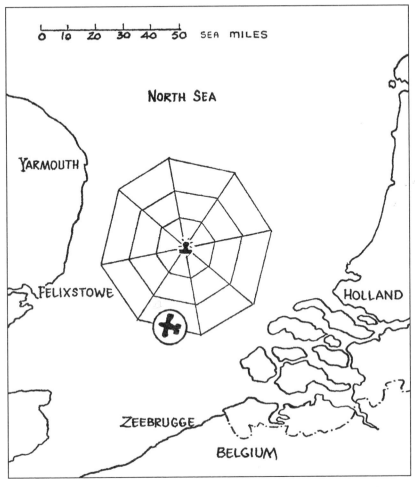

The Spider Web patrol pattern. The circle round the aircraft represents the area covered if the visibility is 5 miles.

In their faster flying-boats, the Large America crews were more fortunate. From mid-April 1917 they began to operate the Spider Web patrols, straddling the main U-boat transit route at the eastern entrance of the English Channel. Centred on the North Hinder light vessel, the aptly named area was octagonal in shape and sixty miles in diameter. Eight radial arms, each thirty miles long, extended from the corners of the octagonal to the centre, and chords further subdivided the area at distances from ten and twenty miles from the centre. By following these track lines, the Large Americas could systematically search all or part of the area of some four thousand square miles enclosed by the octagonal. During the first two weeks in which the Spider Web patrols were in operation, the aircrews sighted eight U-boats and attacked three of them.

On 20 May Flight Sub-Lieutenant C. Morrish was piloting a Large America in the area to the east of the North Hinder light-ship, when one of his crew saw a submarine on the surface. Morrish attacked, and released two 230-pounders, which appeared to explode just in front of the conning tower. The U-boat disappeared from view, leaving a few oil patches on the surface. From German records we now know she was not sunk, although many sources have since misreported the incident. For example, in the 1934 British Official History, *The War in the Air*, H.A. Jones wrote of this attack:

> A post-war comparison with German records, however, has revealed that she was probably the *UC-36*, which never returned to her base. This seems to have been the first direct sinking of a U-boat by aircraft during the war.

Other commentators substituted 'was' for 'seems to have been' in retelling the story, and stated that *UC-36* was the first submarine ever sunk by air attack. Obviously they were ignorant of the *B-10* and *Foucault* incidents. From the definitive German history, *Der Handelskrieg mit U-booten*, by Spindler, which became available after Jones wrote his history, we know that *UC-36* left Zeebrugge on 16 May to lay mines off the Nab light vessel and along the western side of the Isle of Wight. She passed through the Spider Web patrol area and laid the Nab mines, but the minefield west of the Isle of Wight appears not to have been laid. During this period there were instances of German submarine minelayers blowing up on their own mines, and the meagre evidence available suggests that *UC-36* was probably lost from this cause.

Most probably the first 'kill' in the Spider Web area occurred on 22 September 1917. That morning Flight Sub-Lieutenant N. Magor was piloting a Large America in the southern part of the area when he sighted a U-boat on the surface. As he ran in to attack, the German crew attempted to dive to safety, but the two 230-pounders exploded in the water very close to the submarine. The airmen saw the U-boat heel over and sink, and soon afterwards oil and wreckage floated to the surface. The boat appears to have been *UB-32* (Ditfurth), which left Zeebrugge on 10 September and never returned. In any case it was not *UC-72*, credited to Magor on that day in the British Official History, for that boat had been sunk in action with the decoy ship *Acton* two days earlier.

During the summer of 1917 there were, weather permitting, regular anti-submarine air patrols along most of the shipping routes round the coast of Britain. One notable omission, however, was in the area to the south of Ireland, where many ships were lost. The Royal Naval Air Service proposed to establish seaplane bases at Queenstown (near Cork) and Berehaven, but the Queenstown's die-hard naval commander, Vice-Admiral Bayly, resolutely resisted the idea. He wrote:

> If the sloops have to look after them, to rescue or mother them, then the seaplanes will be a hindrance and a serious nuisance; the patrol routes will be dislocated and the submarines will be able to reap a rich harvest during the absence of the sloops. If the seaplanes are not wanted elsewhere, and can look after themselves, they will be useful. If not, they will be an offence.

All of which would have sounded more convincing, were it not that patrolling sloops from Queenstown were unsuccessful both in sinking U-boats and in preventing merchant ship losses. As events had already shown elsewhere, the effectiveness of aeroplanes in reducing the losses to U-boats fully justified the occasional diversion of surface ships to 'rescue and mother' them when they got into trouble.

The year 1917 saw the German submarine arm reach, and pass, its zenith of effectiveness. During October, November and December monthly sinkings averaged 340,000 tons, continuing the previous downward trend. Following the success of the Allied convoy tactics, the U-boats began to leave the previously lucrative hunting grounds in the western approaches to Britain. The submarines now concentrated in the inshore waters, where many ships sailed independently between the convoy dispersal and collection points and the ports. During the final quarter of 1917, two thirds of all ships lost had been within ten miles of the coast when they were hit. The most dangerous waters were off Devon and Cornwall, and between the Tyne and the Humber.

To help counter the new threat, the Commander of the Grand Fleet, Admiral Beatty, requested additional aircraft to cover the coastal areas. In reply Captain R. Groves, the Deputy Controller of the Technical Department of the Air Ministry, suggested a scheme of 'protected lanes' through the danger zones. Groves based his scheme on the premise that no U-boat commander would dare to stay on the surface during the day in areas where there were continuous air patrols. He estimated that if an aircraft passed any given point along the 'protected lane' once every twenty minutes, any U-boats would have to submerge each time and so would be unable to operate effectively. The Captain then went on to suggest that the submarine crews' dislike of aircraft was such that they would be susceptible to bluff: any aircraft, even types without armament, would suffice to force the U-boats down. He reasoned that no submarine commander would stay on the surface while an aircraft made an attacking run, merely to satisfy his curiosity as to whether it carried bombs. The object of Grove's scheme was not to destroy submarines, but rather to make life unbearable for them in areas he wished to protect.

Groves's superiors accepted his recommendations, and the hunt began for an aircraft type suitable for the 'Scarecrow' patrols. They did not have to look far: the aircraft parks contained some three hundred de Havilland 6 two-seaters, aircraft deemed unsuitable for the training role because of their lack of manoeuvrability. The type was simple to fly and – an important factor since its motor was unreliable – it floated well. When the D.H.6 began operating in the 'Scarecrow' role there were several occasions when the motor failed and the crew had to 'ditch'. With the specially developed flotation bags, there were occasions when these aircraft remained afloat for as long as ten hours.

The 'Scarecrow' de Havilland 6 units began forming in May 1918. Soon some two hundred aeroplanes were operating in the role, formed into thirty-four flights operating from airfields spaced around the coastline of Britain. The units had a very low priority, and suffered from shortages of ground crews. Also, the improvised facilities at many of the bases were poor. The aircraft usually operated as single-seaters, in which case they carried a wireless transmitter and a few small bombs. For convoy protection work an observer was necessary, but if one was carried the wireless transmitter and the bombs had to be removed. Some flights had insufficient trained observers, and to make good the deficiency they sent officers to scour the local ports to 'borrow' trawlermen able to signal by lamp.

In spite of their problems, the 'Scarecrow' flights did add to the pressure on the U-boat crews. Between 1 May 1918 and the Armistice in November, D.H.6 crews sighted submarines on sixteen occasions and attacked them on eleven. None of the attacks caused serious damage. More important than any physical damage, however, was the numerous occasions when the U-boats' lookouts saw the aircraft before their boat was seen, and it was forced to submerge.

During the closing months of the war the prodigious Allied air and sea patrol effort, coupled with the movement of most of the shipping in convoys, made life both difficult and frustrating for U-boat crews in the waters around Britain. Between 1 May and 12 November 1918 there were available for this task an average of 190 landplanes, 216 seaplanes, 85 large flying boats and 75 airships. During that six month period these aircraft amassed nearly 90,000 flying hours while engaged on anti-submarine patrols. In addition, the Allied naval anti-submarine forces comprised more than 300 destroyers and escort vessels, 35 submarines and nearly 4,000 auxiliary vessels. All of that, to counter a submarine fleet that at its largest never mustered more than 150 operational U-boats. Indeed, the tying-down of Allied forces was the most significant effect of the U-boat campaign during the last year of the war.

The strength of the anti-submarine forces meant that, from the spring of 1918, the U-boats suffered almost continual harassment while moving to and from, and in, their operational areas. The cruise of the *U-98*, in May and June 1918, illustrates how difficult things had become. She set out from Emden on 14 May, and took ten days to reach her operating area in the Irish Sea. During that time she twice came under attack from British submarines, but managed to avoid their torpedoes. On the 24th, while in St George's Channel, she launched a torpedo at a ship escorted by three destroyers. The torpedo missed, but then *U-98* came under depth-charge attack and lost contact. Her crew spent the next day submerged, unsuccessfully endeavouring to find suitable targets with her periscope. However, on the surface that evening *U-98* found and sank a small Norwegian ship passing through the war zone without escort. The submariners had to abandon an attempt to press home a second attack early the next morning, when a blimp appeared over the horizon. On the night of the 27th *U-98* surfaced and entered Cardigan Bay in search of targets. A British flotilla detected her with hydrophones, however, and the subsequent depth-charge attacks forced the boat to submerge and leave the area empty handed. Early on the following morning the U-boat surfaced, but then had to dive hurriedly to avoid another torpedo attack from a British submarine. At mid-day on the 28th *U-98* made contact with a large convoy, escorted by destroyers, some of which flew flying observation balloons, and aircraft. As she tried to move into position for an attack, a lookout spotted her, and on the approach of two of the destroyers she broke away and lost contact. On 30 May *U-98* left the area for home, and reached Emden on 7 June. During her 23-day cruise she had come under attack five times, and had sunk only one ship of 1,300 tons.

Other U-boat commanders were more resolute – and often more lucky – but the downward trend in merchant ship losses continued throughout 1918. The Allies were over the worst. In June U-boats sank 240,000 tons of shipping, the lowest monthly figure for two years. In September, losses fell to 187,000 tons.

The German submarine crews were not the only ones to suffer from the attentions of aircraft during the final months of the war. Operating from bases in Belgium and the German Friesian Islands, the fast German Brandenburg seaplanes proved particularly unpleasant to the British sailors. For example, on 6 July a flight of five Brandenburgs surprised the British submarine *C-25* on the surface near Harwich. With the famous ace *Oberleutnant* Christiansen in the lead, the seaplanes attacked out of the sun with bombs and machine-guns. The sailors returned the fire, but during the initial exchange their commander and two men with him on the conning tower were killed, and others were wounded. The wounded were helped back into the boat, but the leg of one of the dead men dangled stubbornly through the conning tower hatch, preventing the boat from diving. Attempts to lift the body clear, while the seaplanes continued their strafing attacks, were unsuccessful, and ended after two more sailors suffered fatal wounds. Finally the First Lieutenant took the only course possible: he seized a galley knife, and hacked the leg off his dead comrade. Yet even after this grisly operation ended and the hatch was closed, *C-26* still could not dive. Her electric motors had suffered damage from the exploding bombs, and refused to run. In the end the seaplanes, their bombs and ammunition exhausted, broke off the action. British warships arrived on the scene and took off the wounded, then the riddled *C-25* returned under tow to Harwich. She had been damaged beyond repair, and went to the breakers.

During the final year of war the British airmen received some important new items of equipment. Operating off the choppy waters that surround Britain, the H-12 Large Americas had soon begun to show signs of wear and tear to their hulls. To overcome the problem, Wing Commander Porte designed a more seaworthy hull for the machine. With improved tail surfaces, and fitted with two 350-horsepower Rolls-Royce motors, the new flying-boat entered production as the Felixstowe F-2A. Laden with two 230 pound bombs and fuel for eight hours flying, the type had a maximum speed of 95 mph. When she entered service in the winter of 1917, the F-2A was one of the most expensive aeroplanes in the world; she cost £9,983 ex-works, which included a beaching trolley but not instruments or armament.

A significant pointer to the future was the twin-engined Blackburn Kangaroo, the first large landplane type to fly regular anti-submarine patrols. Land-based aeroplanes are better load carriers than water-based machines because, weight for weight, they do not have the weight and drag penalty of the boat hull. At four tons fully laden, the Kangaroo weighed a quarter less than the F-2A, yet it was able to carry twice the bomb load, at 920 pound. Although the Kangaroo had only two-thirds the power of the flying-boat, it was slightly faster and had a slightly better endurance. The new bomber entered service with No. 246 Squadron at Seaton Carew, near Hartlepool, in May 1918. No other squadron received the type before the war ended, and only rarely were there more than eight Kangaroos available for operations. Yet during the six months up to the armistice these aircraft sighted twelve U-boats, attacked eleven of them, and shared in the destruction of *UC-70* (Doberstein).

British attempts to produce larger blimps, and also rigid airships along the lines of the German Zeppelins, ended in disappointment. The largest of the World War I blimps was the 360,000 cubic foot envelope 'North Sea' Class, featuring an enclosed cabin and designed for patrols of up to twenty hours. But the blimp proved unreliable in service and few were built. The nine British rigid airships built during the war all had poor lifting characteristics, which made them unsuitable for long-range patrols.

During the first three years of the war it was clear that aircraft would never become really potent weapons against the submarine so long as detection depended on the human eye, sometimes aided by binoculars. As early as 1915, British scientists had conducted experiments using hydrophones to detect and amplify the screw noises from submerged submarines. The experiments were successful, and the device entered large-scale service in the Royal

Navy. Both ships and shore stations operated hydrophones to detect U-boats moving in their vicinity. Following this, the notion of fitting a hydrophone to seaplanes or flying-boats was not long in coming. The latter would be able to alight on the water, and listen for submarines moving beneath it. In the spring of 1917 the Royal Navy conducted feasibility trials in the Mediterranean, using small seaplanes. The hydrophones were of the non-directional type, however, and the results were poor. The following year saw further trials using directional hydrophones, which yielded better results.

The next step was to fit a directional hydrophone to one of the large flying-boats. The 27 pound hydrophone was mounted on one end of a ten-foot-long wooden spar, pivoted at the top end to allow the hydrophone to be swung into position below the aircraft when it sat on the water. During flight, the spar was braced in the horizontal position along the fuselage.

Several Large America and Felixstowe flying-boats carried hydrophones during the closing stages of the war; but in service the device achieved little. Before listening could begin the engines had to be stopped, and there was always a possibility that they could not be restarted afterwards. That made crews nervous of using the device in open water. In the event operational hydrophone searches were few and far between, and invariably unsuccessful. Unless a U-boat commander was careless and made a lot of noise, the device rarely had a range greater than a few hundred yards.

During trials in the autumn of 1917, the blimp proved to be a rather more effective platform for the operation of hydrophones. For one thing an airship did not need to alight on the water before listening could begin, though it was still necessary to shut down the motors. A specially designed hydrophone performed satisfactorily, even when the blimp was drifting with the wind at speeds of up to eight knots. At the end of the war hydrophone equipment was on order for all blimps engaged on anti-submarine patrols, but the Armistice intervened before it was delivered.

In itself the use of hydrophones from aircraft during World War I was of no operational significance: there is no record of a U-boat being located by such means. But what was important was that, for the first time, the scientist had attempted to provide the aviator with a device to help him to find submarines out of view of the human eye.

In 1918 no submarine was sunk by aircraft acting independently, though one was damaged so heavily that her captain had to accept internment in Spain. That was *U-39* (Metzger), attacked by French seaplanes in the western Mediterranean. And, as related above, the British *C-25* was damaged so severely by air attacks that she had to be scrapped. British aircraft assisted surface craft to destroy four U-boats, however: *UB-31*, *UB-103*, *UB-115* and *UC-70*. In the first three cases airships had been involved, and in the fourth it was a Blackburn Kangaroo, as already mentioned.

During World War I the German Navy put a total of 573 U-boats into action. Between them, they sank 5,708 ships totalling over 11 million tons – about one-quarter of the world's total tonnage. More than half the ships sunk were British, and two-thirds of the total were in the vicinity of the British Isles when they went down. The combined Allied anti-submarine forces destroyed 140 German submarines, 19 were lost to unknown causes and a further 19 were lost in accidents.

The British Official History, *The War In The Air*, listed six U-boats as having been sunk by aircraft alone, but in the light of information that became available after it was written, it is now known that this figure was too high. Only *UB-32* was probably sunk by aircraft acting alone, while the remaining five were sunk by other means. Four U-boats were sunk by aircraft co-operating with ships.

No nation mounted anything like the large or sustained air effort against the submarine that Britain did, though others did score notable successes. As mentioned earlier, Austrian aircraft sank two submarines – one of them at anchor – and damaged several others. German aircraft damaged several boats, one so badly that she had to be scrapped.

The general stifling effect that aircraft had on submarine operations was well summed up by a British submariner, who wrote after the war:

> Aircraft were an infernal nuisance. You never can be certain if they have seen you or not and the tendency is to take it for granted that they have done so. If you are then in enemy waters you must be on the qui vive for being hunted by the usual methods; if not in actual enemy local waters, you feel that your chance has gone for the day and that, even if a target does come by, she will be well protected and on the lookout for periscopes.

From the submarine-hunting operations mounted by aircraft during World War I, six salient lessons emerged. The first was that any sort of air cover for shipping, no matter how slow or poorly armed the planes, was much better than none at all. But to produce a really worthwhile protection for ships, large numbers of aircraft were necessary.

Secondly, only in very calm seas with perfect weather conditions, and then only with an element of luck, was a submerged boat likely to be seen from the air. Submarines at periscope depth could be seen due to the 'feather' wake of the periscope, but only under favourable conditions. U-boats on the surface were seen at an average range of five miles, though in a rough sea it was easy to miss these small craft. Under average conditions of visibility, an alert submarine watch was likely to catch sight of an aircraft before their own craft was seen.

Thirdly, once the crews of the submarine and the aircraft had sighted each other, it was a race between the submarine getting under water and the aircraft reaching a position to release its bombs. Therefore, other things being equal, a fast anti-submarine aircraft was more likely to make a successful attack than a slower one.

Fourthly, aircraft had proved that they could carry bombs heavy enough to inflict fatal damage to a submarine. But to achieve this the bombs needed to explode very close to, or actually on, the target.

Fifthly, a patrol aircraft with a long endurance could do as much useful work of several planes with only a short endurance. For example, if an aircraft had an endurance of two hours and it was based thirty-five miles from its patrol area, it would spend about one hour flying to and from the patrol area, and one hour on task. An aircraft with an endurance of six hours but with the same cruising speed, flying from the same base to the same area, could spend five hours over the patrol area. Thus a machine with three times the endurance could spend five times longer on patrol. If the patrol area was farther out, the difference between the two aircraft types was even more marked. If there was a fifty-two-mile transit, the out and back flights took about 1½ hours; then the aircraft with the longer endurance could spend nine times as long on patrol as the plane with the shorter endurance.

The sixth and last lesson was that if the convoy system was a powerful countermeasure to submarines in its own right, it was doubly so if the ships had air cover. During the final eighteen months of the war, Allied merchant ships made some 84,000 voyages in convoy. On these, only 257 were sunk while they were in convoy. Yet of those 257, only two were lost when a convoy enjoyed the protection of both aircraft and warships. This was the measure of success of the aircraft as an anti-submarine weapon during World War I. Even though it could sink its prey only rarely by itself, it ensured that only the bravest, or the most foolhardy, of submarine captains would attempt to sink the ships it protected.

CHAPTER 2

The Years Between

1919 to August 1939

We must be prepared for unrestricted attack by submarine against our trade, more particularly by Germany, but we do not visualise that the submarine will constitute the menace which it did in 1914–1918. Our anti-submarine measures . . . together with the assistance afforded by air reconnaissance, should provide adequate protection . . .

Committee of Imperial Defence, November 1937

Following the victory of 1918, the Allies were determined that never again would they permit German submarines to menace their trade. Accordingly, Paragraph One of the 1919 naval peace treaty ordered:

German submarines to the number of 160 (including all Submarine Cruisers and Minelaying Submarines), with their complete armament and equipment, are to be surrendered to the Allied and the United States of America Governments, in ports that will be specified by them. All other Submarines are to be paid off and completely disarmed.

Furthermore, the treaty specifically forbade the construction of submarines in Germany. With no visible threat to justify their retention, the vast sea and air anti-submarine forces diminished to a shadow of what they had previously been.

In 1921 an important conference was held in Washington, with the intention of avoiding a possible repetition of the arms race that had preceded World War I. The largest five naval powers attended: Britain, the United States, France, Italy and Japan. During the discussions Britain – who at that time had the largest submarine fleet in the world – strongly advocated the abolition of her own and everybody else's submarine fleets. She maintained that the submarine was really effective only as a commerce raider, and then only if international law was disregarded and no proper provision made for the safety of the attacked ships' crews. Those nations with smaller fleets refused to accept this argument, however. They said that the submarine was a very effective and perfectly legitimate weapon against warships, and was also very useful for reconnaissance. Moreover, as the US representatives pointed out, there was no intrinsic reason why the submarine should be used contrary to international law, any more than any other type of warship. The discussions ended in deadlock.

Having failed to secure the abolition of the submarine at the conference table, the Royal Navy pressed ahead with measures to counter them.

During the 1920s the Royal Navy devoted considerable effort to the development of a new method of locating submerged submarines – the device we now call sonar (initially called Asdic). The equipment can be thought of as an 'underwater radar'. A sound transmitter emitted a burst of energy, directed into the water in front of the ship in a fan-shaped beam. Any object within the beam – for example a submarine – would reflect energy back to the transmitting source. Since the velocity of sound through water was known, the time delay between the transmission and the reception of the echo gave an accurate measurement of the object's range. By noting the direction from which the returning echo came, an operator could also determine the bearing of the object. All that was possible even when the warship was steaming moderately fast and the submarine was moving as quietly as it could. Thus sonar was a significant improvement over the simple directional hydrophones used by submarine-hunting ships in World War I. In the early 1930s the device entered service in the Royal Navy, and with skilled operators it performed impressively. In Britain the belief grew that the Royal Navy had found 'the answer' to the submarine. By 1935 more than half the destroyers in her fleet carried sonar, all new destroyers and anti-submarine vessels were to have it on completion and a programme was in hand to equip the remainder.

In spite of the limitations imposed by the peace treaty, the German Navy had also kept abreast of the latest ideas in submarine design during the years following World War I. In 1922 German ship-building yards, with the approval of the German Admiralty, set up a clandestine submarine construction office in Holland. This office enabled submarine construction staff to keep itself abreast of modern developments, by carrying out work for foreign navies. In 1928 a company, Igewit, was formed to prepare the way for a rapid construction of the German submarine fleet should the order be given. The firm began work preparing detailed constructional drawings of submarines to German Navy specifications. Between 1927 and 1933, eight boats of German design were built in foreign shipyards – two in Holland, one in Spain for the Turkish Navy and five in Finland for the Finnish Navy. Thus by the autumn of 1933, when Hitler order the re-creation of a German submarine fleet, an efficient design office for these craft already existed.

On 16 March 1935 Germany formally abrogated the Treaty of Versailles, which had confirmed the prohibition of submarines for the German Navy. By this time work was well advanced on the first batch of submarines in heavily guarded sheds at the Germania and Deutsche Works at Kiel, and the *U-1* was launched on 15 June. Three days later Germany entered into a naval agreement with Britain, under which the former voluntarily undertook to restrict its total naval tonnage to thirty-five per cent of that of the British Commonwealth. In return, Germany was permitted to build submarines to a tonnage equal to that of Britain. On 29 June, only eleven days after the signing of the agreement, the German Navy commissioned its first submarine since 1918.

In charge of the first operational flotillas in the new submarine fleet, and shortly afterwards of all German submarine activities, was *Fregattenkapitän* Karl Dönitz. A 44-year-old career naval officer, he had served since 1910. During World War I Dönitz had risen to command the submarine *UB-68*, and had been captured by the Royal Navy in October 1918 following an unsuccessful attack on a convoy in the Mediterranean. Ten months later he was released, and accepted a place in the peacetime German Navy. Now he set about his task of forging the new weapon with energy and enthusiasm. Since his own near-fatal brush with a convoy, he devoted a great deal of thought to the tactics that might defeat them. If the answer to individually attacking submarines was the convoy, the reply to the convoy – Dönitz felt sure – was a co-ordinated attack by a pack of submarines. Training in the new tactics began almost immediately.

As with the idea of the convoy itself, the pack attack was by no means new. As related earlier, during the sixteenth century the Spaniards had put their treasure ships returning from the Americas into convoys (*flotas*) to safeguard them. The French pirates replied by banding their raiders together into squadrons. Others followed their example: during the war of 1585–1604 between England and Spain, of which the destruction of the Spanish Armada was the climax, English naval forces spent many weeks at sea each year cruising in squadrons in an attempt to intercept the *flotas*, overwhelm their escorts and plunder the treasure ships. But by maintaining strong escorting forces, and continually changing their routes, the Spaniards foiled these tactics. Indeed, the attempt to capture treasure ships in one such *flota* led to the only major naval defeat the English suffered during that war.

The aircraft that were to bear the brunt of the aerial anti-submarine operations against Dönitz's fleet in the war to come belonged to Coastal Command of the Royal Air Force. Coastal Command as such was formed in July 1936, and its first commander was Air Vice-Marshal Sir Arthur Longmore. Longmore was one of the pioneering British naval aviators, who had begun his flying career before World War I. In July 1914 he was the first Briton to drop a torpedo from the air.

At its formation Coastal Command bore the marks of many years of financial stringency. It comprised four flying-boat squadrons, equipped with an assortment of obsolescent biplanes. There were two squadrons of Avro Ansons, a monoplane landplane of fairly modern design but unspectacular performance. Its sole striking force comprised a single squadron of Vickers Vildebeest biplane torpedo-bombers.

During the 1930s the reconnaissance and strike capability of Coastal Command, such as it was, was directed mainly against enemy surface vessels. The Royal Navy, with whom the Command would work closely if war came, was at that time very much concerned with the problem of preventing enemy – almost inevitably German – surface raiders getting out into the Atlantic and disrupting trade routes. At that time the submarine threat was a secondary consideration, for it was felt that the sonar-equipped convoy escorts could inflict losses out of all proportion to the success any underwater attacking force was likely to achieve.

With the steadily worsening political situation, Coastal Command engaged in expansion and re-equipment from the time of its formation until the outbreak of World War II. Meanwhile, British scientists were working hard on a device that promised to increase greatly the effectiveness of oversea aerial reconnaissance by night or in conditions of bad visibility. In 1935 work had begun on the development of radar in Britain. In the following year Dr Edward Bowen headed a four-man team working at Bawdsey Manor in Suffolk, investigating the possibility of building a radar small enough to fit into an aircraft. From the start it was clear that there were a couple of formidable problems to be overcome. Firstly, the wavelength of the airborne set had to be considerably shorter than that of the ground sets then under test, otherwise the aerial array would be physically too large to carry in an aircraft. Secondly, there was the problem of reducing the weight and size of the transmitter to a point where it could be fitted into a combat aircraft.

To prove the feasibility of their ideas, Bowen and his team started by fitting an early television receiver modified for the task, and a crude directional aerial system, into an obsolescent Heyford bomber. A radar transmitter on the ground beamed transmissions at the target aircraft, and about ten miles away from the latter, the operators in the Heyford observed the echo signals. The test, albeit a limited one, established that radio energy reflected off one aircraft could be received in another. It also gave the team a lot of encouragement.

By the middle of 1937 Bowen's team had doubled in size, to eight men. And they had built a small radar, complete with high-powered transmitter and a sensitive receiver, working on the then extremely high frequency of 240 MHz. The aerials of the new radar were short enough to be fitted to a combat aircraft – 240 megacycles represented a wavelength of 1.3 metres, so the half-wavelength aerials were about two feet long. Before the set could be taken into the air, however, Bowen had to allay the fears of the flight safety experts. It had been unheard-of to radiate a power of one kilowatt from an aircraft. Might it cause sparks that could ignite the petrol? The scientists were able to show that this was not the case.

In July 1937 the new radar was fitted in a twin-engined Anson aircraft to begin flight trials, and soon the scientists were observing echoes from large ships at ranges of up to five miles. Then, on 3 September, Bowen took off in the Anson in an attempt to find warships known to be exercising off the Suffolk coast. In this he was successful, and he observed clear returns from the battleship *Rodney*, the aircraft-carrier *Courageous* and the cruiser *Southampton*. On the following day Bowen again took off in the Anson, bent on repeating the performance. But on that day the weather had deteriorated sharply, and the Coastal Command aircraft taking part in the exercise were all recalled by radio. The radar-fitted Anson was not part of Coastal Command, however, and it was not maintaining a listening watch on the Command's radio channels. As a result the crew did not hear the recall signal, and continued with their private reconnaissance. Using the radar Bowen again found some of the warships, and afterwards he reported:

> On the morning of 4 September at about 0530 hours, Anson K 6260 was again taken out to sea at about latitude 52 degrees, and echoes were again observed from *Courageous* and one destroyer. Flights were made broadside to the craft at 3,000 ft, 6,000 ft and 9,000 ft [altitude].

On the return flight, through solid cloud cover up to 12,000 feet, Bowen used the radar to assist the navigator to make a landfall. All in all the new radar had, with some nursing, worked extremely well. An enthusiastic Bowen was able to inform his superiors that '. . . these results encourage the hope that it will ultimately be possible to discover and locate ships at sea at distances up to about ten miles from an aircraft.'

Yet in spite of this success, endorsed by Sir Henry Tizard (chairman of the Committee for the Scientific Survey of Air Defence), work on the new radar progressed only slowly: in 1937 the early-warning radar chain for the British Isles absorbed the lion's share of the limited available research and development effort.

Following the success of the feasibility trial, the next thing to be decided was the best radiation pattern that could be obtained using an aerial array that would be aerodynamically acceptable. Obviously, the ideal would have been sets of directional aerials pointing in all directions from the aircraft. But such an arrangement would have caused considerable drag, and might possibly have affected the aircraft's handling characteristics. After much experimenting Bowen's team settled for a forward-looking aerial system, in which the transmitted energy was concentrated in a fan-shaped beam in front of and below the aircraft. Two separate receiver aerials, one under each wing looking outwards at an angle of thirty degrees, provided an indication of the direction of the source of the echo signals. When he observed signals on his screen, the radar operator instructed the pilot to turn the aircraft until the signals picked up by two receiver aerials were equal in strength. When these coincided, the target was dead ahead. By the early part of 1939 this aerial system had been proved in trials.

During the spring of 1939 airborne radar was still a 'hothouse flower', requiring the care of, and operation by, skilled scientists. And even with this treatment it often failed to produce consistent results. As yet it was neither simple enough nor reliable enough to be introduced into service.

If airborne radar was a ray of hope for Coastal Command during the last days of peace, its anti-submarine weaponry represented the rain clouds. Only when war became inevitable was there a serious attempt to cure the faults that dogged these weapons.

The British anti-submarine bombs used during World War I had been poor in shape and bad ballistically. In 1924 the Admiralty initiated the design of a new family of light-cased bombs for this purpose. The work culminated in the three anti-submarine bombs available to the British services at the beginning of World War II: the 100, 250 and 500 pound weapons. In each case the explosive charge made up approximately half the bomb's weight. The fuse protruded six inches in front of the weapon, and became 'live' when the airflow rotated a small propeller a given number of turns after release. The double-action fuse was a complex device. If the bomb struck a submarine on the surface, the charge was to detonate instantaneously. If, on the other hand, the bomb fell in the water, there was a short delay before detonation.

The first of the new anti-submarine bombs began trials in 1931, some seven years after the project began. From the start there was considerable trouble with the special fuse: water often leaked into the mechanism, causing it to fail. The weapons' other failings took longer to reveal themselves. Not until the summer of 1935 were the bombs' underwater trajectories examined. This revealed the disquieting fact that the fuse protruding from the nose caused the bombs to follow unpredictable paths through the water. A fez-shaped ballistic cap fitted over the nose went some way towards solving that problem. The protracted series of trials with the bombs, and resultant modifications, continued until February 1938. Then the worsening political situation demanded that the designs be frozen – although the fuse was still not satisfactory – so that mass production of the anti-submarine bombs could begin.

Even if the anti-submarine bomb functioned correctly, it needed to detonate close to the hull of a submarine if it was to inflict lethal damage. The largest, 500 pound, weapon needed to detonate within about eight feet to cause that degree of damage. Delivering the bomb to that point was no simple matter, however. The Mark IX bombsight fitted to Coastal Command aircraft required a steady bombing run from 3,000 feet or above. That requirement was almost impossible to meet against a fleeting target like a submarine, which was likely to disappear from view within half a minute of the crew sensing danger. Lacking an effective bomb-sight, aircrews could attack submarines only by going to very low altitude and lobbing their bombs at the target 'by eye'.

In order to increase the chances of damaging the target a number of bombs, say four or six, could be dropped at regular intervals in a 'stick'. In that case the ideal spacing between bombs was twice the 'lethal diameter' of the weapon, plus the width of the sub-marine. Of the aircraft available to Coastal Command in the summer of 1939 only the American-built Lockheed Hudson – then on the point of entering service – carried a delay unit to release the bombs in such a stick. Therefore, when Coastal Command entered the war, its anti-submarine equipment was in a lamentable state. It had anti-submarine bombs of doubtful quality, no proper anti-submarine bombsight, and most of its aircraft were fitted with an unsatisfactory bomb release gear. Yet it would be unfair to place the blame on those who had the unenviable task of developing these weapon devices. Between 1925 and 1935 Britain's annual Air Estimates never exceeded £19 million; and during none of those years was there more than half a million pounds available for government-sponsored research into aviation and weaponry. Full-scale, properly instrumented weapon trials are a costly item, and there simply was not enough money to conduct those. With so many other demands on its limited resources, it is easy to see how the Royal Air Force's effort to counter the submarine had been allowed to recede into the background. And had not the Royal Navy said, loudly and repeatedly, that in any future war the sub-marine would achieve little when confronted with sonar-equipped convoy escorts ?

In the summer of 1937 Air Chief Marshal Sir Frederick Bowhill was appointed head of Coastal Command, and under him the previously initiated expansion continued. But the many years of financial cheese-paring had left their mark. In common with the rest of the Royal Air Force, the Command was critically short of modern aircraft in the summer of 1939. On the eve of war its front-line force comprised nineteen squadrons. There were ten squadrons of Avro Ansons, of which four were still undergoing training, and one squadron of Lockheed Hudsons, which was not fully operational. There were six squadrons of flying-boats, two with Short Sunderlands and four with obsolete Saro London or Short Stranraer biplanes. Finally there was the so-called 'striking force' comprising two squadrons of obsolete Vickers Vildebeest torpedo-carrying biplanes dating from 1930. In all there were about three hundred aircraft, with fully trained crews for about half of them.

Only the Hudson and the Sunderland could be considered up-to-date combat aircraft. Despite its modern appearance, the aircraft that made up the backbone of the Command, the Anson, was not in all respects an improvement over the Blackburn Kangaroo of 1918: the Kangaroo carried four 230 pound anti-submarine bombs, while the Anson carried only four 100-pounders; also, the Kangaroo had a better endurance. The Hudson, which was to replace the Anson, carried four 250 pound bombs and had a six-hour maximum operational endurance – figures the Kangaroo matched almost exactly.

At this stage, mention should also be made of the aircraft operating from the Royal Navy's six operational aircraft carriers during the summer of 1939. Between them these ships carried some 150 Swordfish and 25 Skua aircraft that could be used for anti-submarine operations. The Swordfish was a slow biplane designed as a general-purpose machine for torpedo dropping, bombing and reconnaissance, while the faster Skua monoplane was designed primarily as a dive bomber. When operating in the anti-submarine role, these aircraft used the same weapons as those employed by Coastal Command. Being confident in the ability of its sonar-equipped destroyers and escorts to deal with enemy submarines, the Royal Navy did not place anti-submarine training high on the list of requirements for its aircrew.

None of the aircraft in service in 1939 carried ship-search radar, though the device was by then in an advanced state of development. No flying-boats carried hydrophone listening equipment, nor were there any blimps that in 1918 had 'dunked' hydrophones to listen for submerged submarines. The World War I hydrophones had not been efficient, but they did at least provide a limited capability against boats under water; now aircrews were back where they had been in 1917, limited to making visual searches for enemy submarines, with or without the aid of binoculars.

The Royal Air Force and the Royal Navy entered the war in 1939 with better anti-submarine aircraft than those of any of the other belligerents. But that was because the other nations had devoted even less effort to combating enemy submarines. The French Navy operated a hotchpotch collection of obsolescent flying-boats for oversea reconnaissance. The *Luftwaffe* had a mixed bag of flying-boats and landplanes, some of them modern machines, but its anti-submarine patrols were confined to the Baltic and the waters immediately off the north-west coast of Germany.

During the final years of peace the German Navy, having heard the British claims regarding the effectiveness of sonar, also entertained serious doubts as to whether the submarine would ever again become a major offensive weapon. Under the so-called Z-Plan of January 1939, that service aimed at building a battle fleet designed to fight large-scale fleet actions in mid-Atlantic against the Royal Navy. Its battleship strength was to be brought up to eight modern ships, supported by four aircraft-carriers. The plan also called for the building of 233 submarines, but their construction was to be spread out over six years.

In the event the outbreak of war overtook the Z-Plan before it began to show results. In the summer of 1939 the Germany Navy had 56 U-boats in commission. Of those, 46 were combat ready and 22 were suitable for operations in the Atlantic. However, it is interesting to note that those submarines of 1939 were not greatly superior in general performance to those the service had used in 1918, as a comparison between boats built in these two years shows. In general the advances in submarine design between the wars had been confined to improvements in underwater handling, silent running, and a tougher structure, which gave the ability to dive deeper. Also the newer boats were longer ranging. In 1918 a range of 5,500 sea miles was regarded as 'ocean-going', but in 1939 a range of 6,500 sea miles was considered only as 'medium-range'.

In the new torpedoes, with their greatly increased range and striking power, the German Navy believed it had achieved a major improvement over what had gone before. Finally, ships' radio equipment had improved greatly during the years between the wars. And good radio communication was the cornerstone of Dönitz's planned anti-convoy tactics.

In August 1939, as the twenty-one years of peace neared their end, few people could say with certainty whether the submarine was still an effective weapon of war. Or would the sonar-fitted convoy escorts – perhaps with air support – be able as predicted to deal savagely with any submarine crew foolhardy enough to attack an escorted convoy? Such questions could be answered only after the hard school of war had taught its inevitable lessons.

Comparison of U-boat types, 1918 and 1939

	U-114, 1918	*U-53 Type VIIB, 1939*
Surface displacement (tons)	798	763
Oil capacity (tons)	122	108
Maximum speed, surface (knots)	16.9	17.2
Maximum range, surface (nm)	6,600 @ 12.6 kts	6,500 @ 12 kts
Maximum speed, submerged (knots)	9.8	8
Maximum range, submerged (nm)	60 @ 3 kts	72 @ 4 kts
Minimum diving time (sec)	60	60
Maximum safe depth (ft)	160	660
Torpedo tubes	4 bow, 2 stern	4 bow, 1 stern
Torpedo calibre, warhead,	600 mm, 396 pound	633 mm, 770 pound
Torpedo range	1,100 yards at 40 kts	2,700 yards at 50 kts
Deck guns	one 105 mm; some had an 88 mm as well	one 88 mm

CHAPTER 3

The Long, Hard Road

September 1939 to June 1941

Courage alone is not enough – in technical warfare of this nature we must also have the best possible weapons and, above all, be so well trained as to be able to use those weapons effectively.
                                        General Douglas MacArthur

A week before German troops marched into Poland, on 23 August 1939, Coastal Command of the Royal Air Force implemented its previously laid war contingency plan. Aircraft began patrolling over the North Sea, their crews searching for German warships and submarines moving out into the Atlantic. It was, however, already too late: by that time the heavy cruisers *Graf Spee* and *Deutschland* had sailed and were clear of the areas under patrol. That was also true of many of the forty-six U-boats that were available for operations.

At mid-day on 3 September 1939, Great Britain and France declared war on Germany. Now the patrolling Coastal Command aircraft carried live anti-submarine bombs, and U-boats were to be attacked on sight. The early attempts to do so were, however, almost uniformly unsuccessful.

Coastal Command had been at war for two days when, on 5 September, an Anson of No. 233 Squadron surprised a submarine on the surface off the west coast of Scotland. The crew dropped two 100 pound bombs as the boat was submerging. Released from low level, the bombs struck the surface of the sea but then 'skipped' back into the air like a couple of flat stones. As the fuse was designed, however, the impact with the sea had initiated the time delay. After a short pause the two bombs detonated, in the air beneath the Anson. Flying splinters pierced its fuel tanks and petrol streamed from the holes. Unable to regain their base, the crew set the machine down in St Andrew's Bay. The men boarded their dinghy, which was fortunately still intact, and were soon rescued. Only later did the Anson's crew learn the measure of the fiasco that they had been lucky to survive: the submarine they had attacked was HMS *Seahorse*. The bombs caused no damage to the boat, but she suffered slight hull damage when she struck the bottom in her effort to escape from her attackers.

The first attack on a genuine U-boat, just over a week later, went no better. On the 14th two Skua dive-bombers from the aircraft-carrier *Ark Royal* attacked *U-30* as she was in the act of submerging. Once again the bombs exploded in the air, both aircraft suffered shrapnel damage and crashed. His boat unscathed, *Oberleutnant* Lemp surfaced, took on board the two British survivors, dived, and left the area. On the next day another Anson was damaged by its own bombs, following an unsuccessful attack on a submarine.

During the first few months of war the British anti-submarine bombs caused minor damage to one or two U-boats. Yet during this period these weapons did more harm to the British cause than to that of her enemy, and caused more damage to the dropping aircraft than to the submarines. The fact was that the splinters from the bombs, exploding after glancing off the surface, were more effective against the dropping aircraft than was their blast effect against U-boats. The aircrews were in an unfortunate position. With no proper bombsight for use against submarines, they could only overcome this lack by attacking from low altitude and releasing their bombs 'by eye'. But if they did this they ran a severe risk of being knocked down by their own bombs.

Nor were the other British anti-submarine measures as effective as the pre-war exercises had led many to believe. The U-boats did not suffer the heavy losses that some Germans naval officers had feared. Near the end of September 1939 Dönitz, recently promoted to Kommodore, commented in his War Diary:

It is not true that Britain possesses the means of neutralising the menace of our submarines. Our experience confirms that the British anti-submarine measures are not so effective as had been claimed. Without doubt the enemy's technique has improved; but so has that of the submarine, which now moves more quietly; the firing of a torpedo no longer leaves a tell-tale splash . . . Great advances have been made in communications, so that it is now possible to control the movements of widely dispersed submarines and concentrate them for attacks on convoys.

Not that Dönitz was without problems. The new German torpedoes were fast and they carried a heavy warhead. But their depth-keeping mechanism was unreliable, and frequently their magnetic firing pistols failed to function. Because of this, the U-boats missed many opportunities. After reading his captains' reports, which contained many graphic descriptions of juicy targets that had escaped because of torpedo failures, Dönitz noted in the War Diary:

> I do not believe that ever in the history of war have men been sent against the enemy with such a useless weapon.

Had he known the truth about the anti-submarine bombs used against his boats, the German commander might perhaps have been a little less emphatic.

Despite the high incidence of torpedo failures, the U-boats scored some successes during the first two months of the war. On 17 September *Kapitänleutnant* Schuhart in *U-29* torpedoed and sank the aircraft-carrier *Courageous*, herself on an anti-submarine patrol in the Western Approaches. During the first two months of hostilities the U-boats sank sixty-eight merchant ships totalling 288,686 tons. The attackers also suffered losses, however: Dönitz lost seven U-boats, one-eighth of his available force. Mines had destroyed three of the submarines, and British naval forces accounted for the other four. Following this brisk initial skirmish, the U-boats returned to their bases.

If there was one lesson the Royal Navy had learnt well from World War I, it was the need to institute the convoy system as soon as possible after the outbreak of hostilities. This was done, and from the middle of September 1939 most merchant ships moved in convoy.

Dönitz had developed his special method of co-ordinated attacks by U-boats – the so-called 'Wolf Pack' – as a means of defeating the convoy tactic. But this tactic required several U-boats for their success, and at the beginning of the war the German submarine fleet was far too small. The first attempt to mount a 'Wolf Pack' attack on a convoy was on 18 October; only three submarines were available for the operation. These sank one ship each, before the arrival of air cover forced them to break off the action. A second such attack, the following month, also ended inconclusively. Following this, Dönitz temporarily shelved his ideas for massed attacks. When he had more U-boats available for action, he would try again.

In the closing months of 1939 it was Coastal Command's intention to operate one aircraft over each convoy during the day, for as long as the convoy was within range of the Command's airfields. But there were too few aircraft available to meet all the demands made on them. To overcome this, Air Chief Marshal Bowhill reintroduced the 'Scarecrow' patrols that had been part of the anti-submarine effort in 1918. This time the planes were unarmed Tiger Moth trainers and Hornet Moth touring aircraft, with ex-reservist pilots at the controls. Designated the Coastal Patrol Flights, the first 'Scarecrow' aircraft began operations in December 1939. Each flight operated about nine aircraft, from an airfield situated near the coast.

As in World War I, the 'Scarecrows' caused no U-boat sinkings. But, as in the previous conflict, they added their weight to the general aerial harassment of the U-boat crews and helped save ships that would otherwise have been sunk. The patrols continued until the late spring of 1940, when the changing German strategy would render them ineffective.

During the first four months of the war, to the end of 1939, Coastal Command crews sighted U-boats on 57 occasions. They delivered forty attacks and caused damage to eight boats. No U-boat had yet been sunk by aircraft, or even with their help. The air patrols were becoming stronger with each month that passed, however, and a 'kill' could not be long in coming.

The first U-boat sinking during World War II for which an aircraft could claim some credit, took place on 30 January 1940. *Kapitänleutnant* Heidel in *U-55* had attacked a convoy moving round the north-western tip of France, and sank two ships; but the surface escorts then counter-attacked. Heidel would almost certainly have escaped, had not the crew of a Sunderland of No. 228 Squadron found him again after each attempt. Because of this the warships could maintain the pursuit until *U-55*'s batteries were exhausted. At that point Heidel ordered his men to scuttle the U-boat and abandon her.

Two months later an aircraft operating alone destroyed a U-boat. The distinction of achieving the first aerial 'kill' during World War II fell not to an aircraft of Coastal Command, but to one of RAF Bomber Command. The weapons it used were not the specially designed – if not very successful – anti-submarine bombs, but ordinary 250 pound general-purpose bombs.

On 11 March 1940 Squadron Leader Miles Delap was piloting a Blenheim bomber of No. 82 Squadron engaged in an armed reconnaissance of the Heligoland Bight. The aircraft was flying in and out of cloud at 6,000 feet when Delap caught sight of a U-boat on the surface on his starboard side, about ten miles away. He pulled the Blenheim back into cloud and turned towards the submarine. When he reached a position that he estimated was just short of the U-boat, Delap broke cloud once again and saw his prey still on the surface and in front of him. The bomber pilot pushed down the nose of his aircraft and dived into attack. Because the bombs were fused to explode on impact, Bomber Command standing orders stated that they should not be released from altitudes below 1,000 feet. But in the heat of the moment, in his eagerness to sink the U-boat, Delap took the Blenheim well below this safe height. When he felt he could not miss, he released the bombs in a concentrated salvo. Delap then pulled his bomber up to get clear of the blast; even so, the aircraft suffered a shaking and there was some damage from bomb splinters. As Delap climbed away he had the satisfaction of hearing that the risks had not been in vain: the rear gunner, Corporal Richards, said he had seen one, possibly two, bombs score direct hits on the U-boat's hull. Delap turned the aircraft to get a better look, and he and his crew watched the boat slide beneath the waves. They were sure they had sunk her. The airmen were not mistaken: the submarine was *U-31* (Habekost), which had been engaged in sea trials following a refit. A large part of the boat's crew comprised dockyard workers, and there were no survivors. The submarine sank in fifty feet of water, and shortly afterwards a German Navy salvage team raised her (after repairs she re-entered service, but was finally sunk by HMS *Antelope* in November 1940).

Just over a month later, on 13 April, during an action in Narvik Fjord, the Swordfish floatplane from the battleship *Warspite* caught *U-64* (Schulz) at anchor and sank her with a pair of 100 pound anti-submarine bombs.

The German anti-submarine aircraft were considerably less numerous, and somewhat less effective, than their British counterparts. They were, however, able to 'take into custody' two Royal Navy submarines that had previously suffered damage. The first of these was the minelaying boat HMS *Seal*, which had suffered severe damage after striking a German mine on 4 May 1940. Only one diesel motor still ran, and that had its gear train jammed in reverse. The boat's rudder was locked hard to starboard. Lieutenant-Commander Lonsdale, *Seal*'s commander, attempted to reach Sweden. The following morning, however, Arado 196 floatplanes found the crippled submarine. After strafing her and causing injuries to several members of the crew, the aircraft directed warships to the scene. Since his boat could no longer dive to safety, Lonsdale was in a hopeless position; he surrendered his battered submarine.

Two months later, on 5 July, Lieutenant P. Buckley in HMS *Shark* made a lone attack on a German convoy off the coast of Norway. During the subsequent counter-attack, however, *Shark* suffered a severe shaking, which put her motors out of action. She regained the surface, but was dead in the water. Early the next morning an Arado found her, and after a series of damaging attacks Buckley surrendered. Soon afterwards two German warships arrived on the scene to take charge of the prize and remove the crew. As the last British sailors were leaving their boat, however, one of them opened the valves to flood the ballast tanks. It was some time before the captors realised what had happened. By the time it was clear that *Shark* was sinking, it was too late to do anything about it. The German sailors had to watch, helpless, as their trophy slid out of their grasp.

Following its exertions during the first two months of the war, the U-boat arm settled down to a long war of attrition. During the seven-month period from the beginning of November 1939 to the end of May 1940, it sank just over 560,000 tons of merchant shipping – an average of about 80,000 tons per month. For the Allies those losses were uncomfortable, but they were not serious. The U-boat fleet was still too small to have a serious effect: in May 1940 there were only about thirty boats available for operations. Because of this, the U-boat's massive potential threat was not appreciated.

Then, in June 1940, the war took a decided turn for the worse for the Allies. Following Hitler's successful *Blitzkrieg* in the West, the bulk of the British forces in France had had to be evacuated from Dunkirk. On 11 June Italy entered the war on the side of Germany, and on the 26th France surrendered.

On the day of the French armistice, a long convoy of vehicles set out from the German naval base at Wilhelmshaven. The lorries carried torpedoes, torpedo stores, air compressors and the para-phernalia necessary to support U-boat operations from the newly captured ports along the west coast of France. Dönitz, now a *Konteradmiral*, fully appreciated the value of the prize that had fallen into his lap: no longer would the U-boats have to make the long journey round the north of Scotland to reach their hunting areas in the Atlantic.

The German Navy wasted little time. On 6 July the commander at Lorient declared the base there ready for use by U-boats. The next day *Kapitänleutnant* Lemp took *U-30* into the port to load torpedoes. Almost overnight, the North Sea – which the short-ranging British air patrols had been able to cover – lost much of its significance in the battle to protect the trade routes.

U-boat crews would later refer to the months immediately following the capture of France as 'the Happy Time'; that was when many ace commanders made their names. Between the beginning of June and the end of December 1940 the U-boats sank 343 merchant ships grossing more than 1,700,000 tons, an average of about 240,000 tons per month. The magnitude of this loss to the British cause can be seen from the amount of military equipment that might be carried aboard a single 6,000 ton freighter: twenty-one tanks, eight 6 inch howitzers, forty-four medium artillery pieces, twenty anti-tank guns, twelve armoured cars, twenty-five tracked weapon carriers, 2,550 tons of ammunition, three hundred tons of rifles and parts, two hundred tons of tank parts and a thousand tons of general stores.

The losses now inflicted on the convoys forced them to abandon the route to the south of Ireland, and instead take the longer route round the north. The German Navy achieved this with a very small force of submarines: at the end of August 1940 there were only twenty-seven operational U-boats, compared with forty-six at the beginning of the war. Since the passage to and from the convoy routes was much reduced, however, the submarines were able to spend much longer in their operational areas. Now Dönitz felt that the time was ripe to reintroduce his 'Wolf Pack' tactic, and this time his crews were much more successful. During the second half of October 1940, for example, a 'Wolf Pack' sank thirty-eight ships from two eastbound Atlantic convoys. Nearly three-quarters of the successful torpedo attacks were made at night by U-boats operating on the surface, when they could exploit their greater speed. Still lacking radar, the convoy escorts found this tactic very difficult to counter (sonar did not detect submarines on the surface).

During the summer of 1940 the British anti-submarine aircraft had only limited success against U-boats operating in the Atlantic: on 1 July a Sunderland assisted surface warships to sink *U-26* (Scheringer), and the following month another aircraft of the same type caused serious damage to *U-52*.

In the Mediterranean theatre, however, British aircraft enjoyed somewhat greater success against the Italian submarines. Also, without knowing it, they were able to nip in the bud two attempts to attack warships in the port of Alexandria. Under conditions of great secrecy before the war, Italian naval officers had developed a two-man 'human torpedo' for attacks on enemy fleet anchorages. The device received the cover letters SLC (for *Silura a lunga corsa*, long-range torpedo). These craft were carried in special containers mounted on the upper deck of a parent submarine, which carried them to within ten miles of their target. While the submarine waited outside the harbour, the SLC crews were to take their craft right inside and attach limpet mines to the enemy ships, before returning to their parent submarine.

The Italian Navy planned its first such SLC attack for the night of 25 August 1940, against the British fleet anchorage at Alexandria. For the raid the Italian stepping-off base was the sheltered bay at Bomba, on the coast of Libya near Tobruk. On the morning of the 21st, Lieutenant Brunetti took the SLC-modified submarine *Iride* into Bomba Bay, in company with the depot ship *Monte Gargano* and the torpedo boat *Calipso*. The three vessels tied up together, and on the following morning *Iride* received her complement of four SLC craft. While the force was thus moored, it was spotted by the crew of a British reconnaissance aircraft.

Shortly before noon three Swordfish aircraft of No. 818 Squadron of the Fleet Air Arm took off from Ma'aten Baggush to launch a torpedo attack on the ships reported in Bomba Bay. Captain Oliver Patch, Royal Marines, led the attacking force in from the seaward side and the Swordfish achieved complete surprise. The first target to come into view was *Iride* herself; she was running into deeper water, to test the containers with the SLC craft in position. Patch made straight for the submarine and released his torpedo. The weapon struck *Iride* forward of the conning tower, and the explosion blew a large hole that cut the submarine almost in two. She sank immediately, leaving fourteen of her crew bobbing on the surface. Meanwhile the other two Swordfish opened out, and attacked the two Italian ships at anchor from nearly opposite directions. One torpedo hit *Monte Gargano*, which blew up and sank; *Calipso* survived the attack.

The Italian Navy launched a second attempt to attack the anchorage at Alexandria using SLC craft early in September 1940. This venture also came to grief. On this occasion Royal Navy ships and aircraft caught the parent submarine *Gondar* when she was still about a hundred miles from her launching point, and after a long combined hunt they sank her.

In neither case was there any indication that the submarines attacked were in any way special. (In December 1941 the SLC craft would finally get inside the anchorage at Alexandria, where they caused serious damage to two battleships, a destroyer and a tanker.) In addition to the SLC parent boats, British aircraft sank two conventional Italian submarines and assisted surface ships to sink a third.

To return to the Atlantic: there was one other air attack in the autumn of 1940 that deserves mention here. On 25 October three Hudsons of No. 233 Squadron were conducting an armed reconnaissance off Norway when they stumbled upon a U-boat on the surface. The bombers slid into line astern and dived on their prey from out of the sun. First to attack was Pilot Officer Maudsley, who straddled the submarine with his stick of ten 100-pounders. The second Hudson then attacked the boat, which was now partly hidden under a dense cloud of black smoke. Pilot Officer Walsh, in the third Hudson, saw the stern of the U-boat rise up through the smoke then sink with a distinct list to port. The submarine was *U-46*, and she had suffered a direct hit from a 100 pound bomb on her stern The weapon had detonated correctly, and punched a ten-foot-long hole through her outer plating. The hole was just to the rear of the pressure hull, however, and the latter did not split. As a result *Kapitänleutnant* Endrass was able to get his U-boat back to port. The incident showed that even when the British 100 pound anti-submarine bomb struck its target and functioned according to plan, the results were not necessarily lethal.

During 1940 aircraft had caused no more than a mild harassment to enemy submarines. Certainly there were very few successes to show for the many tens of thousands of flying hours spent on patrol. Clearly, improved weapons and new detection and location devices were needed, if aircraft were to perform with any greater chance of success. As the year drew to its close, several such avenues were being explored in Britain.

Air Chief Marshal Bowhill quickly realised the ineffectiveness of the anti-submarine bombs in use in his Command, and he made vigorous demands for more lethal weaponry. A completely new weapon might take two years or more to perfect and produce in quantity; that was far too long. Bowhill asked the obvious question: was there anything else readily available that could be converted for the task? The only other anti-submarine weapon available in Britain was the drum-shaped naval 450 pound depth-charge, which had been in service with few changes since 1918. During trials held in the winter of 1939–40, naval depth-charges were dropped from the air. The weapons detonated satisfactorily, provided the aircraft was not flying too fast or too high. By the late spring of 1940 the trials spawned a makeshift weapon for use by anti-submarine aircraft: a standard Mark VII naval depth-charge, with a rounded fairing fitted to the nose and fins at the rear to stabilise it during its passage through the air. The modified naval depth-charge offered three major advantages over the anti-submarine bombs it replaced. First, its simple hydrostatic pistol, which detonated the weapon as it passed a previously set depth, was more reliable than the complex fuse fitted to the bomb. Secondly, nearly three-quarters of the weight of the thin-cased depth-charge comprised high explosive, compared with half in the case of the anti-submarine bombs; thus, weight-for-weight, the former produced a somewhat more powerful blast effect. Thirdly, the hydrostatic pistol would not detonate the main charge until the depth-charge had fallen to the depth previously set. So there was no risk of the aircraft suffering damage during the subsequent explosion (in contrast to the anti-submarine bombs, which, as we have observed, were liable to 'skip' off the surface and explode in the air).

There were two major disadvantages to the modified naval depth-charge in aerial use, however. Firstly, if one of these weapons hit on a U-boat on the surface, the best that could be hoped was that it would not break up but would drop over the side and explode underneath the boat. Secondly, the depth-charges could not be released from altitudes greater than one hundred feet or speeds greater than 115 mph, or they were likely to suffer damage on impact with the sea.

The advantages of the depth-charge far outweighed its disadvantages, however, and in August 1940 Coastal Command obtained seven hundred of these weapons from the Admiralty. After modification these were carried on the larger anti-submarine aircraft. Later, the 250 pound Mark VIII depth-charge was produced to replace the 100 pound and 250 pound anti-submarine bombs.

★   ★   ★

In the autumn of 1939 a version of Dr Bowen's experimental radar set went into production for Coastal Command. The device had a minimum of refinement, for speed of production was of the essence. Pye Radio Ltd built the first two hundred airborne radar receivers, while E.K. Cole Ltd built the transmitters. The device received the designation Air-to-Surface-Vessel Mark I, or ASV I for short (that designation differentiated it from the other airborne radar then under development, the airborne interception, AI, for night-fighters).

In November 1939 the first production ASV Mark I sets began trials, including one aimed at discovering the effectiveness in locating submarines. That trial did not pass without incident. Beforehand the captains of the radar-fitted Hudson and the Royal Navy submarine worked out a system of signals using aircraft identification lights and flares. At the appointed time and place an aircraft duly appeared, and the submarine crew let off their recognition signals. For their pains they came under attack from bombs,

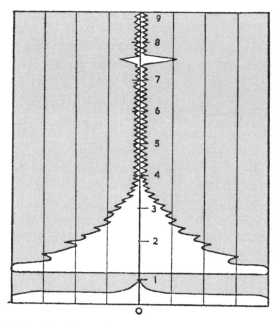

The ASV Mark II radar picture shows a contact ahead and slightly to the right, range 7½ nautical miles. Note the patch of sea clutter extending from the minimum range of the set at 1.2 nautical miles, to 4 nautical miles. The sea clutter would conceal the echo signals from a boat in that area.

for the approaching aircraft was German. The submarine dived, and when it resurfaced the Hudson had flown through the area and was searching elsewhere. Eventually another aircraft approached. and the sailors again fired their signals. This time it was British, a fighter that ran in and machine-gunned the boat. Once more it was forced to dive. Only later did a very suspicious and wary submarine commander make contact with the puzzled crew of the Hudson, and the trial began.

The maximum range of ASV against the submarine was found to be 5½ miles, when the aircraft flew at 3,000 feet. But at that height the echo signals from the target were lost in the mass of echoes reflected off the surface of the sea ('surface clutter') at ranges less than 4½ miles. If the aircraft flew at 200 feet, the effect of surface clutter was greatly reduced. At that altitude the maximum location range was 3½ miles, and the target could be observed down to a minimum range of half a mile. Yet under average daylight conditions, visual lookouts aboard the aircraft should have done rather better than that. The trial's main value was that it demonstrated that a greatly improved radar was necessary, if the device was to play a major role in the war against submarines.

While ASV Mark I was only barely effective in locating submarines, it was valuable for other tasks. The radar was of considerable help in assisting aircraft to rendezvous with the convoys they were to escort; and it could observe a large ship or a convoy of smaller ones at ranges in excess of twelve miles. Also, the device was a useful aid to navigation, for it could detect coastlines more than twenty miles away.

By the middle of January 1940 twelve Hudson aircraft had been fitted with ASV, shared between Nos 220, 224 and 233 Squadrons. Thus Bowen's airborne radar set had moved, in the remarkably short period of only four months, from the experimental laboratory into active service. As one might expect, that gave rise to severe problems. The equipment was still far from reliable. Also, test equipment, spares and instructional manuals either did not exist or were in short supply. The struggle to make good those deficiencies should be seen against the general background of wartime shortages. As one firm concerned with ASV production complained in a letter to the Air Ministry:

When we inform sub-contractors that a matter has urgent priority, they are inclined to laugh and say "Yes, so has everything else we are making . . .

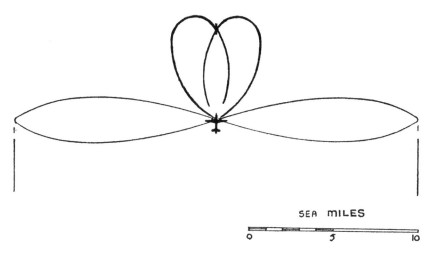

An ASV Mark II shows the area covered by the forward- and sideways-looking aerials. The radar operator could select either the forward- or the sideways-looking aerials, but not both at the same time. The normal method of search was to use the sideways-looking aerials, which enabled the operator to cover a twenty-four-mile-wide strip of water; when contact was made, the aircraft turned through 90 degrees towards it and homed in using the forward-looking aerials.

As soon as they had seen ASV Mark I into service, Dr Bowen and his team began work on an improved Mark II version. The Mark I's operating frequency of 214 MHz caused interference on certain other radio devices then in use, so its frequency was reduced to 176 MHz. A more powerful transmitter, and a more sensitive receiver, promised to give an improved range against submarines. Most important of all, the new set was engineered for mass production, and was more robust and reliable than its predecessor. In the spring of 1940 Pye Radio and E.K. Cole received orders to build four thousand ASV Mark II sets, the first to be delivered during that August.

To go with the ASV Mark II, scientists at the Telecommunications Research Establishment designed a new aerial array with separate, sideways-looking aerials mounted on the aircraft fuselage. This radiated the radar transmissions at an angle perpendicular to the line of flight, alternately to port and to starboard. The larger array focused the radiated power into a beam somewhat narrower than produced by the forward-looking aerials, giving a much increased search range. The sideways-looking aerial varied in its design, depending upon the type of aircraft that carried it. Typically, it comprised eight radiating elements on either side of the rear fuselage, which used the aircraft skin as a reflector. A further eight horizontal reflectors, mounted above the fuselage on four posts, each four feet high, served to give the radar beam a slight downward tilt.

Using the new system the crew would carry out a general search using sideways-looking aerials. When they found an object of interest, the pilot turned the aircraft through ninety degrees to head towards it. The crew then finished the homing using the forward-looking aerials.

During tests with the sideways-looking aerials fitted to a Whitley bomber with a modified ASV Mark I radar, the new array gave a significant improvement in search range. From 2,000 feet altitude, a submarine broadside on was observed at twenty miles, and bows-on at twelve miles. When the Whitley flew at 1,000 feet the ranges were ten and seven miles respectively. Because the aerial array switched the radiations alternately to port and to starboard, in each case the area either side of track swept for submarines was double these figures (that compared with a five-mile-wide area swept by the original, forward-looking, aerials). The ASV Mark II radar, coupled with the sideways-looking aerial system, augured well for the future.

Even before the end of 1940, an exciting new advance in radar technique overshadowed even those developments. The choice of frequency for the Mark I and Mark II ASV radars had been limited to that around 200 MHz, because with the components available in Great Britain in 1939 it was not possible to generate sufficient power at higher frequencies. The great breakthrough came in February 1940, when Professor J.T. Randall and Dr H. Boot built the first high-power 'magnetron' oscillator in the Nuffield Research Laboratory at Oxford. This remarkable device generated 500 watts of power at the unprecedentedly high frequency of 3,000 MHz, corresponding to a wavelength of 10 centimetres (for that reason these were called 'centimetric' wavelengths). In the summer of 1940 scientists at the Telecommunications Research Establishment built an experimental centimetric radar for ground use, which could detect aircraft at a range of six miles and a submarine conning tower at four miles. During the months that followed the power of the magnetron, and with it the range of the radar using it, steadily rose.

In August 1940, as the Battle of Britain was approaching its climax, Sir Henry Tizard had journeyed to the USA at the head of a technical mission aimed at improving scientific co-operation between that country and Great Britain. By that time Britain was leaning heavily upon the USA for weapons supplies, and it was clearly in her interest to ensure the greatest possible interchange of technical information between the two nations. One of the members of the British party was Dr Bowen, now working at the Ministry of Aircraft Production, and he took with him three examples of the new magnetron. In America the new invention caused quite a stir: the US Navy had also experimented with centimetric radar transmitters, but they had been unable to generate a power greater than 10 watts. At one stroke the British contribution increased the power of their radar by a factor of one thousand. As one US historian later commented, the magnetron was '. . . the most valuable cargo ever brought to our shores'.

The Massachusetts Institute of Technology began development work with the magnetrons in its newly opened Radiation Laboratory, which was to become one of the most important centres involved in the development of centimetric radars.

Back in Britain, during the closing months of 1940, Telecommunications Research Establishment scientists set up an improved centimetric radar at the coast and used it to observe the movements of a surfaced submarine seven miles away. In March 1941 an example of the new radar was flown for the first time.

While Coastal Command cast covetous eyes at the new radar, that was all it could do for the time being. The night blitz on Britain was still in progress, and Fighter Command's urgent need for a centimetric radar for its night fighters took first priority.

During 1940 it was difficult enough to locate U-boats on the surface sufficiently accurately to deliver attacks by day. At night it was almost impossible. The ASV radars then available or projected had an important weakness: their minimum range was somewhat greater than the maximum range at which a U-boat could be seen visually at night. Thus U-boats were almost immune to air attack when they surfaced during the hours of darkness.

The reason for the minimum range problem was as follows. When a radar transmitted its brief high-powered pulse, the sensitive receiver had to be 'switched off' or it would suffer damage. For that reason the receiver did not pick up echo signals from objects closer than about three-quarters of a mile. If the sea was rough the echoes reflected from waves (surface clutter) would blot out targets at even greater ranges.

Before the war British scientists had experimented with flares, either suspended from parachutes or towed, to provide illumination so that aircraft could attack ships at night. But in neither case did these offer much hope of success against a submarine, which was likely to disappear from sight within half a minute if it felt threatened.

In September 1940 Air Chief Marshal Bowhill had sent a circular to units in his Command, asking personnel to submit any 'bright ideas' that they thought might help combat the submarine menace. In the circular he commented: 'For instance, somebody may think of a new way of killing U-boats at night – a very difficult problem.'

At that time Squadron Leader Humphrey de Verde Leigh was an administrative officer at Coastal Command headquarters at Northwood. He had been a pilot during World War I, and had flown numerous anti-submarine patrols over the Mediterranean. One day Squadron Leader Sydney Lugg came into the office where Leigh worked, to settle an administrative matter. One of Leigh's colleagues asked Lugg about the 'Special Duties' title of Lugg's post at the headquarters. What did that mean? Lugg replied, 'It's ASV.' He then he went on to describe the workings of the device. Leigh listened spellbound. From his experience more than twenty years earlier, he knew that submarines operating in areas that were intensively patrolled usually surfaced at night to charge their batteries. Could they, he asked, be located at night using ASV? 'Yes.' Then, remembering his C-in-C's cry for help, he asked if it was possible to attack the U-boats at night. 'Well, no.' Lugg explained why the submarine disappeared off the radar tube when the aircraft was within about one mile, and why a successful night attack was almost impossible unless there was a clear night and a great deal of luck.

At this stage it must be stressed that Leigh's post was purely administrative; he did not need to know of the existence of the highly classified ASV radar, let alone of its limitations. Technically, Lugg's detailed explanation constituted a breach of security. Nevertheless, as will become clear, Lugg's 'breach of security' would be a major service to his country.

During the weeks that followed Leigh's thoughts began to crystallise on a solution to the problem of bridging the all-important final mile to the submarine: a searchlight mounted on an aircraft, which could be switched on and trained on the U-boat during the final stages of the attack. In October 1940 Leigh submitted a paper to his superiors, in which he outlined his 'Proposal for Attacking Enemy Submarines by Night'. His suggestion was to fit a 90 cm searchlight 'either in the nose or the underside' of a Wellington bomber. Leigh's reason for choosing this aircraft was that several had been modified to explode magnetic mines from the air. For this purpose the aircraft carried a 48-foot-diameter circular magnetic loop beneath the wings and the fuselage, energised by current from an auxiliary generator driven by an additional engine mounted in the fuselage. Some of these so-called DWI Wellingtons were no longer in use and were lying idle. Leigh wanted the magnetic loop to be removed, but he needed the auxiliary generator to power his searchlight.

As almost any inventor will testify, basic ideas are ten-a-penny – it is getting them to work that is the problem. Leigh went into some detail in his paper:

> The electrical generating equipment used in the DWI Wellingtons employed by this command earlier in the year consisted of either a Gypsy Queen engine and a 90 kW generator or a Ford V-8 engine and a 35 kW generator, either of which would give ample power for the searchlight.
>
> The searchlight would not be fixed but would be mounted in a swivel ring to allow at least 20 degrees downward or sideways movement. The 15 cwt 90 cm Army-type searchlight as at present used for ground defence gives an effective beam of about 5,000 yards with 2 degrees dispersion. It is suggested that a searchlight of not less than this power . . . would be most suitable for this purpose.

The success of Leigh's searchlight scheme would depend upon the solution of several unrelated problems. How difficult would it be to illuminate a small U-boat? When the latter was picked up, could it be held in a movable beam projected from an aircraft? Would the back glare from the searchlight temporarily blind the pilot and the light operator? Would the electrical striking-up of the arc cause interference on the ASV radar? Indeed, could such a lamp be made to work in an aircraft at all?

The last of those questions was not a trivial point. The carbon arc of the lamp gave off dense fumes. These had to be carried away from the light by a scavenging airflow, which also prevented the arc from getting too hot. If the airflow was too fast, it was likely to blow out the flame or else cause it to fluctuate. The difficulties of getting this through-current of air correct – not too fast and not too slow, regardless of where the light was pointing – was to be one of the most difficult problems to overcome.

In general Leigh's paper was well received at Coastal Command headquarters, the more so when the Commander-in-Chief to put his weight behind the idea. In his covering letter Bowhill wrote:

> I am fully aware that in a matter of this nature no certain results can be promised, but having regard to the fact that our shipping losses from submarine action are running in the neighbourhood of 200,000 tons per month, the matter is so urgent that no possible means of countering this must be neglected . . .

Scientists at the Royal Aircraft Establishment at Farnborough were less enthusiastic about Leigh's scheme. They thought the suggested light would be too large to fit into a turret of a Wellington. Instead they suggested a smaller Mercury vapour lamp, but: 'These lamps are, however, in the process of development and it is not certain that a reliable lamp can be obtained . . .' Their letter of reply went on to outline the official Farnborough thinking on the matter:

> We do not know if you are aware of the trials of towed flares for the reconnaissance of shipping, made in 1928. Briefly the method was to use two aircraft flying up to 14 miles apart. One, or both, aircraft tows a 4-inch training flare, weighing 9 pound and burning for about 2½ minutes. Length of tow 250 feet. Objects on the water are picked up in silhouette against reflected light from the water, remaining visible for about 3 seconds at 1,000 feet when flare, object and observer are in line . . . We are of the opinion that the towed flare scheme would work well for the purpose you have in mind and that it would be put into operation more quickly than any scheme involving searchlights.

The copy of this letter, received by Leigh on 12 November 1940, still exists; at the bottom he had pencilled:

It would not.

i. the submarine would have submerged long before 'flare, object and observer' were in line. There is no time for a 'search'.

ii. 3 seconds from 1,000 feet is useless.

iii. Flares cost £7 each.

iv. If the submarine was anywhere near a convoy the position would be given away.

Leigh's superiors knew full well that the towed flare idea would not work, and sided with him. Leigh was allowed to work on his light full time, and set about overcoming each objection to his scheme. Instead of the 90 cm Army searchlight, he now chose the smaller naval 24 inch (61 cm) searchlight carried by destroyers. The latter could fit into a retractable mounting, which could be lowered through the hole in the fuselage originally made for the under-belly gun position of the Wellington. Using a very precise hydraulic system that the Frazer Nash car company had designed for the control of bombers' gun turrets, the light beam could be controlled accurately in angle and elevation. So accurate was this system that a favourite trick of gunners was to insert a pencil into a machine-gun barrel and sign their name on a card held in front of the turret.

Leigh overcame the difficult problem of ventilation by ducting air through a hollow fairing on the underside of the aircraft, then through a cleverly designed labyrinth of holes at the top of the mounting. The removal of the fumes called for no less ingenuity, and he accomplished this by means of a rotating cowl kept pointing rearwards by the slipstream.

On 22 November Leigh attended a conference at the Vickers company, which finalised the details of the modification work necessary to convert a Wellington to carry his light. A few days later a DWI Wellington arrived at the firm's Brooklands factory for conversion. The device was named the 'Leigh Light' after its inventor, and in March 1941 the prototype installation fitted in a Wellington was ready to begin its flight trials. The initial trials showed that the high-powered searchlight could be installed in an aircraft, and it worked successfully. The next step was to fit the aircraft with ASV radar as well, and test the two devices together during a mock attack on a submarine. By 24 April this further work had been completed, and the Wellington flew to Limavady in Northern Ireland for the second series of trials.

The first full-scale night test of Leigh's ideas took place a week later. It ended in failure. The Wellington's crew was unable to place the searchlight beam on the British submarine *H-31*. Only on the following day did the disappointed Leigh find out what had gone wrong. The submarine commander told him that during one of the runs the Wellington had passed right over his boat, and on two other occasions it had passed within four hundred yards. The light came on, but in each case the operator switched it off too early. The sailors were convinced that had the light been on for a little longer, their boat would have been illuminated.

For the next test, during early-morning darkness on 4 May, Leigh himself operated the searchlight. The crew homed on the submarine using radar, and at a range of one mile Leigh switched on his light – and left it on. After a short wait the submarine came into view, and he was able to hold the beam on the target until it passed below the aircraft. Following that initial success, the Wellington made repeated illuminating runs on the submarine. Those present during the trial were very enthusiastic about what they had seen. One Royal Navy officer who had watched the Leigh Light test, Commander G. Hoare-Smith, afterwards wrote:

> The aircraft was not heard by the submarine until it [the submarine] had been illuminated, and was able to dive and attack down the beam for 27 seconds before being pulled out at 600 feet. This effort was most impressive, and there seems no doubt that, given an efficient aircraft crew and good team work, this weapon would be invaluable in attacking U-boats on the surface at night and in low visibility.

To those concerned with the Limavady trial, it seemed that the value of the Leigh Light searchlight was proved beyond reasonable doubt. All the more stunning, then, was the blow that fell a few weeks later: for the entire project came within a hair's breadth of being axed.

The reason was that in May 1941 Leigh's system was not the only airborne searchlight undergoing trials for the Royal Air Force. Group Captain Helmore had designed another type of searchlight for carriage in aircraft, to illuminate an enemy bomber so that an accompanying single-seat fighter could then attack it. Helmore submitted that Coastal Command aircraft could also make use of his light to illuminate submarines on the surface.

Since there has been some confusion between the two systems, it is important to review the differences between Leigh's Light and

Helmore's. The Leigh Light used 10½ kW of electrical power. Helmore's light was thirteen times as powerful, and required a battery of accumulators that took up the whole of the aircraft's bomb bay. Leigh's light shone from below the aircraft fuselage, so the operator's eyes were some six feet above the top of the beam; Helmore's light occupied the whole of the nose of the aircraft, which meant the pilot looked along the length of the beam. The advantage of the former arrangement can be seen on any foggy day: lorries have fog lamps that are positioned some six feet below the driver's eye level, where they give little back-glare and the view ahead is adequate even under quite bad conditions. Car drivers, on the other hand, are much closer to their fog lamps, with the result that there is considerable back glare and driving is more difficult. Most important of all, Leigh's light gave a narrow beam four degrees wide – later widened to twelve degrees by means of a spreader lens – which could be steered in both azimuth and elevation; Helmore's light gave a very wide beam, fixed to point straight ahead of the aircraft.

Air Chief Marshal Joubert, who took over command of Coastal Command in June 1941, later described why he had come close to rejecting Leigh's searchlight:

> When I first took over at Coastal Command, having been so closely associated with the Helmore Light, I thought it might be given a general application by being used against U-boats as well. I thought that its wide beam and great illuminating power would be valuable. I therefore gave instructions that Squadron Leader Leigh was to return to his duties as Assistant Personnel Officer. After some two months I found, as I do not mind admitting, that I had made a mistake. I found out that the Helmore light was unnecessarily brilliant for use against U-boats and otherwise unsuitable. I then came to the conclusion that Leigh's light was preferable for use against the U-boat, and decided to drop the Helmore Light and concentrate on the Leigh Light.

In mid-August 1941, after a two-month hiatus, Leigh resumed full-time work on his system. Now that his crude 'lash-up' had proved the feasibility of the system, the time had come to 'freeze' the design and engineer the parts properly. That process took several months; the method of beam control, in particular, needed a lot of work before Leigh was satisfied with it. Also there was a fundamental change in the method of powering the light; the previous motor-driven generator system was unnecessarily big and heavy. Leigh decided that a battery of seven standard RAF 12-volt accumulators, trickle-charged from a small extra generator driven from one of the aircraft's engines, would do the task just as well. As the trials had shown, no single running of the light needed to exceed half a minute (the time a Wellington took to fly one mile), and the accumulators could provide the necessary current for that long. In its final form the Leigh Light installation weighed about 600 pound. Now the device was ready to go into production.

When the new version of the ASV radar and the Leigh Light entered service, the U-boats would lose their near-immunity to air attack by night. But, unless the sea was exceptionally clear, they were still safe from attack from above while fully submerged. During 1941 British scientists attempted to produce an airborne magnetic detector that would indicate the presence of a submerged submarine, but it proved too insensitive for the task.

With his airborne searchlight, Humphrey Leigh had shown how a comparative outsider could make a major contribution to the defeat of the U-boat. Yet it is difficult to find other examples of this; almost invariably, the ideas and schemes of those not closely involved with anti-submarine work were of little or no value. For example, in April 1941 Mr Churchill received a letter from his scientific adviser, Professor Lindemann, which stated:

> It has been suggested that a large number of small magnets, fitted with lights, could be projected even from aeroplanes or destroyers to the region in which the submarine was suspected. Any of these striking the submarine would prob-ably stick, and the idea is that they would show its position. Though this very simple scheme would probably not work, it seems possible that other types of signal might.
>
> For instance, the magnet might carry a suitable device containing calcium phosphide, or a similar substance, which in contact with the water produces a self-igniting gas; the salvo would produce bubbles of gas that would catch fire when they reached the surface of the sea, thus providing a useful marker. If any magnets hit the submarine they would stick to it, and as it moved away it would betray itself by a track of bubbles catching fire as soon as they reached the surface.

A certain amount of investigation and design is of course involved, but I think in some such form the idea is worth pursuing.

The Prime Minister disagreed, and a few days later he expressed his disapproval in true Churchillian fashion:

This seems to be rather far fetched. If the aeroplanes or destroyers were as close to the submarine as necessary it would surely be better to throw explosives by bomb or depth-charge. The complication of fitting these new gadgets and apparatus into the few aeroplanes we have on this service will be tiresome. I do not think I wish to associate myself with the matter.

As anti-submarine warfare became more complex, there grew a need to have people with brilliant minds to advise those who fought, to devise ways of getting the utmost from the available equipment. In March 1941 Professor Patrick Blackett (later Lord Blackett, President of the Royal Society), had become scientific adviser to Air Chief Marshal Bowhill. In the following summer he formed an operational research section for Coastal Command. One of the first to join the team was Professor E.J. Williams, whose previous job at Farnborough had involved him in work on a magnetic proximity fuse designed to detonate a bomb as it passed through the water close to a submarine.

The purpose of the operational research section, as Blackett saw it, was to provide scientific advice for operational staff officers on matters not normally handled by the service establishments. A year earlier he had organised a similar section for the Army's Anti-Aircraft Command, and he knew such a team could be of great potential value to Coastal Command. As Blackett later wrote:

'New weapons for old' is apt to become a very popular cry. The success of some new devices has led to a new form of escapism, which runs somewhat thus: 'Our present equipment doesn't work very well; training is bad, supply is poor, spare parts non-existent. Let's have an entirely new gadget!' Then comes the vision of the new gadget, springing like Aphrodite from the Ministry of Aircraft Production, complete with spare parts, and attended by a chorus of trained crews.

One of the tasks of an Operational Research Section is to

make possible at least an approach to a numerical estimate of the merits of a change-over from one device to another, by continual investigation of the actual performance of existing weapons, and by objective analysis of the likely performance of new ones . . .

In general, one might conclude that relatively too much scientific effort has been expended hitherto in the production of new devices and too little in the proper use of what we have got. Thus, there is a strong general case for moving many of the best scientists from the technical establishments to the operational Commands, at any rate for a time. If, and when, they return to technical work, they will be often much more useful by reason of their new knowledge of real operational needs.

One of the first projects undertaken by the new team at Coastal Command was an analysis of attacks made on U-boats to date. With his recent work on the proximity-fused anti-submarine bomb fresh in his mind, Professor Williams set about the task with enthusiasm. It was to result in one of the classic examples of the value of operational research for a fighting service.

Although the depth-charge was a clear improvement over the inefficient anti-submarine bombs it had replaced, the results it achieved were still unsatisfactory. Only one per cent of the attacks made by British aircraft on submarines had resulted in an assessment of 'definitely sunk', while a further two and a half per cent had been assessed as 'probably sunk'. There were two ways in which the effectiveness of a depth-charge of a given size and weight could be increased. First, the power of the high-explosive charge could be increased by the use of an improved type; this was in hand, and an improved explosive – Torpex, which contained powdered aluminium – was soon to be introduced for depth-charges. Secondly, the explosive could be set off closer to the hull of the submarine; the projected underwater proximity-fuse was aimed at bringing this about.

To have a fair chance of causing a fracture of the hull, a 250 pound depth-charge needed to explode within about twenty feet of a submarine. Air-dropped depth-charges were set to explode when they sank to a depth of between 100 and 150 feet. That was the *average* depth that a U-boat would reach, if it commenced its dive at the *average* distance at which an aircraft was likely to be seen. As he investigated the figures, the fallacy of that reasoning became clear to Williams. At the close of a report he wrote on the subject, he commented:

> In as many as about 40 per cent of all attacks, the U-boat was either visible at the instant of attack or had been out of sight for less than a quarter of a minute. It is estimated from such statistics, and the rate at which the uncertainty in the position of a U-boat grows with time of submersion, that the U-boat that is partly visible or just submerged is about ten times more important a target, potentially, than the U-boat that has been out of sight for more than a quarter of a minute. The very small percentage of U-boats seriously damaged or sunk in past attacks is probably largely the result of too much attention having been given to the long submerged U-boat . . .

As Williams pointed out, although the *average* submarine was about 125 feet deep when the attacking aircraft passed overhead, such a U-boat was unlikely to be damaged because of the great horizontal distance between it and its diving swirl. The only submarines likely to be depth-charged accurately were those caught on the surface, or were in the act of submerging. Until now the depth-charges had exploded too far beneath these 'easy' targets to cause fatal damage – when a Type VII U-boat was on the surface, the base of the pressure hull was about twelve feet below sea level. That was why several submarines caught on the surface and accurately straddled had survived, albeit with a severe shaking. The fault had existed for a long time. It will be remembered that during World War I, the anti-submarine bombs had been set to explode at a depth of sixty to eighty feet beneath the surface. It is of interest to speculate how many German submarines had escaped destruction because of this. Williams's analysis showed that the requirement was not a completely new weapon in the form of the proximity-fused anti-submarine bomb – a difficult and expensive device to develop and manufacture – but a more realistic setting for the depth-charges already in use.

Williams calculated that the ideal setting for the aircraft depth-charges should be a detonation at about twenty feet below the surface. But that was not possible with the firing pistol then in use; the latter had been designed originally to be dropped from surface warships, and for safety reasons its minimum depth setting was fifty feet (warships engaged surfaced submarines with gunfire, not depth-charges). Following this recommendation, Coastal

Command immediately adopted the minimum fifty-foot setting for its depth-charges. At the same time, work began at the highest priority to produce a shallow-setting hydrostatic pistol for this weapon.

By itself, the discovery of the incorrect depth setting on the air-dropped depth-charges would have justified the formation of the Operational Research Section at Coastal Command. But Blackett and his team did not rest on their laurels.

Since the very beginning of aerial anti-submarine warfare, a mutual sighting usually culminated in a race: while the submarine crew sought to dive to a safe depth, those in the aircraft attempted to deliver their attack before their quarry could do so. Unless visibility was poor, or the attack came from out of the sun, or the U-boat's lookouts were not alert, the odds were greatly in favour of the boat being wholly submerged before the attack could take place.

Could anything be done to make the aircraft less conspicuous? For most of the time an aircraft is seen as a dark object, against the somewhat lighter background of the sky. The only exception is when light from the sun is reflected off the aircraft and at the observer – a rare occurrence. The Whitleys and Wellingtons flown by Coastal Command had previously operated in the night-bomber role, and so they had retained their black undersurfaces. That brought the questions: would lighter undersurfaces bring about a worthwhile reduction in the range at which these aircraft could be seen? A trial was run, using a Wellington repainted with white undersurfaces and one with the normal black undersurfaces, in which both aircraft flew a series of runs past observers on the ground. The trial showed that, on average, the white-painted aircraft was first seen at ranges twenty per cent less than the black-painted one.

Using this numerical result, Williams calculated that a white-painted aircraft was likely to catch a submarine on the surface on thirty per cent more occasions than a black-painted one could. Because – other things being equal – the number of U-boat sinkings was directly proportional to the number of successful attacks, the former promised to increase by the same ratio. Certainly that difference was worth the effort of repainting the anti-submarine aircraft in Coastal Command. During the final months of 1941 maritime patrol aircraft began to appear with white undersurfaces. It was a tacit recognition of the advantages of the colour scheme that gulls and other sea birds had adopted some millions of years earlier.

⋆   ⋆   ⋆

While the fighting men fought, the commanders commanded and the scientists researched, a further group of men went soundlessly about their part of the Battle of the Atlantic: the electronic eavesdroppers who painstakingly recorded the immense volume of their opponents' signals traffic sent in Morse code. The operators' logs were then passed to others, who wrestled with the mind-twisting task of bringing meaning into the strings of enciphered characters. When there were successes in this field, it was necessary to devise schemes to conceal the source of the information. As with Aladdin's cave, there might be no end to the treasures one might pilfer, so long as one held the magic combination that swung the guardian rock clear of the entrance. The moment an enemy learned of the intrusion, however, he was certain to seal off the opening and alter the combination. Then the business of cracking the cipher would have to begin again, perhaps never to succeed.

The first to enjoy a major cipher-breaking success during World War II was the German Navy's cryptoanalysis service, the *B-Dienst*. By April 1940 it had broken the Royal Navy's Cypher No. 1, and was reading without serious delay nearly half of the intercepted radio traffic. In August 1940 the Royal Navy introduced its Naval Cypher No. 2. Against that system the *B-Dienst* had little success until September 1941, but for the remainder of that year it read much of the Royal Navy's traffic.

Those noteworthy German successes were eclipsed, however, by the work of the British cipher-breaking specialists working at Bletchley Park in Buckinghamshire. Much has been published on the cracking of the Enigma system, but the salient parts of the story are as follows. Beginning in the spring of 1940, the code-breakers were able to read a small but growing volume of German Army and *Luftwaffe* messages enciphered using Enigma. From February 1941 it was also possible to read large numbers of messages encrypted using the German naval Enigma. The organisation to exploit this massive Intelligence coup built up rapidly. Soon there were many of thousands of men and women engaged in receiving the German radio transmissions, deciphering them, and combining the information with that from other Intelligence sources to build up a detailed picture of the enemy and his intentions.

Each U-boat carried an Enigma cipher machine, similar in appearance to an ordinary typewriter with a standard keyboard. When a key was pressed, the electrical circuitry printed a different letter. For example, if the key for the letter 'V' was pressed, the enciphered equivalent 'B' would be printed. Between each letter conversion the electrical circuit changed, so that the next time the key for 'V' was pressed the enciphered equivalent would be different, perhaps an 'H'; and so on. Each letter of the secret message was typed out in turn on the Enigma machine, and the resultant jumble of letters was transmitted in Morse code. At the receiving end the operator wrote down the enciphered message characters, retyped then one at a time on his Enigma machine, and reproduced the original plain-language text.

To ensure the security of the Enigma system, the settings of the machines were altered at frequent intervals. Thus the capture of an Enigma machine would not by itself compromise the system. Unless the receiver operator knew the correct settings for each limited time period, the messages could not be deciphered.

The cracking of the Enigma ciphers was judged to be so important to the British, and later the Allied, cause that extraordinary measures were taken to ensure its secrecy. As Winston Churchill pointed out at the time, it was far better to lose even a battle than to compromise this vitally important source of Intelligence. A special security classification, Top Secret Ultra, was introduced for all information obtained from, or relating to, cracked enemy ciphers.

Enigma machines were in large-scale use in all three German armed services, as well as in the civilian administration. Thus the defeat of this cipher system had far-reaching effects on the course of the war. In this book, however, the relevance of the story is confined to the effect it had on operations against the U-boat arm of the German Navy.

By its very nature, the 'Wolf Pack' tactic hinged on having good communications between *Grossadmiral* Dönitz's headquarters and the U-boats at sea. Only in that way could he exercise centralised co-ordination of their activities. He would order a dozen or more U-boats to form a patrol line in mid-ocean, hoping to ensnare a passing convoy. When one of the boats made contact with the convoy, it followed on the surface and broadcast a series of sighting reports. The other boats in the pack then received instructions on when and where to converge on the convoy to deliver their concerted attack. These signals were read by the Royal Navy Intelligence officers, in some cases within a short time of their transmission. It was almost as if they could peer over the enemy Commander-in-Chief's shoulder, and observe each decision as it was made. Rarely, if ever, in the history of warfare, has one side received such continuous, accurate and immediate information on the intentions and activities of its foe.

One immediate effect of the Enigma decrypts was that it allowed the Royal Navy to plot the approximate positions of many of the U-boats at sea. By re-routeing convoys round known U-boat patrol lines, several of the former avoided attack altogether.

If the pattern for future aerial anti-submarine operations was becoming clear, for the present the available resources were insufficient in both quantity and quality. In the middle of 1941, when Air Chief Marshal Joubert took control of Coastal Command, the force comprised some four hundred maritime patrol aircraft – only one-third more than it had had in September 1939. In the meantime there had been a thoroughgoing re-equipment programme: in place of the Ansons there were many more of the newer and more effective Hudsons, Whitleys and Wellingtons. The biplane flying-boats had given way to the more effective Sunderlands and also some thirty modern American Catalina flying-boats. About three-quarters of this fleet of aircraft carried ASV radar, and all of them now carried 250 or 450 pound depth-charges set to explode at as shallow a depth as their pistols would allow.

The greatest single shortcoming in the Command's order of battle at this time was the lack of an aircraft with the range to provide an effective escort for convoys in mid-Atlantic. The Hudson could patrol effectively out to nearly 500 miles from base, while the Whitleys and Wellingtons could spend about two hours on task at this distance. Only the modern flying-boats, of which there were comparatively few available, could go much farther: the Sunderland could spend about two hours on patrol 600 miles from base, the Catalina a similar time at more than 800 miles from base. But that was not enough. In the mid-Atlantic there existed a yawning abyss some 300 miles wide, where no effective air cover was possible. This was the so-called 'Atlantic Gap', where U-boats could manoeuvre at will on the surface and launch attacks on convoys with no interference from the air. *Grossadmiral* Dönitz concentrated his boats in that part of the ocean, where they operated to great effect. Despite the often successful re-routeing of convoys round the German patrol lines, based on Ultra decrypts, during the first six months of 1941 the U-boats sank 1,400,000 tons of merchant shipping.

★   ★   ★

Whatever the uncertainties before the war, there could now be no doubt that in the war on trade the submarine was a highly dangerous weapon. Now the German Navy was commissioning new U-boats with clockwork regularity: on 1 July 1941 it had fifty-three boats operational, fifty-eight undergoing trials, and forty-two U-boats engaged in the training of new crews. Clearly the German Navy was on top of events. With the steady expansion of the force, its senior commanders had little reason to doubt that victory in the shipping lanes would be only a matter of time.

CHAPTER 4

The Conflict Widens

July 1941 to June 1942

Nothing is so hard, as to give wise council before events. And nothing so easy as, after them, to make wise reflections. Many things seem true in reason, and prove false in experience; many, that are weakly consulted, are executed with success.

Sir William Temple

In the Atlantic, the strengthening air patrols from bases in Great Britain, Iceland and Canada had driven the U-boats to operate against the convoys in mid-ocean, in the so-called 'Atlantic Gap'. That shift forced a change in Coastal Command tactics. The only immediate remedy was to strengthen the air patrols over waters within reach of its aircraft through which the U-boats had to pass, namely the transit routes through the Bay of Biscay and between Scotland and Iceland.

The majority of U-boats were based in France, and passed through the Bay of Biscay to reach their hunting grounds. So the air patrols over the Bay were strengthened, as aircraft swept the area methodically in a manner similar to the 'Spider Web' patrols of a quarter of a century earlier. And, like the patrols over the German transit routes during World War I, initially those over the Bay of Biscay achieved little.

When the air patrols over the Bay of Biscay became troublesome, however, the U-boats would cross the dangerous waters submerged during the day. At night they would resume their passage on the surface, when they were almost immune from air attack (Humphrey Leigh's airborne searchlight was not yet ready for operational use).

One of the few successes of the air patrols over the U-boat transit routes during the summer and autumn of 1941 came at the end of August. And on that occasion the RAF crew did not sink the boat

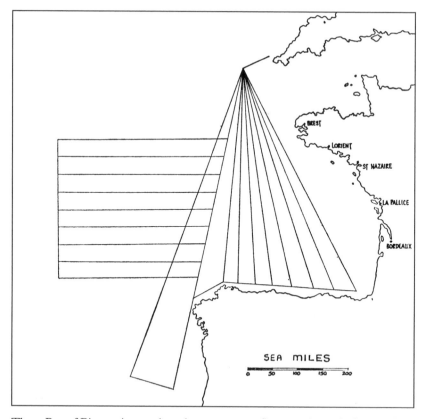

These Bay of Biscay air patrol track routes are as flown at the end of 1941. The
U-boat bases along the west coast of France are marked.

but went one better: they captured it. Early on the morning of the
27th, a U-boat was sighted submerging in a position some eighty
miles south of Iceland. The sighting aircraft immediately flashed
details of the encounter to its headquarters, and soon other aircraft
were converging on the scene.

Unaware of the hornet's nest she had stirred up, *U-570*
continued submerged towards her patrol area. Above her the seas
were rough, and many of her less-experienced crewmen were
suffering from seasickness. Shortly before 11.00 hours the boat
resurfaced. As her commander, *Korvettenkapitän* Hans Rahmlow,
climbed out through the conning tower hatch he was aghast at the
sight that met his eyes: a Hudson, bomb doors open, running in at
low altitude to attack his boat. Rahmlow bellowed an order to dive,
but it was too late. The Hudson pilot, Squadron Leader J.

Thompson, accurately straddled her with his stick of four 250 pound depth-charges.

The explosions shook the boat savagely: they smashed many of the instruments, extinguished the lights, and cracked the hull, allowing seawater to leak into the battery compartment. That produced the submariners' nightmare – poisonous chlorine gas trapped inside the boat. Convinced that all was lost, Rahmlow countermanded the order to dive. As the boat resurfaced he ordered his men to don life-jackets and prepare to abandon her.

During his attack Thompson had expended all his depth-charges, and now he had only the plane's machine-guns to strafe the submarine wallowing beneath him. Rahmlow had no way of knowing that, however, and to him it seemed only a matter of time before the Hudson delivered another attack that would finish off the boat. The German commander decided to surrender. He ordered his sailors to hold up a large white cloth, a move that made their intentions clear enough to a surprised Thompson and his crew. The Hudson's wireless operator signalled the news to an equally surprised headquarters in Iceland.

Soon there were aerial reinforcements heading into the area. Relays of aircraft then orbited the prize until that evening, when destroyers and armed trawlers arrived on the scene to take the boat in tow. On the following afternoon *U-570* was run aground on a beach on the south coast of Iceland. Although the German crew had smashed their secret equipment – including the Enigma machine – and dumped their codebooks over the side, there was much else of value to British Intelligence. After repairs in Iceland and a detailed examination, *U-570* was commissioned into the Royal Navy as HMS *Graph*.

During 1941 Air Chief Marshal Joubert, and other British officers involved with the operational use of radar, were able to keep up to date with new developments during the weekly Sunday meetings held at the Telecommunications Research Establishment at Swanage. These meetings, the so-called 'Sunday Soviets', brought the establishment's scientists into contact with interested parties ranging from Cabinet Ministers to junior officers straight from the various battle fronts. There were some extremely frank exchanges between those who designed the equipment and those who had to use it in action. And on more than one occasion a senior officer had 'his ears pinned back' by an over-enthusiastic junior.

The 'Soviets' fulfilled an important function, bringing a touch of reality to the scientists, who were sometimes in danger of becoming mesmerised by the sheer technical brilliance of the systems they had produced. They gave senior officers a clear idea of how the new devices really performed in action, and of weaknesses in their organisations that needed to be eradicated. They also provided operational crews with useful advice on how to get the utmost from their equipment.

Significantly, the German Navy had no similar 'information exchange'. That would later lead to a gap in trust between the scientists and the sailors, which would create a host of troubles. We shall follow the course of this, in a later chapter.

Nearer to home, the radar equipment operated by Joubert's own Command had given disappointing results since its introduction. By the middle of 1941 three-quarters of his aircraft carried ASV Mark II. Theoretically the device should have detected surfaced U-boats at ranges greater than the human eye could, whatever the visibility state. Yet the great majority of U-boats were being detected not by radar, but visually: of the seventy-seven sightings in August and September, only thirteen followed an initial pick-up by ASV. Clearly, the crews were missing much of what they should have seen on the radar.

In November 1941 Joubert set up a working party to find out what was going wrong. Its members did not need to search for long. They found that the biggest single problem was the poor serviceability of the equipment. The ASV set had been designed and built hurriedly under the stress of war, there were chronic shortages of test equipment and spare parts, and many of the ground technicians had received no proper training. In the air a quite different set of problems militated against its success. In the aircraft the ASV was 'nobody's child': either the navigator or the wireless operator would operate it, but that was in addition to their normal duties. As a result they operated the radar only when they had time to spare from their primary tasks. Moreover, in each case the ASV operator's position had been added to the aircraft as an afterthought. Usually it was poorly designed and uncomfortable, with the result that operating the radar was an unpopular task. In the Whitley, for example, the operator worked mid-way down the cold, dark, tunnel-like fuselage, facing athwartships, seated on the closed lid of the aircraft's lavatory – which he had to vacate if anybody needed to use it for its primary purpose!

Air Chief Marshal Joubert was quick to act on his working party's findings. He launched programmes to improve the training of ground technicians and aircrews, and improved the supply of spare parts and test equipment. Responsibility for operating the ASV was allocated to the wireless operator, and an extra crewman was to be carried to share in this task. It was more difficult to improve the ASV operators' positions in aircraft types already in service, but Joubert ensured that those in future aircraft types would be much better.

Even while Joubert's working party was in session, he received the first report of successful air attacks following the radar detection of a U-boat. On 30 November the ASV operator in a Whitley of No. 602 Squadron detected a surfaced boat five miles away, and guided his pilot into position for a visual attack; the latter was successful, and resulted in the destruction of *U-206* (Opitz). It would be the sole kill by the Bay of Biscay air patrols during the whole of 1941.

U-206 had been part of a powerful reinforcement for the U-boat force in the Mediterranean, involving more than twenty boats. Soon her compatriots were running the gauntlet of British defences at the Straits of Gibraltar. They planned their runs to pass through the Straits on the surface at night at their best speed, a method that had kept boats safe from air attack in the past. This time it would be different, however.

No. 812 Squadron of the Fleet Air Arm had disembarked at Gibraltar, from the carrier HMS *Argus*. Each night the unit flew anti-submarine patrols over the Straits. No. 812 Squadron's crews were highly proficient in the use of ASV radar, and the Swordfish proved almost ideal for the night hunting role. Its open cockpits allowed the pilot and observer an excellent view of the sea around them, the aircraft was very manoeuvrable and it could be flown with great precision.

On the evening of 1 December the commander of 812 Squadron, Lieutenant-Commander Woods, attacked *U-96* to such effect that she had to abandon her attempt to pass through the Straits and return to France. During the three weeks that followed, the Swordfish delivered night attacks on four more boats attempting to pass through the Straits. In each case they inflicted damage sufficient to force the boats to return to France for repairs: *U-202* (Linder), *U-432* (Schultze), *U-558* (Krech) and *U-569* (Hinsch).

Now 812 Squadron was getting into its stride, and on 21 December one of its crews achieved the distinction of making the first ever night 'kill' of a submarine from the air. From the rear cockpit of his Swordfish, on patrol to the west of the Straits, Lieutenant L. Plummer observed a radar contact just over three miles away. His pilot, Sub-Lieutenant P. Wilkinson, turned towards it, looking for the telltale lights of a fishing boat or a small coaster. But the night was dark, with no moon and a choppy sea. He saw nothing. Wilkinson took the Swordfish down to 300 feet and manoeuvred so that he approached the contact from the west. If this was indeed a U-boat aiming to pass through the Straits, that would position him behind it and ready to deliver an attack. As the range closed the radar echo merged into the sea clutter, and Plummer could only direct his pilot to maintain the previous heading. Now both men were peering into the blackness below them, searching for signs of movement. Just over a minute later the crew's attention to detail rewarded them with the sight of the distinctive wake of a U-boat on the surface. Their attack took *U-451* (Hoffmann) by surprise, and the stick of three 450 pound depth-charges straddled the submarine. She broke up and sank.

During the last day of November and the first three weeks of December 1941, 812 Squadron's night attacks resulted in one U-boat sunk and five seriously damaged. Yet in spite of these successes, fifteen boats had passed safely into the Mediterranean. Dönitz, now a *Vizeadmiral*, now had sufficient U-boats in that area, and there would be no further attempts to run through the Straits for several months.

One obvious method of providing air cover for convoys out of reach of land-based aircraft was to use aircraft-carriers. Yet in 1941 the Royal Navy had far too few of these precious ships to employ them for general convoy escort work. There was a clear need for a simple, second-rate aircraft-carrier that could be produced rapidly and cheaply. The answer was to convert merchant ships for the role, fitted with flight decks, arrester gear and simple crash barriers. The first of these so-called 'escort carriers' appeared in the summer of 1941: HMS *Audacity*, converted from a captured German 5,500 ton freighter.

From September 1941 *Audacity* formed part of the escort of convoys passing between the United Kingdom and Gibraltar. On this route the primary danger to convoys was from enemy bombers, so the escort carrier's complement of aircraft comprised six Martlet fighters armed only with machine-guns. The ship had no hangar, and so all servicing work had to take place in the open on the flight deck.

During her first three voyages, *Audacity* drove away or shot down German reconnaissance aircraft attempting to shadow the convoy. On her fourth voyage she demonstrated that she could also make things difficult for attacking U-boats.

On 14 December the thirty-three-ship convoy HG 76 set out from Gibraltar for the United Kingdom. In addition to *Audacity*, the escort comprised three destroyers and ten corvettes and sloops. Also, during the first three days of the voyage, aircraft based at Gibraltar provided cover.

On the evening of the 16th, following a sighting report from a reconnaissance aircraft, *Grossadmiral* Dönitz ordered nine U-boats into position to intercept the convoy. By the following morning the attackers were closing in: a Martlet pilot sighted a U-boat on the surface twenty-two miles away, and forced it to dive. The escort commander despatched five warships to hunt down the boat, and following a damaging attack with depth-charges *Kapitänleutnant* Baumann brought *U-131* to the surface and tried to make good his escape. There followed a hectic chase, during which two destroyers gained remorselessly on the boat. A Martlet also joined in and made a strafing attack, but the U-boat's gunners promptly shot it down, killing the pilot. It was the first time a submarine had shot down an aircraft. The German crew did not have long to savour their victory, however. Soon afterwards they came under accurate fire from the destroyers, and Baumann scuttled his boat.

During her outbound voyage *Audacity* had lost two Martlets, and as there had been no spare ones at Gibraltar, she began her return voyage with only four fighters. Now she was down to three. The problem of keeping the vitally needed survivors serviceable, on the open deck of the carrier in December, placed a severe strain on the servicing crews. On one occasion a Martlet over-ran the arrester wires and smashed into the barrier, buckling its propeller. Lacking a spare, the sailors heated the metal blades with blowlamps, and bent the propeller back into something approximating to its original shape. The Martlet was returned to operations and flew several more sorties. By such means, *Audacity* maintained regular air patrols round the convoy for the next four days. The Martlets forced down shadowing U-boats, and also fought off attempts by reconnaissance aircraft to shadow the convoy.

By dusk on the 21st, however, the U-boats were closing in to deliver their attack. A torpedo struck one of the ships in the centre of the convoy, and then, not long afterwards, *Audacity* herself came under attack from *U-751* (Bigalk). The latter loosed off two salvoes of torpedoes and scored several hits, and *Audacity* sank bows first. On the following morning, 22 December, convoy HG 76 came within range of patrol aircraft based in Britain. *Vizeadmiral* Dönitz had to call off his boats, and the ordeal of HG 76 ended.

During that action, as well as *Audacity*, U-boats sank a destroyer and two merchantmen. Yet in exchange they had lost four of their number. Had the aircraft-carrier not been present, there can be little doubt that the convoy would have suffered far more heavily. The Martlets had had an effect on the U-boats out of proportion to their number, or the ability of their four-machine-gun armament to harm them. In the section of his War Diary describing the action, *Grossadmiral* Dönitz noted:

> The worst feature was the presence of the aircraft-carrier. Small, fast, manoeuvrable aircraft constantly circled the convoy; and boats that did make contact had repeatedly to dive or else withdraw. Also the enemy aircraft prevented any continuous shadowing or homing by our aircraft. The sinking of the aircraft carrier is therefore of great importance . . . in all future convoy actions.

During the final months of 1941, even as *Audacity* had been proving the concept of this type of warship, other vessels were being converted for the purpose. Yet, as we shall observe, several months would elapse before more of these useful craft would be available.

On 7 December 1941, Japanese naval aircraft delivered a massive attack on the US Navy fleet anchorage at Pearl Harbor. Later that day, Japan declared war on the United States and Britain. Four days later Adolf Hitler sided with his new ally and declared war on the United States. Now the conflict was truly global in extent.

The sudden entry of Japan and the USA into the war took *Vizeadmiral* Dönitz and his staff by surprise, yet they recovered quickly. The U-boat commander-in-chief recognised the need to get boats into the western Atlantic as quickly as possible, before the ships plying the various routes could be organised into convoys. He knew his crews were combat hardened and thoroughly proficient in the use of their weapons. It would take time for the US Navy to reach that state – and in the mean time there would be easy pickings to be made.

In mid-January 1942, the first wave of five U-boats arrived off the eastern seaboard of the USA. There they found the American shipping vulnerable beyond the wildest German dreams. At any one time there were more than a hundred ships plying through those waters; but there were no convoys, no organised shipping routes, and few escorting ships or aircraft to hinder the attackers.

The US Navy paid heavily for its disregard of lessons it should have learnt more than twenty years earlier. During the second half of January thirteen ships were sunk, but these grossed out at nearly 100,000 tons. The U-boat crews were offered so many potential targets that they would expend their precious torpedoes only against the larger ones. The risk of retaliation was so slight that often boats would surface, to finish off a damaged ship using gunfire.

One may gain an impression of this sort of war from the log of *Kapitänleutnant* Hardegen's boat, *U-123*. On the evening of 18 January she surfaced off Cape Hatteras in North Carolina and within two hours she had sunk a freighter. The next three ships passed by out of torpedo range, and were followed by a small coaster that the German captain judged not worth attacking. He then noticed that the channel was marked by light buoys, which ships left to port. By following the line of buoys, Hardegen found more targets than he could engage. He sank a second freighter, then observed a line of five brightly lit merchantmen coming from astern. The leading ship, an 8,000 ton tanker, Hardegen engaged with his deck gun and set on fire. He then torpedoed and sank a further freighter, before finishing off the damaged tanker with torpedoes. On his return to France, Hardegen reported:

> It is a pity there were not a couple of large minelaying U-boats with me the other night . . . or ten or twenty submarines instead of just one. I am sure all would have found targets in plenty. Altogether I saw about twenty steamships and a few small tramp steamers, some undarkened, all of them hugging the coast. The buoys and the beacons in the area had dimmed lights; however, they were visible at ranges of between two and three miles.

The British anti-submarine organisation had had its weaknesses in the autumn of 1939; but compared with the state of affairs now prevailing in the western Atlantic it had been a paragon of preparedness. The US Navy entered its fifth week of hostilities against the nation with the most powerful submarine fleet in the world with no centralised organisation responsible for fighting submarines.

In the United States the Army Appropriations Act of 1920 decreed that the Army Air Corps, as it then was, should control land-based aviation. The US Navy would look after sea-based aviation (seaplanes, flying-boats, aircraft based on carriers and also airships). Thus there arose a situation where, in the words of the official US Navy historian:

> The Army Air Force, which controlled almost the entire supply of United States military land-based planes in 1941, did not expect to include anti-submarine warfare among its duties. Army pilots were not trained to fly over water, protect shipping or bomb small moving targets like submarines. And the Navy did not have the planes to fill the role so successfully assumed by the British Coastal Command.

The US Navy possessed few anti-submarine vessels. And, after the transfer of several squadrons to the Pacific, there remained on the east coast only some sixty Catalina and Mariner flying-boats, a single squadron of Hudsons and four blimps.

One way to exert some pressure on the U-boats was to introduce 'Scarecrow' air patrols, similar to those employed earlier off the coast of Great Britain. Characteristically, the world's richest nation turned to the owners of private aircraft for help. Their pilots enrolled in the Civil Air Patrol as an act of patriotism. The pilots received no pay for the work, merely subsistence and a mileage allowance for the patrols flown. Thus an odd assortment of brightly coloured aircraft, ranging in size from twin-engined company machines to small runabouts, began patrolling the shipping lanes close to the east coast.

During the early months of 1942 the US Navy and Army Air Force made strenuous efforts to improve the defences against the U-boats. But the reader has seen that the formation, equipment and training of effective sea and air anti-submarine units are not something that can be accomplished in a few weeks. In April the US Navy belatedly introduced the convoy system off the east coast of the USA. But when the pickings became less there, the U-boats shifted their attack to the Gulf of Mexico and the Caribbean, where ships were still being routed independently.

During this period, U-boat losses off the US coast were minimal: four submarines lost up to the end of May. Two of them fell to air attack – *U-656* (Kroening) and *U-503* (Gericke), both sunk by Hudsons of US Navy Patrol Squadron 82 in March.

Only at the beginning of June did convoys become almost universal in the western Atlantic. With that the U-boats returned to their previous happy hunting grounds in mid-Atlantic, where they were beyond the reach of air patrols.

In February 1942 the Allies suffered two further major reverses in the war against the U-boats, this time on the cryptographic front. First, the German Navy introduced a modification to its version of the Enigma ciphering machine to make it more secure. At a stroke, that rendered the mass of signals to and from U-boats operating in the Atlantic and the Mediterranean unreadable to the cryptographers at Bletchley Park. The rest of the German Navy, the other fighting services and government organisations continued using the older coding system, which meant that information on the U-boat arm was sometimes divulged indirectly. But although those glimpses were often useful, it meant the Royal Navy had nothing like the strong grip on U-boat movements it had had before.

The effect of that blow was compounded by another, which coincidentally occurred within a few days of the first. The *B-Dienst*, the German Navy's cryptographic department, finally succeeded in reconstructing the Royal Navy's Cipher No. 3, which carried the bulk of its communications concerning north Atlantic convoys. For the next several months *Grossadmiral* Dönitz would receive a mass of detailed information on movements of convoys, while his enemy received nothing like that level of high-level Intelligence on the dispositions of his force.

During the early part of 1942 the maritime conflict widened eastwards, too. In June 1941 German troops had invaded the Soviet Union. The British government – and that of the USA, too, when that nation entered the war – committed themselves to providing supplies and equipment for their remote ally.

There were many routes along which war materials could be sent to the Soviet Union, but by far the quickest was that round the northern tip of Norway and on to the ports at Murmansk and Archangel. This meant that the merchant ships had to sail far beyond the cover of the Coastal Command aircraft based in Great Britain. Moreover, as well as the U-boat threat, the ships would come within range of the German torpedo- and dive-bomber units based in Norway.

In spite of the dangers, the first convoys to sail the Arctic route did so with deceptively little reaction from the German Navy or the *Luftwaffe*. In the spring of 1942, however, losses began to mount. The convoy that made the passage at the end of March, PQ 15, lost five ships out of twenty. The May convoy, PQ 16, lost eight out of the thirty-five. The next convoy, whose tattered remnant arrived early in July, was the most disastrous of them all: PQ 17 lost twenty-three out of the original thirty-seven merchant ships to attacks from U-boats and aircraft.

From the beginning of July 1941 to the end of June 1942, U-boats had sunk more than three and a half million tons of Allied merchant shipping. Of this, some three million tons had been lost during the first six months of 1942, most of it off the coast of America. During the same period the Allies destroyed fifty-five German and Italian submarines. Of these, eleven had been sunk (and one captured) by aircraft operating alone, and three by aircraft co-operating with warships.

It was a hard fight, and the Allies were getting the worst of it. Well might a German news broadcaster gloatingly comment early in July, as details of the PQ 17 convoy action were announced:

> Great things, which you cannot always see or hear, are happening all the time. Do you hear the striking of this gong? It strikes every second. Now imagine that you are on a floating raft on the sea, on a sort of little island. A ton of goods sinks at every stroke of the gong. Wool, cotton, bacon, grain, innumerable tons of oil, other fuel, sugar, ammunition, canned goods, spare parts for aircraft – every second another ton drops to the bottom of the sea. This gong, the striking of which may begin to get on your nerves, goes on and on. Think of it when you wake up tonight. It means that during every one of these seconds a ton of goods has been sunk. As has been announced, our U-boats and the *Luftwaffe* have sunk another 156 ships totalling 866,000 gross registered tons.

Meanwhile, on the Allied side, a series of new anti-submarine measures were about to enter service. 'Great things' were indeed happening, but not all of them were going to be to the taste of the U-boat service.

CHAPTER 5

The Crow Begins to Peck

June 1942 to January 1943

The aeroplane can no more eliminate the submarine than the crow can fight a mole.

Grossadmiral Karl Dönitz, August 1942

Throughout the first half of 1942, as the US Navy had striven to erect a defence against marauding U-boats off the US east coast, its British allies intensified the air patrols over the northern and Biscay transit routes used by the boats. Yet we have seen that the submarines avoided the worst attentions of the patrolling aircraft by surfacing only at night, and moving submerged by the day. Since Humphrey Leigh's searchlight was not yet in service to illuminate U-boats for attack, the twin-engined aircraft of Coastal Command could not emulate the successful night attacks made by the nimble Fleet Air Arm Swordfish biplanes over the Straits of Gibraltar.

The immunity to night attack in the Bay of Biscay was not to last much longer, however. By the beginning of June, No. 172 Squadron of the RAF had five Leigh Light Wellingtons ready for action, and crews trained in the difficult and precise flying necessary to use the system.

The early hours of 4 June 1942 saw the 1,076 ton Italian submarine *Luigi Torelli* rumbling on the surface, in the south-western corner of the Bay of Biscay. The boat had set out from La Pallice on the previous day, and was heading west towards her patrol area off Puerto Rico. There was no moon and the night was very dark. Suddenly the men on watch in the conning tower were horrified to find themselves in the glare of a brilliant white light, which seemed to be coming from an aircraft heading in their direction. There was no time to dive, so the officer of the watch ordered the helm put hard to port to escape the attack, which could not be long in coming. Then, some twenty seconds later and before anything else happened, the light went out.

The light had indeed come from an aircraft, a Wellington of No. 172 Squadron flown by Squadron Leader Jeaff Greswell. The Leigh Light was being used in action for the first time. The plane's radar operator had picked up the boat on ASV at a range of just over six miles, and he guided the aircraft up to the contact. With the Leigh Light lowered into position below the fuselage, Greswell brought the Wellington down gradually until his altimeter read 250 feet. When range countdown from the radar operator reached one mile, Pilot Officer Triggs in the nose had switched on the light. As he had done so many times during the training runs, Triggs twisted the control handle to bring the light beam slowly up to the target. The beam rose higher and higher, and he saw . . . nothing.

Triggs brought the beam down again and then, after some searching, he and Greswell glimpsed a submarine disappearing under the port wing. By then the Wellington was too close to the boat to attack it on that run, so Triggs turned off the light. From bitter experience, Greswell knew the enemy boat would now have plenty of time to submerge before he could make a second attack run.

The view of the submarine had been fleeting, but it was enough to show why the attack had failed: the Wellington had been too high. The 250 foot altitude for the Leigh Light attack was critical, but when the light had come on the aircraft had been at least 100 feet higher than that. Thus when Triggs aimed the light at a point that should have been below the target, the beam was already pointing above it. When he then raised the beam, that made matters worse. Greswell knew that he had brought the Wellington down precisely to 250 feet indicated on the pressure altimeter. Clearly the altimeter reading had been too high – and the reason was not difficult to fathom. It was dark outside the aircraft, and Greswell had no way of accurately measuring the sea-level pressure over the Bay of Biscay. In fact the forecast pressure given to him prior to take-off had been in error by about 3 millibars, corresponding to 100 feet. As he climbed away, Greswell swiftly reset his altimeter.

In the meantime, the conning tower of *Luigi Torelli* became the scene of an animated discussion. To the sailors it seemed that the light must have come from a friendly aircraft. What else could explain why there had been no attack? To make sure, they fired the recognition colours for the day.

As he swung the Wellington through a semicircle to line up for a further attack run, Greswell was amazed to see red, green and white fireballs sailing up into the sky. Now the intercom in the RAF aircraft became alive, with an argument closely paralleling that in the submarine. Might it be a British submarine? Then Greswell remembered: British submarines did not fire recognition flares into the air, they burnt coloured candles on the surface. The discussion was closed, they would attack again.

The boat's fireworks gave Greswell a precise heading on which to bring his aircraft, and before the glow of the flares died away the radar operator had regained contact. Again the Wellington closed in and, again at an indicated altitude of 250 feet and at a range of just under a mile, Triggs switched on the light a second time. He then brought the beam slowly up in the normal way and there, exactly where it should have been, lay the submarine. Greswell heard a call, 'Target ahead', and began his attack. Pilot Officer Pooley, manning the nose gun, opened fire and watched a stream of tracer bullets climb up the boat to the conning tower. Greswell brought the aircraft down to 60 feet, and when nearly overhead the boat, he released his four 250 pound depth-charges at intervals of 35 feet.

It was a good straddle. The depth-charges went off almost underneath *Luigi Torelli*, and she suffered badly: her gyrocompass was smashed and her steering gear damaged. Moreover, the batteries had received a severe shaking, which caused a small fire. To prevent an explosion, the ammunition magazine had to be flooded. Clearly the boat was in no fit state to continue her war cruise, and her commander, *Tenente di Vascello* Augusto Migliorini, decided to head for the nearest friendly haven, the little French port of St Jean de Luz in the extreme south-eastern corner of the Bay.

The early morning of 5 June saw the shaken Italian submarine making her way back to France at 15 knots, running eastward and about six miles away from, and parallel to, the north coast of Spain. There was patchy coastal fog in the area, and the partially inoperative compass system failed to indicate that the boat's bow had swung round a little too far to starboard. Suddenly Migliorini was horrified to see the rocky Spanish shore of Cape Penas emerge from the mist just over a hundred yards in front of his bow. He shouted for full speed astern on the diesel motors, but to no avail: *Luigi Torelli* continued on and her hull crunched upon the rocks.

It took a couple of tugs to free the battered submarine, and tow her into the small Spanish port at Aviles. There the authorities made the position clear: under international law a combatant warship was allowed to remain in a neutral port for only twenty-four hours, after which she was liable for internment. If *Luigi Torelli* was not clear of Spanish territory by midnight on 6 June, she would not be allowed to leave at all.

So it was that late that night *Luigi Torelli* limped out of Aviles at a sedate four knots. Once clear of the port she turned eastwards and, with great care, followed the line of the coast just outside the three-mile limit.

At almost exactly the same time as the submarine set course, Pilot Officer Egerton of No. 10 Squadron Royal Australian Air Force lifted his Sunderland flying-boat off the water at his base at Mountbatten in Devonshire. His orders were to carry out an anti-submarine and anti-shipping patrol down the length of the Bay of Biscay, as far as the Spanish coast.

On the morning of the 7th the flying-boat was nearing the Spanish coast, flying at 1,800 feet, when one of the crew spotted the *Luigi Torelli* five miles away and to starboard. Egerton ran in to attack. But as the range closed the submarine's gunners engaged the plane with their 100 mm deck gun and 13 mm machine-guns, causing minor damage to the flying-boat and wounding two of her crew. Despite this, Egerton pressed home the attack, and his stick of eight 250 pound depth-charges fell across the wounded boat. Again *Luigi Torelli* disappeared in a cloud of spray, but when this cleared she remained on the surface, though her steering gear had suffered damage.

Still the luckless submarine's ordeal was not yet over. Even as Egerton climbed away after delivering his attack, another Sunderland arrived in the area from the same squadron. With Flight Lieutenant Yeoman at the controls, the fresh aircraft orbited the boat before running in to attack. And again *Luigi Torelli*'s gunners struck the first blow: they opened fire on the Sunderland and caused damage to her tail. Angered by this show of aggressiveness, Yeoman continued his attack. During the run in there was a further exchange of fire, and the tail of the flying-boat suffered further damage. Then Yeoman put down his stick of eight depth-charges close to the submarine, and the explosions appeared to lift her almost clear of the water. There was a bright flash and some black smoke, and from Egerton's aircraft it appeared that Yeoman's Sunderland had been hit. But not so – the flash had come from *Luigi Torelli*.

The two Sunderlands, both damaged and with their depth-charges expended, now broke off the action and headed back for Mountbatten. They left behind them a very sorry *Luigi Torelli*, drifting on the surface with her diesel motors stopped. After a quarter of an hour her engine room staff succeeded in getting the diesel motors running again, and the battered craft set off for the Spanish port of Santander. By now she had developed a heavy list, and it was necessary to line up her crew on deck on the high side in an effort to counter this. In this condition the submarine reached port and her commander ran her onto a sandbank near the main pier. This time there could be no question of the unseaworthy *Luigi Torelli* leaving neutral territory, and on the following day Spanish officials declared her to be interned.

That would not be the end of the *Luigi Torelli* saga, however. After temporary repairs in the outer harbour at Santander, just over a month later, the Italian crew was ordered to man the boat when she was towed into the inner basin for more permanent repairs, prior to her handover to the Spanish Navy. Halfway across the harbour one of the submarine's motors was started, and a sailor ran down the deck and cast off the line to the tug. *Luigi Torelli* then made a dash for freedom, taking with her the pilot of the port of Santander and a senior Spanish naval officer. Once in open water, the unwilling passengers were told that unless they cared to go to Bordeaux they should board one of the boats fishing nearby. Under voluble protest, the Spaniards complied. The submarine reached the French port without further problems. (Even that did not end *Luigi Torelli*'s adventures. A year later she sailed to the Far East, to deliver examples of German military equipment and key personnel to the Japanese. The boat was at Singapore when Italy surrendered, and was handed to the German Navy, becoming the *UIT-25*. She was still there when Germany surrendered in May 1945, and the Japanese Navy commissioned her as the *RO-604*. When Japan capitulated, the submarine fell into US hands; her sixth and final owner scuttled her in 1946.)

Although the depth-charges carried by RAF aircraft were now fitted with hydrostatic pistols designed to detonate them at a depth of 25 feet, it still seemed that too many were exploding some way beneath that. Therefore they failed to inflict lethal damage on surfaced submarines – as had been the case with the *Luigi Torelli*. Tank tests revealed that the air-dropped depth-charges hit the water hard and sank rapidly. As they plunged they dragged down with them a large bubble of air, which slowed the entry of water into the hydrostatic pistol and thus delayed firing.

The answer was to fit these weapons with a different nose, shaped concave instead of convex, and a specially weakened tail that broke off on impact with the water. These changes caused the depth-charges to sink broadside on and much slower than previously. The redesigned depth-charges with the 'genuine twenty-five foot setting' would take a few months to come into general service, and during this time other submarines survived attacks that would otherwise have been lethal.

Following Greswell's unsuccessful first attack run on the *Luigi Torelli*, No. 172 Squadron's Wellingtons were hastily equipped with radio altimeters. This device measured altitude by radio means, making it possible to fly the accurate altitude run-in necessary for attacks using the Leigh Light.

Just over a month after the attack on *Luigi Torelli*, Pilot Officer W. Howell – an American who had joined the RAF before his country entered the war – made the first U-boat kill using the Leigh Light. Early on the morning of 5 July his radar operator observed a contact to starboard, and Howell followed the directions towards it. At a one-mile range the searchlight was switched on, to illuminate a U-boat on the surface heading east. The Wellington's depth-charges straddled the boat, and when the spray had settled a dark patch of oil began to spread across the sea. That marked the end of *U-502* (Rosentiel), returning from a successful foray in the Caribbean.

Eight days later, on 12 July, Howell caught another U-boat, *U-159*, also returning from the Caribbean. When the searchlight came on, *Kapitänleutnant* Witte ordered his gunners to try to shoot it out. But in the dazzling glare of the beam the sailors were unable to score hits. The stick of four depth-charges shook the submarine badly and fractured several battery cells. Witte dived the boat to safety and regained his base, but the subsequent repairs kept her out of action until the following October.

Initially only five searchlight-fitted Wellingtons were available for operations. But their eleven sightings and six attacks during June and July 1942 had an effect on the U-boat service that went far beyond the one submarine sunk and two damaged that resulted. The immunity enjoyed by U-boat crews traversing the Bay of Biscay on the surface at night had gone; instead, they were now liable to sudden air attack without warning. German sailors soon coined their own name for the Leigh Light: *das verdammte Licht* – that damned light.

[The after-attack] interrogation should take the form of a round-table discussion and the whole attack thrashed out in the light of the evidence of the various members of the crew and of the photographs. Any unusual incidents should be given special care and the most accurate description possible obtained of any oil or bubbles, wreckage or any other after-effects which may be seen after the attack . . .

Coastal Command Booklet
Submarine and Anti-Submarine, 1942

Grossadmiral Dönitz had no way of knowing that only five aircraft were involved in the night attacks, and in retrospect it is clear that he overreacted to the initial reports he received. On 16 July he ordered a reversal of the previous procedure for crossing the Bay of Biscay, running submerged during the day and on the surface at night:

Because the danger of attacks without warning from radar-equipped aircraft is greater by night than by day, in future U-boats are to surface by day . . .

That change of tactics gave the daylight air patrols over the Bay of Biscay a chance they had never had before: compared with only fourteen U-boats sighted in June and sixteen in July, after Dönitz's order came into force there were thirty-four sightings in August and thirty-seven in September. Still not many submarines were being sunk in the Bay: between the beginning of June and the end of September there were only four sinkings. Yet even that was an improvement, for during the previous five months there had been none.

Towards the end of September, however, the rate of U-boat sightings in the Bay of Biscay started to fall: the submariners had introduced an effective counter to the night attackers. The German Navy had known about the British ASV radar for a long time – in 1941 German engineers had fitted a captured ASV set into a Focke-Wulf Kondor aircraft and conducted flight trials with it. Yet until the Leigh Light attacks began, the device had not been considered to pose a serious threat to U-boats. Now all that had changed, and Dönitz pressed for a suitable counter-measure.

The answer was a simple radio receiver that would detect the ASV transmissions from patrolling aircraft. In the U-boat's radio room, the wireless operator heard the radar transmissions as a buzz in his earphones. Thus warned of the approach of the aircraft, the boat could dive to safety before an attack could develop. Early in August 1942 the first three such receivers underwent sea trials on U-boats. Until a permanently mounted pressure-tight aerial system could be developed, German naval signals experts devised a simple wood-framed aerial that was clipped on the conning tower. A cable ran through the open conning tower hatch to the radio room, and before the boat dived a sailor had to unclip the aerial and take it and the cable below.

U-boat crews commented favourably on the new receiver. It picked up radar signals in the band 113–500 MHz, and thus covered ASV transmissions between 176 and 220 MHz. The device picked up transmissions from aircraft more than thirty miles away – much further than the ASV operator could detect a submarine. *Grossadmiral* Dönitz ordered that all operational boats be fitted with the new listening receiver, with the utmost urgency.

By the middle of 1942 the German radio industry was heavily committed to supplying the needs of the nation's armed services. There was no spare capacity to meet the rush order from the Navy. As a result, two French firms, Metox and Grandin, both located in the Paris area, were ordered to produce the receiver in quantity. The set was designated the R 600A, but more usually it was called 'the Metox'. In introducing the new receiver the emphasis was on speed of production, quantity and simplicity; there was no time for refinements.

By mid-September 1942 several U-boats had been fitted with Metox receivers, and those with the device acted as escorts for those without it when crossing the dangerous Bay of Biscay area. By the end of the year nearly all boats carried the receiver. Because of its cross-shaped wooden frame, the Metox aerial was known affectionately to U-boat crews as the *Biskayakreuz* – the Biscay cross. It meant that, once again, the boats enjoyed near-immunity from air attack as they traversed the Bay on the surface at night.

During September 1942 there were only two night sightings of U-boats by aircraft over the Bay of Biscay, and in October only one. Adolf Hitler was delighted to hear of the success of the Metox, as *Luftwaffe Generalfeldmarschall* Milch recounted at the time:

> The Führer has told me that since they have had the equip-ment in the U-boats the Navy hasn't lost a single boat in the Bay of Biscay, whereas before they lost several. They were located without knowing it, and then the enemy set about them. But now the submarine commander knows 'Aha, now somebody has ideas about me'—just in the same way as a young lady notices when a man is looking at her.

Nor was this the only measure taken to assist U-boats crossing the Bay of Biscay. In September 1942 the *Luftwaffe* began sending long-range fighters to mount patrols by day over the Bay, as Dönitz, now a full *Admiral,* had requested. The unit involved, the Fifth *Gruppe* of *Kampfgeschwader 40*, flew some thirty Junkers 88C fighters, based at Kerlin Bastard near Lorient and Merignac near Bordeaux. Within a short time the Ju 88s had began to make their presence felt over the U-boat transit areas, and when they came upon the lumbering anti-submarine aircraft they usually made short work of them.

The RAF's answer to the new threat was predictable: long-range Beaufighters, and later, Mosquitoes, moved to bases in Cornwall, and they too began patrols over the Bay of Biscay. Initially the fighters patrolled in pairs, but gradually each side increased the size of its formations until they hunted in packs of as many as eight. When the two sides met, a running battle often ensued.

Towards the end of 1941 Coastal Command had gained a powerful addition, in the shape of No. 120 Squadron, which had recently formed with the four-engined American B-24 Liberators. These aircraft had been specially modified for the long-range anti-submarine role, with the installation of ASV radar and their fuel capacity increased to 2,500 gallons. With that amount of fuel these aircraft could spend up to three hours on patrol in an area 1,100 miles from base; its maximum endurance was about sixteen hours. The aircraft carried an armament of four 20 mm cannon firing forwards from a tray under the fuselage, six movable 303-in machine-guns and, typically, six 250 pound depth-charges. The aircraft were from an early production batch and had their share of teething troubles, but by the middle of 1942 many of these had been cured.

The shift of the main U-boat effort back to mid-Atlantic in the summer of 1942 gave added importance to No. 120 Squadron, whose Liberators were then the only aircraft able to reach into the area from land bases. And this period also saw the star of the top-scoring RAF anti-submarine pilot – Squadron Leader Terrence Bulloch – in the ascendant.

An Ulsterman, Bulloch had flown Ansons and Hudsons on anti-submarine operations earlier in the war. He then moved to No. 120 Squadron when it formed with Liberators. There can be no doubting his skill as a pilot: by the end of July 1942 he had logged 2,300 flying hours and was officially assessed as 'Exceptional' as a pilot and 'Above the Average' as a navigator. Such qualities, though admirable, did not of themselves guarantee success as a U-boat hunter. In Bulloch's case, however, they combined with three others. Firstly, he had exceptionally keen eyesight. Secondly, he was intensely interested in new gadgetry, and strove to get the utmost out of his equipment. And thirdly, and perhaps most important of all, the loss of a brother killed in action had left him with a burning hatred and a thirst for revenge.

Bulloch's enthusiasm for hunting submarines was a rare phenomenon, for most crews regarded it as the most boring type of flying imaginable. The Ulster pilot appreciated that crew co-operation was the key to success, and he set about welding those who flew with him into a well-knit team. Results were not long in coming. Bulloch and his crew had made their first attack on a submarine in October 1941, and by the second week in August 1942 they had made seven sightings and converted three of these into attacks. Considering that many Coastal Command crews flew an entire tour of duty at this time without getting a glimpse of a submarine, those figures are remarkable. Bulloch's emphasis on search technique, both visual and radar, was paying off handsomely. And, of course, each success gave crew morale a powerful boost.

On 16 August 1942, while operating in support of a convoy off the Azores, Bulloch's depth-charges straddled *U-89* (Lohmann) as it was returning from patrol off the east coast of the USA. The boat suffered damage, but once again the lack of a proper shallow-setting depth-charge saved her. Two days later Bulloch repeated the performance against *U-653*, as she attempted to engage a convoy in the same area. The boat was damaged so seriously that *Kapitänleutnant* Feiler had to break off the action and return to his base.

Still a 'kill' eluded Bulloch and his crew, but now the modified depth-charges with the 'genuine twenty-five foot setting' were becoming available. Given the opportunities the crew had had before, that 'kill' could not be long in coming. In any case, Bulloch was not going to take any chances. At this time it was the practice for Coastal Command crews to attack submarines at an oblique angle across their length. That gave the best chance of inflicting damage, although it inevitably meant that at least half the depth-charges fell beyond lethal range from the target and so were wasted. Bulloch now decided to attack the next submarine he met along its length. He also reduced the spacing between his depth-charges to 25 feet – the minimum possible – so that every one would achieve maximum effect. Those settings demanded a skilful pilot if they were to succeed, for they allowed very little margin for error.

Mid-day on 12 October found Bulloch and his crew operating from Iceland, flying close escort for Convoy ONS 136 as it passed to the south-west of their base. It was then that one of the crew sighted the wake of an unidentified craft some eight miles away to starboard. Bulloch curved round after it, and closed on the vessel from out of the sun. As he straightened out and began his attack run, he caught sight of the wake of a submarine. He lined up on the U-boat and attacked almost exactly along her length. As the craft disappeared under the aircraft nose, Bulloch let go of his depth-charges in a closely spaced stick. Two depth-charges failed to leave the bomb bay, but the remaining six splashed into the water with great precision. One depth-charge exploded near the stem, two went off on each side of the hull, and the sixth exploded next to the bow. Pieces of metal from the boat flew high into the air, and one chunk narrowly missed the Liberator's rear turret. Her pressure hull ruptured in several places, *U-597* (Bopst) broke up and sank.

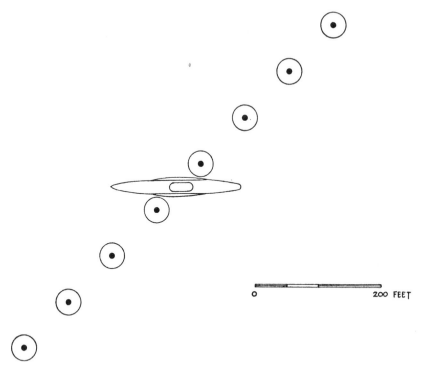

The normal method of attacking a submarine uses a stick of eight depth-
charges released at 100-foot intervals; there is a good chance that at least one
and possibly two of the depth-charges will detonate within lethal range of the
target. The large circles represent the 26-foot effective radius of the 250 pound
depth-charge.

During the next three weeks Bulloch and his crew sighted four
more U-boats, and attacked two of them without inflicting lethal
damage.

Then, on 5 November, the crew was sent to the support of
Convoy SC 107. On the previous day this convoy had come under
concerted attack from the thirteen-boat *Veilchen* group. It suffered
a fearful mauling, losing fifteen ships totalling 88,000 tons. The
first U-boat Bulloch's crew sighted dived before it could be
attacked. But the lookouts on the next boat seen, *U-132*
(Vogelsang) were less vigilant. Bulloch made one of his deadly
attacks down the length of the boat, from bow to stern, and that
was the end of her. Later in the day he sighted another U-boat, and
attacked her with his two remaining depth-charges shortly after she
submerged. The boat escaped unscathed.

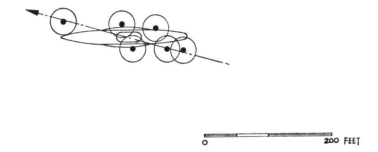

Bulloch's closely spaced stick of depth-charges explode round *U-597* (taken from the after-attack report and based on photographic evidence). Two out of the intended stick of eight depth-charges failed to leave the aircraft, but any one out of the other six would probably have sufficed to destroy the U-boat.

During the following month, December 1942, Bulloch and his crew provided a dramatic example of the effect a single well-handled aircraft could have in nullifying the German 'Wolf Pack' tactics. On the 7th *Admiral* Dönitz ordered the *Draufgänger* and *Panzer* groups, totalling more than twenty boats, into action against the eastbound Atlantic convoy HX 217 moving through the 'Atlantic Gap'. The convoy comprised twenty-five ships with five escorts. A shadowing U-boat was maintaining contact with the convoy, while the remaining boats moved into position to attack before dawn on the following day.

During the early morning darkness of 8 December the first U-boats made contact with the convoy, and torpedoed and sank a merchantman. Shortly afterwards Terrence Bulloch arrived on the scene to provide close escort. He later recalled:

We arrived over the convoy just as it was beginning to get light. We knew that there were U-boats around, and we were keeping our eyes skinned. The visibility wasn't too good. There was a sort of half-light, and the hailstorm didn't improve things. I started my patrol by making a wide sweep round the convoy and almost at once we struck lucky. Astern of the ships and on the Liberator's port beam I spotted a submarine travelling fast on the surface. It was going all out to catch the convoy.

Bulloch attacked the boat with six of his eight depth-charges, but it had a lucky escape. Just over an hour later Bulloch sighted two

U-boats about 300 yards apart, both heading at high speed towards the convoy twenty miles away. He attacked one of the boats with his two remaining depth-charges, but the submarine had submerged when the Liberator released its weapons and there was no evidence of damage. The other U-boat also dived.

Although the Liberator's depth-charges were now expended, Bulloch had plenty of fuel left and he continued with the patrol. The crew settled to their routine tasks, while one of the gunners cooked a lunch of steak and potatoes on the galley stove. Then, in Bulloch's words:

> I was sitting in the cockpit with a plate on my knee, with 'George' [the automatic pilot] in charge. I was going to enjoy that steak, but another U-boat popped up. The plate with its steak and potatoes went spinning off my knee as I grabbed the controls and sounded the alarm, and there was a clatter of plates back in the aircraft as the rest of the crew jumped to it, forgetting how hungry they were.

Bulloch dived on the submarine and strafed it with cannon fire; it dived to safety. Then followed a period during which, he recounted:

> . . . the submarines kept bobbing up all over the place. We'd no sooner finished one attack and got all the details logged than another would show up.

Twenty-three minutes after the 'lunchtime' attack Bulloch made another, thirty-five minutes after that another, fifty-four minutes after that another, and twenty-four minutes after that yet another; on each occasion he strafed the boats with his cannon and forced them to dive. In a space of just over five and a quarter hours he made eight sightings, seven of which he converted into attacks. After seven and a quarter hours with the convoy the Liberator reached its prudent limit of endurance and the crew set course for Iceland. They reached Reykjavik after having been airborne for 16 hours 25 minutes.

As Bulloch left HX 217, another Liberator from the same squadron took over the close escort task. Squadron Leader Desmond Isted and his crew sighted five U-boats and attacked four of them.

Together, Bulloch and Isted had made thirteen sightings of

U-boats, and attacked eleven of them. Although they failed to secure a 'kill', in their primary task of safeguarding the convoy the two Liberator crews had been brilliantly successful. They had broken up what would otherwise have been an overwhelming attack on HX 217. In the words of the U-boat War Diary account of the engagement:

> Following an analysis of this action, Flag Officer U-boats stated that the results were poor due to the strength of the escort . . .

Certainly it had seemed to the U-boat crews that many more than two aircraft had been hounding them that day.

> Following the action around convoy HX 217, Bulloch left No. 120 Squadron for a rest tour: during his year and a half with the unit he had sighted U-boats on twenty-three occasions and delivered sixteen attacks. He had sunk two U-boats and inflicted damage on two more. And he had not finished yet.

During the final months of 1942, there were also some noteworthy attacks on U-boats off the north coast of Africa. On the evening of 7 November British and US troops landed in French Morocco and Algeria. The German Navy's reaction to the landings was characteristically vigorous: fifteen U-boats headed immediately for the Moroccan coast and were joined shortly afterwards by others that had been engaged in anti-convoy operations in the Atlantic. While it was too late to interfere with the initial landings, if U-boats could get at the ships carrying reinforcements they could do considerable damage. By the time the main body of U-boats reached the operational area on 11 November, however, the Allied defences were ready for them. Of more than a hundred ships off the coast of Morocco, the U-boats were able to sink only three, and that was at a cost of two of their number.

Meanwhile, a force of seven U-boats passed through the Straits of Gibraltar unscathed. That brought the number of boats in the Mediterranean to twenty-five, the highest ever. In addition, ten Italian boats put out from Cagliari and headed for the invasion area.

In the series of actions that followed, the RAF maritime patrol squadrons in the western Mediterranean were heavily committed:

No. 179 with Leigh Light Wellingtons, Nos 48, 233 and 500 with Hudsons, and Nos 202 and 210 Squadrons with Sunderland and Catalina flying-boats respectively. Initially these units operated from Gibraltar, but after the capture of airfields in French North Africa some of the squadrons moved there.

On the morning of 14 November the commander of No. 500 Squadron, Wing Commander Denis Spotswood, caught *U-595* on the surface to the north of Oran. The exploding depth-charges lifted the U-boat, then she settled in a cloud of spray. The Hudson made two firing runs on the wallowing submarine, but during the second of these *Kapitänleutnant* Quaet-Faslem's gunners replied in kind: their bullets punctured one of the aircraft's fuel tanks and severed the aileron control runs, with the result that the crew had to break off the action. By then, however, other Hudsons from the same unit were converging on the scene. Flying Officer Green and Pilot Officer Simpson arrived almost simultaneously. Green attacked first, and went down to 30 feet to place his depth-charges close to the bow of the U-boat. Again the boat's gunners fought back defiantly and scored several hits: they riddled the fuselage with holes, knocked out the gun turret and set fire to the signal cartridge locker. Almost blinded by smoke, Green was forced to break off the action. Then Simpson, and Flying Officer Lord in yet another Hudson of No. 500 Squadron, delivered their attacks, the latter's aircraft suffering extensive damage from return fire. Although *U-595* was damaged and unable to dive, she was still far from subdued. After an hour's respite Squadron Leader Mike Ensor, also flying a Hudson of No. 500 Squadron, regained contact with the submarine. He braved the defensive fire and put down his depth-charges accurately alongside her hull. For the already crippled *U-595*, that was the last straw. Quaet-Faslem ordered his men to destroy the U-boat's secret equipment and throw her documents overboard, then he ran her aground on the north coast of Africa; soon afterwards American troops took the survivors prisoner.

The action round *U-595* illustrated yet again the resilience of the submarine as a target, especially if it was on the surface at the time of the attack. Quaet-Faslem's ability to fight back against aircraft was due in no small measure to his own extensive flying experience – earlier he had piloted one of the floatplanes aboard the battle-cruiser *Scharnhorst*. During this action he had handled his boat with great skill, and his gunners had inflicted serious damage on three of the attackers.

On the following day Ensor was in action again: he surprised a U-boat on the surface, dived to attack her and placed his depth-charges accurately across her. Precisely what happened next will never be known with certainty, for the boat, *U-269* (Koepke), exploded with great violence. Possibly the shock from one of the exploding depth-charges had detonated the warhead of one or more of the torpedoes.

The blast from the explosion wrecked Ensor's aircraft, too. It blew in the cockpit floor and most of the windows, uprooted much equipment, tore off the elevators and rudders and bent the final few feet of each wing tip vertically upwards. By rights the broken bomber should have spun into the sea there and then. Almost certainly it would have done so, had Ensor not regained control in masterly fashion: he steered the aircraft by making differential throttle settings on the engines, and achieved fore-and-aft trim by using his crew as 'movable ballast' walking up or down the fuselage. By these means Ensor climbed the crumpled Hudson to a safe altitude and headed for base. To get the Hudson to climb he had to close the engine cooling gills, however, and that finally brought an end to the precarious flight. One of the engines over-heated and spluttered to a stop. Without rudders to hold it straight, the aircraft banked out of control. Ensor ordered his crew to bail out, and he followed. In spite of everything, by a savage twist of irony two of his crew were then killed. The parachute of one failed to open; the other hit the fuselage as he fell clear and was knocked unconscious, and subsequently drowned. Ensor and the fourth man parachuted into the sea without injury and were picked up soon afterwards. For a display of airmanship and cool-headedness that can have few equals in the history of flying, Squadron Leader Michael Ensor later received the DSO.

No. 500 Squadron's run of successes continued. Two days later, on 17 November, Squadron Leader Patterson sighted *U-331* running on the surface. Commanding the boat was *Kapitänleutnant* Baron Hans-Diedrich von Tiesenhausen, who earlier had been awarded the Knight's Cross for penetrating a destroyer screen and sinking the Royal Navy battleship *Barham*. Now the submarine's successful career was fast drawing to a close, for the young and inexperienced lookout on her starboard quarter failed to notice the approaching aircraft until it was too late. Only when Patterson was well into his bombing run did *U-331* begin her dive, and her conning tower was still visible when the stick of depth-charges exploded across her.

What Patterson later termed 'a good straddle' reduced an
efficient fighting submarine to a hulk within a fraction of a second.
The boat's batteries received a severe shaking and one of the diesel
motors was almost wrenched from its mounting. But it was the
third wound that very nearly spelt disaster for *U-331*, immediate
and complete: the shock blew out the boat's forward hatch and
jammed it in the open position. By then the foredeck was under
water, and a torrent poured into the craft. Von Tiesenhausen had
not gained his reputation for nothing, however. Taking stock of the
situation, he abandoned the dive, and ordered the forward
compartment to be abandoned and sealed. The German
commander's quick thinking had saved his boat, but the reprieve
was only temporary.

Already other Hudsons of No. 500 Squadron were converging
on the scene from all directions. The next to attack, piloted by
Flight Lieutenant Barwood, wrecked the submarine's depth
gauges and compasses and smashed her steering gear. Von
Tiesenhausen ordered all the crew, except for those necessary for
the immediate running of the boat, on deck in case it became
necessary to abandon the craft. Many of them were blown overboard shortly afterwards when Squadron Leader Young made his
attack. In between the attacks with depth-charges, the angry
Hudsons strafed the boat with their machine-guns. For von
Tiesenhausen there was no way out. He had done all mortal man
could to save his boat; now his duty was to his crew. Reluctantly
he ordered the white flag run up above the conning tower.

The triumphant Hudson crews proudly orbited their prize,
mightily pleased with their success. Already the destroyer *Wilton*
was speeding to the scene to consolidate the capture. That elation
only served to increase the crews' feelings of disappointment at
what followed, however. A lone Albacore torpedo-bomber from
the aircraft carrier *Formidable* suddenly appeared on the scene,
made a beeline for the U-boat – and torpedoed and sank her. The
survivors, who included the German commander, were rescued
shortly afterwards.

While Allied aircraft intensified their battle against the
U-boats, scientists in Great Britain and the USA had been hard at
work developing an assortment of new devices to assist in their
detection and destruction. Throughout 1942 the new centimetric-
wavelength ASV radar, the Mark III, had continued to improve in
both reliability and performance. During trials it demonstrated

that it could detect large convoys at a range of forty miles, and submarines on the surface at twelve miles. In the USA, too, work was well advanced on a similar radar for this purpose.

As we observed earlier, the German Metox warning receiver had, to a large extent, neutralised the metric-wavelength ASV Mark II. This gave the new centimetric-wavelength radars an even greater importance, for these operated in a part of the frequency spectrum far outside the coverage of Metox. If the new radars could be kept secret, they offered the chance of inflicting a great victory over U-boats crossing the Bay of Biscay. Air Chief Marshal Joubert made strong demands to get the new radar fitted into his aircraft; but the radar's progress, although rapid by modern peacetime standards, proved infuriatingly slow at the time.

By the autumn of 1942 US scientists were well advanced with their work on a quite different device for locating submarines from the air: the magnetic airborne detector (MAD). Before the war mineralogists had used sensitive magnetic detection devices, magnetometers, to plot distortions in the earth's magnetic field to locate underground mineral deposits. But these devices, though sensitive enough for mineral exploration, could not readily detect a small object like a submarine.

The breakthrough in magnetic detection from the air came late in 1940, with the work of Victor Vacquier of the Gulf Research and Development Company in the USA. Vacquier produced a new type of magnetometer that was between two and three times more sensitive than the previous types, for use in mineral prospecting. Yet that intention was soon overshadowed by its potential for detecting submarines: unlike radio waves, magnetic fields are unaffected by their passage through the air/sea interface. Early in 1941, the US National Defense Research Committee assumed sponsorship of the device.

Even with Vacquier's sensitive magnetometer, however, the detection of a submarine from the air presented a difficult practical problem: the device measured the minute distortion caused to the earth's magnetic field by the presence of a small ferrous metallic object – a submarine. The strength of the earth's magnetic field varies with latitude, but typically is about 50,000 gammas. The distortion of that magnetic field by a typical World War II submarine was of the order of 10 gammas at a distance of 400 feet from the measuring system. That field strength decreased rapidly with distance, so that 800 feet away it was only 1.25 gammas. Yet another problem was caused by the interference caused by ferrous

metals in the aircraft itself; though this could be reduced to acceptable level by fitting the magnetic detector in the extreme tail or a
wing tip, and by replacing ferrous metallic components in the
vicinity with non-ferrous ones.

Even if all worked well, the short range of the MAD device
meant the aircraft had to fly at an altitude of about 100 feet, and
pass directly over the boat, if it was to locate a submarine at a depth
of 300 feet. Early in 1942 two US firms, Western Electric and the
Airborne Instruments Laboratory, began work on an operational
magnetic submarine detection equipment for aircraft. During that
spring the first trial sets took the air in US Navy patrol aircraft and
airships. Later in the year the device entered service in units
patrolling the eastern seaboard of the USA.

The range of the MAD detector was so short that the operator
obtained an indication of the submarine only when he was almost
immediately over the boat. Yet if he released depth-charges then,
the weapon's forward speed as they left the aircraft would carry
them safely clear of the target. So a special type of bomb had to be
designed for use with the MAD locator – one that fell vertically
when released from an aircraft flying at 100 mph. To meet that
requirement the California Institute of Technology designed the
so-called 'retro-bomb', a 35 pound bomb with a solid-fuel rocket
fitted into the tail. When the MAD equipment indicated a sub
marine below, the aircraft operator pressed a button to fire a salvo
of retro-bombs. The rockets propelled the bombs *backwards* off
their launching rails and rapidly brought them to a stop in mid-air.
The rockets then ceased burning, and the bombs fell vertically into
the sea. The weapons were fitted with impact fuses, so they
detonated only if they struck a submarine. Otherwise the boat's
crew still had no indication that the craft was under attack.

A Catalina flying boat carried twenty-four retro-bombs, twelve
under each wing on special launching rails. When the operator
pressed the button to fire the bombs, the first salvo of eight roared
off their rails immediately; half a second later the second salvo of
eight followed, and half a second after that the third salvo fell clear.
The retro-bomb launchers were divided into eight groups of three,
each group being set at a slightly different angle; as a result the
bombs from each salvo hit the water in a line about 100 feet long,
perpendicular to the aircraft's line of flight. The half-second delay
between salvoes gave a spacing of about 90 feet between successive lines. Prior to attacking the submarine with bombs, the aircraft
crew tracked its movement with smoke markers; as a result they

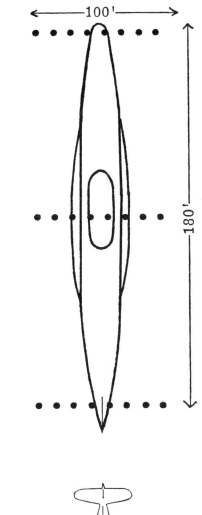

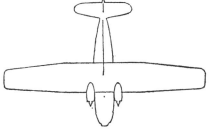

Retro-bomb pattern.

would be able to attack the boat along its length, and thus stood a good chance of scoring a potentially lethal blow with their retro-bombs.

One weakness of the MAD device was that it could not tell the difference between a small metallic object like a submarine at short range, and a far larger wreck lying on the seabed. The need to resolve that problem hastened the development of another new device – the sonobuoy. This consisted of a small floating radio transmitter, beneath which hung a length of cable attached to a hydrophone. The latter listened for sounds in the water around, and passed them to the transmitter, which relayed the sounds to the aircraft flying nearby.

In March 1942 the US Navy conducted a feasibility trial, using sonobuoys placed in the water from a motor launch. A submarine ran through the area, while a blimp hovered overhead carrying a receiver tuned to the transmissions from the buoys. During the trial the radio operator in the blimp heard the submarine's propeller beats at ranges up to three miles from the nearest buoy. Some weeks later the scientists repeated the trial, this time using buoys released from a blimp. In July the US Navy carried out the first 'fast' sonobuoy drops, releasing them at 120 mph from a Douglas B-18 bomber. Both trials were successful in demonstrating the feasibility of the device.

In the autumn of 1942 the sonobuoy entered production. Designated the AN/CRT-1, it comprised a cylindrical buoy 3 feet 9 inches long, 4 inches in diameter and weighing 14 pound. A parachute attached to the top of the buoy slowed its fall. On impact with the sea the hydrophone dropped from the base of the buoy, and sank to the limit of the 24-foot connecting cable. That separation between the hydrophone and the buoy was necessary, to prevent the noises from waves lapping against the buoy from swamping the faint propeller noises from the submarine. The impact of hitting the sea also switched on the buoy's transmitter, and after a warming-up period it began transmitting the sounds picked up by the hydrophone.

For the hydrophone to detect the submarine, the latter had to be travelling at cavitating speed. That is to say, the boat's propellers had to be rotating at a sufficiently high speed to cause the release of bubbles of air, which popped to give a distinctive sound. The speed at which cavitation occurred varied with depth – the deeper the submarine ran, the faster it could go without cavitating. When a submarine ran underwater at 'silent speed' (i.e. when it was not cavitating) it could not be detected by the early sonobuoys. Under ideal conditions the pick-up range of an early sonobuoy could be as high as 3½ miles, if the submarine was moving at seven knots at a depth of 60 feet in a calm sea. That range fell to about 90 yards, if the boat ran at three knots at a depth of 250 feet in a rough sea.

The early sonobuoys were non-directional devices. That is to say, although the operator had an indication of a submarine nearby, there was no indication of the direction from which the noises were coming. To prevent the sonobuoy being captured the enemy, it was fitted with a soluble bung. The latter began dissolving when the buoy entered the water and after about four hours it had dissolved completely. That allowed water to flood into the buoy, and it sank.

To exploit to the full these new-found capabilities to locate submerged submarines, US Navy scientists developed a formidable new weapon, the air-launched homing torpedo. Officially known by its cover-name 'Mark 24 Mine', it was also referred to more endearingly as 'Fido' and 'Wandering Annie'. Like the sonobuoy, the homing torpedo needed the submarine's propellers to be cavitating if it was to home on its prey. As in the case of the sonobuoy, the torpedo's homing ability varied greatly with conditions: at best – against a submarine moving noisily at high speed just beneath the surface – it could home from about three-quarters of a mile. Under operational conditions that optimum was also the most likely, for when an attack was threatened a U-boat commander invariably tried to get clear of the tell-take diving swirl as quickly as possible. If the new homing torpedo promised great things against an unsuspecting foe, however, its Achilles' Heel would be all too clear once an enemy knew of its existence: since the weapon could home only on cavitating propellers, a U-boat commander would be safe if he went against his instincts and slowed down after diving. Hence the exaggerated security precautions that surrounded all aspects of this weapon.

At the end of 1942 the new homing torpedo was nearing the trials stage; if the tests were successful it would go into production. It was not planned to continue production beyond the end of 1943, however; by that time the enemy would almost certainly know about it, and the U-boats would act accordingly.

★ ★ ★

Another promising new anti-submarine weapon being developed for airborne use in Great Britain during 1942 was the rocket projectile. A partially submerged target was set up on the Pendine Sands, Wales, to represent the pressure hull and superstructure of a U-boat. Then Swordfish and Hudson aircraft flew a series of trials to observe the effectiveness of this weapon in the anti-submarine role. The anti-submarine version of the projectile weighed 66 pound, of which 25 pound comprised the solid warhead made of mild steel. After launch the rocket accelerated rapidly, to reach an all-burnt velocity close to the speed of sound. The carefully shaped nose of the warhead governed the rocket's path when it travelled under water: if it struck at an optimum angle of about 13 degrees, the missile took an upward-curving path. Never going more than about eight feet beneath the surface, it emerged from the water some eighty feet from its entry point with about half its entry speed. The object was to punch a hole in the U-boat below the water line, and to achieve this the ideal place to aim the rockets was at a point on the water some twenty yards short of the target. Trials showed that a single hit by a rocket anywhere on the pressure hull was likely to prove lethal.

This weapon was due to become operational in the spring of 1943, and the aircraft were modified to carry a battery of eight launchers under their wings.

Continuing the description of the new anti-submarine devices about to enter service at the end of 1942, there was the high-frequency radio direction-finding equipment – 'Huffduff'. We have seen that a weakness of the 'Wolf Pack' tactics was the U-boats' reliance on high-frequency radio communications. During one convoy action, the escorts noted more than a hundred U-boat transmissions in their area during a seventy-two-hour period.

The Allies had set up a chain of shore Huffduff stations, and in the summer of 1942 these were instrumental in bringing about the destruction of a U-boat that made one transmission too many. This was *U-158* (Rostin), pinpointed 130 miles west-south-west of Bermuda by direction-finding stations on Bermuda itself, Jamaica, British Guiana and on the east coast of the USA. On 30 June a US Navy Mariner flying boat was directed to the area, caught her on the surface and sank her.

The shore Huffduff stations could not give accurate bearings on transmissions coming from more than three hundred miles away, however. During 1942 a small shipborne Huffduff set entered service, and eventually it became standard equipment on Allied ocean-going escort vessels. German Navy planners had long recognised the danger from the shore direction-finding stations (which in any case were ineffective in plotting transmissions from mid-Atlantic). Yet they ignored the possibility that such equipment could be fitted into ships giving an accurate bearing on a U-boat transmitting nearby. By plotting two or more Huffduff bearings it was possible to get a 'fix' on the source. Then warships or an aircraft could be directed to the area to sink the boat, or force it to submerge and so lose contact with the convoy.

What had happened to the escort carriers, which should by now have been providing invaluable air cover for the convoys in mid-Atlantic? Late in 1941 the American-built *Archer* had been commissioned into the Royal Navy, but she and the other vessels in her class suffered frequent machinery troubles, and several months elapsed before she became operational.

In September 1942 HMS *Avenger* provided fighter cover for a convoy to the Soviet Union. Then, in November the Royal Navy's *Dasher*, *Avenger* and *Biter*, together with the US Navy's *Sangamon*, *Suwannee* and *Santee*, provided air cover for the invasion of North Africa. Although several escort carriers became operational in 1942, on no occasion did their aircraft engage U-boats. This was a hazard the German submariners would have to face, but later.

During the last six months of 1942 about half of the German and Italian submarine losses had resulted from air attack, caused by aircraft operating either alone or in concert with warships. As the year ended the U-boats were still causing their greatest destruction in mid-Atlantic, an area that could be patrolled only intermittently by the very-long-range Liberators of No. 120 Squadron.

Had more of these aircraft had been allocated earlier, the 'Atlantic Gap' would have ceased to exist. Numerous other accounts have covered the controversy on whether it was right that the strategic bombing offensive was allocated the lion's share of these heavy bombers, leaving so few for the anti-submarine units. It is not intended to repeat that involved argument on these pages. Suffice it to say that by the early part of 1943, production of these aircraft reached levels that allowed several more anti-submarine units to re-equip with Liberators.

*　　*　　*

At the end of 1942 two new centimetric-wavelength radars were about to enter service in the Royal Air Force: the H2S ground-mapping radar for Bomber Command, and the technically similar ASV Mark III for Coastal Command. In view of the discussions described above, it will not surprise the reader to learn that the former had the higher priority.

Admiralty and senior Coastal Command officers fought hard to delay the operational use of H2S, at least until a sizeable proportion of Coastal Command aircraft carried the centimetric-wavelength ASV radar. They argued that since H2S was to be fitted to the Pathfinder aircraft that led the bombing attacks, by its very nature it had to be used over enemy territory. Therefore it would be only a matter of time before an example of the radar was captured. Forewarned of the new development, the German Navy would almost certainly build a listening receiver to detect its signals. Then Coastal Command would lose the element of surprise with the new ASV radar: it would be the ASV II and Metox story all over again.

In the final month of 1942 the debate reached its climax. The radar pioneer Sir Robert Watson-Watt wrote a lengthy paper on the probable effect on the war at sea if the Germans captured an H2S radar. He said there was no hard evidence on whether the enemy knew, or did not know, of Allied work on centimetric-wavelength radar. On the other hand, the German monitoring service had had ample opportunity to pick up such signals: for over a year two large ground stations had been operational on the south coast of England, and RAF night-fighters had been using centimetric-wavelength radar for several months. Moreover, the battleship *Prince of Wales* was carrying two such radars when she was sunk in shallow water off Malaya. It was known the Japanese Navy had buoyed the wreck, and it was possible they had removed the sets. There was a strong possibility, therefore, that the Germans already knew about the new radar. If this was so, the capture of an example of H2S would make little difference to the U-boat war. If, on the other hand, the Germans knew nothing about this type of radar they could, in Watson-Watt's opinion, design and manufacture a simple receiver for submarines 'within a period of two or three months at the most' of the discovery of the existence of an Allied centimetric-wavelength radar.

Watson Watt's conclusions were discussed at a meeting of the Chiefs of Staff Committee on 22 December, with Mr Churchill in the chair. Following a lengthy discussion, the Prime Minister ruled that the new H2S radar was cleared for use over enemy territory from the beginning of 1943 – even before ASV Mark III could became operational.

At the end of January 1943, RAF Bomber Command began operations over Germany with H2S. During the second attack in which the new radar was used, on 2 February, a night-fighter shot down an H2S-fitted Stirling and the wreck fell near Rotterdam. The event Allied senior officers directing the Battle of the Atlantic had dreaded, the compromise of the new centimetric-wavelength ASV radar, was now a fact.

Watson-Watt had predicted that it might take German scientists two or three months to design and manufacture a suitable search receiver, even if they had to start from scratch. Yet he could not predict the difficulties and diversions they would meet on the way. In the event it was to take far longer than this for the German Navy to get a proper centimetric-wavelength search receiver into service.

In December 1942 there was a further twist in the war between the cipher makers and the cipher breakers. In the previous February, it will be remembered, the German Navy had introduced a modified Enigma machine, and this had equipped most of the U-boat force. This had brought a precipitate end to the decryption of a large part of the U-boat radio traffic.

Now, after several months' mind-bending work, Bletchley Park was once more able to break into the system and decipher much of the U-boats' signals traffic. At first there were frequent delays in deciphering the signals, with the result that the Intelligence they contained often became available too late for it to be of immediate tactical use. Later, with the introduction of more powerful decryption machines, the average times between the reception and decryption of messages were greatly reduced. Bletchley Park would maintain its ability to read the U-boat traffic for the remainder of the war.

All in all, there could be no doubting that the Allies were amassing a formidable effort to counter the U-boat. Yet, for the present, the situation did not look at all bad from the viewpoint of the German Naval High Command. During the final six months of 1942 U-boats had sunk about three million tons of Allied merchant shipping, continuing the rate of success achieved during the first half of the year. Admittedly the Axis submarine losses were nearly three

times greater during the second half of the year than during the
first half – eighty-one German and Italian submarines lost,
compared with twenty-eight in the earlier period. Yet it was clear
that they were still winning their war of attrition against the Allied
merchant fleets.

The current plans for U-boat production, and the training of
crews to operate them, would ensure a steady increase, month by
month, in the number of boats available for action. During
February 1943 the daily average number of operational boats in
the Atlantic reached 116, of which 60 were deployed in the north
Atlantic. Many more boats were undergoing working-up in the
Baltic, and these too would soon join the battle.

To enable U-boat crews to fight back against attacking aircraft,
the German Navy began modifying boats with a platform aft of the
conning tower to carry anti-aircraft guns. Initially the weapon of
choice was the 20 mm cannon, with a maximum rate of fire of 150
rounds per minute and a maximum effective range against aircraft
of about a mile. Many commanders thought that if these weapons
fired tracer ammunition they would deter aircraft crews from
pressing home attacks. It remained to be seen whether this theory
would be proved in action, however.

As the reader will have observed, at the beginning of 1943 a series
of new weapons, new detection systems and new developments
were about to come into play in the Battle of the Atlantic. In
subsequent chapters we shall observe the effects of these on the
way the battle was fought.

CHAPTER 6

Blow for Blow

February to April 1943

*As of today I take over the post of Commander-in-Chief of the
Navy, by order of the Führer. I thank the submarine arm, which
I have been permitted to command hitherto, for its death-defying
readiness to fight, which it has shown at all times, and for its
loyalty. I shall continue to retain command of the U-boats. I will
command the Navy with the same hard, soldierly spirit. I expect
from each one unconditional obedience, the highest courage, and
devotion to the last. In that lies our honour. Gathered round our
Führer, we shall not lay down our arms until victory and peace
have been achieved.*

Order of the Day from Grossadmiral Karl Dönitz,
30 January 1943

On 30 January 1943 Karl Dönitz was promoted to *Grossadmiral*,
and assumed command of the entire Germany Navy. Three days
later came the first scarcely perceptible shudder, the ill-defined
herald, of the earthquake that would shake the U-boat service to
its foundations. The twisted remains of the centimetric-
wavelength H2S radar came as a complete surprise in German
scientific circles. The experts gazed, wide-eyed in astonishment, at
its many – and ominously unfamiliar – new features: the high-
powered magnetron oscillator, the plan position indicator display
and the scanning system employing a small reflector dish little
more than three feet across. The device was named after the city
near which it had been found, 'Rotterdam'.

Why had the German radio monitoring service failed to provide
a warning that the enemy had developed such a radar? As Robert
Watson-Watt had said in Britain a couple of months earlier, there
had been ample opportunity. The answer gave scant comfort to
those whose lives depended upon such Intelligence: the monitors
had simply not bothered to search the centimetric end of the

wavelength spectrum for radar signals. German scientists had calculated, erroneously, that on theoretical grounds a centimetric-wavelength radar would not work because of the phenomenon of 'super-reflectivity'. That is to say, after hitting a target the radar signals would not be reflected back to the radar, but would instead bounce away from it at a flat angle – in the same way as a tennis ball bounces away from the server after an ace service. In fact this phenomenon did occur with the new radar, but the German experts' calculations greatly exaggerated its extent. Now it was clear that the experts had been wildly wrong, and had lost their grip on the situation. As Hermann Goering commented after reading the report on 'Rotterdam':

> I expected the British and Americans to be advanced, but frankly I never thought that they would get so far ahead. I did hope that even if we were behind, we could at least be in the same race.

In an effort to make up some of the leeway the head of the Luftwaffe signals organisation, General Wolfgang Martini, immediately ordered that a special 'Rotterdam Commission' be set up, under the chairmanship of Dr Leo Brandt of the Telefunken company. Brandt's terms of reference were to 'combine the knowledge on centimetric-wavelength working, in the research teams and in industry, in order to bring into operation as quickly as possible the necessary countermeasures to the Rotterdam device.'

The first meeting of the 'Rotterdam Commission' (*Arbeitsgemeinschaft Rotterdam*) was held on 25 February, at the Telefunken factory at Berlin. The Commission decided that with the greatest possible despatch the Telefunken company should build six radar sets based on the captured 'Rotterdam', to serve as the prototypes of a mass-produced version for the German armed services. In addition, the members discussed plans for the production of a special receiver that would detect signals from the enemy radar; this device received the code-name 'Naxos'.

There was little doubt that the new type of radar could be used to locate U-boats, if it was not already in use for this. With the success of the Metox receiver fresh in his mind, the German Navy representative at the meeting, Engineer Bockelmann, spoke of his service's requirement for a version of Naxos; the version of the receiver to be specially designed for use by submarines was given the code-name 'Naxos-U'.

If the German radar experts were worried for the future, that fact had not yet filtered down to the U-boat crews. Ever since the large-scale introduction of the Metox receiver into the German submarine arm, in September 1942, Allied aircraft had had little success against U-boats in the Bay of Biscay. In January 1943 Coastal Command units operating in that area were almost back where they had been before the introduction of the Leigh Light, with only four day and nine night sightings. None of them resulted in a 'kill'.

During February 1943 the air patrols over the Bay were re-organised. Between the 4th and 16th the aircraft of Air Vice-Marshal Geoffrey Bromet's No. 19 Group of Coastal Command flew Operation Gondola: a rectangular stretch of sea in the Bay of Biscay, chosen so as to run across the main U-boat transit routes, was patrolled intensively. During this operation Bromet had control of Nos 1 and 2 Squadrons of the US Army Air Force, both equipped with the Liberators. Although these aircraft did not carry the extra fuel tanks or other modifications to suit them for the very-long-range role, importantly they carried the new American SCR 517 centimetric-wavelength radar.

In the course of 'Gondola', No. 19 Group flew just over three hundred sorties, which resulted in nineteen sightings and eight attacks. Significantly, the only 'kill' was by a Liberator of the American No. 2 Squadron: *U-519* (Eppen).

It did not take the German Naval High Command long to receive confirmation of the expected Allied use of centimetric radar. In March the first British squadron to operate with the new ASV Mark III, No. 172 with Leigh Light Wellingtons, began patrolling over the Bay of Biscay. During the early-morning darkness of the 5th, one of these aircraft illuminated *U-333* as she was moving out to her operational area. But the resultant action was not one-sided: the German sailors opened up with accurate 20 mm cannon fire and shot down the Wellington. The U-boat's perceptive commander, *Oberleutnant* Schwaff, considered the action significant enough to warrant a signal to headquarters:

At [map reference] BF 5897 I was attacked by an enemy aircraft at night, but without receiving any previous warning. Little damage done. Enemy aircraft shot down in flames.

The entry in *Grossadmiral* Dönitz's War Diary for that day struck a sombre note:

The enemy is making use of radar on frequencies outside the coverage of the present search receiver [i.e. Metox]. Until now the only confirmation of this is from an enemy aircraft shot down over Holland, which apparently carried a device with a wavelength of 9.7 centimetres . . .

At the second meeting of the Rotterdam Commission, held on 17 March, the German radar experts learned of these developments. They also heard that the Telefunken company was having difficulty in producing the all-important crystal detectors for the Naxos receivers. Because of this, none of the new receivers were yet available for trials. In view of the danger from the new Allied radars the naval representative at the meeting, *Fregattenkapitän* Dr Becker, requested that his service should have first call on these receivers when they did become available; General Martini agreed to this. It was clear, however, that for the time being the U-boat crews would have to make do without any effective search receiver operating on centimetric frequencies.

Between 20 and 28 March, Air Vice-Marshal Bromet mounted his second all-out operation against the U-boats crossing the Bay of Biscay: Operation Enclose. Earlier in the month he had lost operational control of the two US Army Air Force squadrons equipped with 'centimetric' radar; these had moved to Morocco to cover American shipping in that area. But now Bromet could muster thirty-two Leigh Light Wellingtons equipped with the centimetric-wavelength ASV Mark III; these belonged to No. 172 and the Canadian No. 407 Squadron. In addition there were, of course, the several other squadrons equipped with the old ASV II radar.

From German records we know that during the Enclose operation, forty-one U-boats crossed the Bay of Biscay on the way to or from their patrol areas. From Allied records, we find that the aircraft made twenty-six sightings, and fifteen attacks. The sole boat sunk, *U-665* (Haupt), fell to a Wellington of No. 172 Squadron on the 22nd.

In his War Diary, *Grossadmiral* Dönitz noted on 23 March that movement through the Bay of Biscay was becoming increasingly dangerous. Although few U-boats had been sunk in this stretch of water, several had returned from patrol with hair-raising stories of narrow escapes. Since February, he noted, the effect of the air patrols had increased to an alarming extent, especially when large numbers of boats were returning from the major convoy operations. He concluded his remarks with 'there will be further losses'.

Between 6 and 13 April Air Vice-Marshal Bromet mounted a repeat of the Enclose operation, Enclose II. During this, twenty-five U-boats passed through the Bay area; there were eleven sightings, and four attacks. Again only one boat, *U-376* (Marks), was sunk, but again it fell to a Wellington of No. 172 Squadron.

Immediately after Enclose II, No. 19 Group mounted its fourth intensive patrol operation, Operation Derange, in a different part of the Bay. For the first time Air Vice-Marshal Bromet had a reasonably large force of aircraft with centimetric-wavelength radar at his disposal: about seventy Wellingtons, Liberators and Halifaxes.

The increase in the strength of the air patrols did not pass unnoticed at U-boat headquarters. Faced with a growing number of reports of surprise attacks at night, or in daylight in bad visibility, Dönitz reacted as he had the previous summer. On 27 April he ordered U-boats passing through the Bay of Biscay to run submerged during the night, and surface during the day only long enough to recharge their batteries. He commented grimly:

> The enemy has at his disposal a radar device, especially effective in aircraft, against which our U-boats are powerless . . .

Robert Watson-Watt's predicted three-month time limit for the German Navy to introduce a new type of warning receiver to receive signals on centimetric wavelengths had now expired. Yet still the difficulties of mass-producing the Naxos receiver had not been solved. For a few months longer, U-boat crews would have to take their chances without it.

Before we continue with the long-drawn-out phase leading to the climax of the battle in the Bay of Biscay, however, there are other aspects of the conflict that warrant attention.

At this point, a glimpse into the command structures of the opposing forces might not be out of place.

The command structure of Coastal Command had been settled at the beginning of the war, and would remain essentially unchanged until the end of hostilities. In February 1943 Air Marshal Sir John Slessor assumed command of Coastal Command in place of Sir Philip Joubert; from his headquarters at Northwood in Middlesex, he worked in close co-operation with his Royal Navy opposite numbers. The Royal Navy held the responsibility for the overall strategy and direction of the British effort during the Battle of the Atlantic. It therefore held operational control of the maritime reconnaissance and shipping strike aircraft of Coastal Command. Essentially the Royal Navy, as predominant partner, decided on the maritime air task, and Coastal Command was responsible for carrying it out.

The headquarters of the four Coastal Command Groups in the United Kingdom were in each case combined with that of a Naval Command, with the senior naval officer in overall charge (Naval C-in-C Western Approaches, at Liverpool, with RAF Headquarters No. 15 Group; C-in-C Chatham and 16 Group; C-in-C Rosyth and 18 Group; and C-in-C Plymouth and 19 Group). In general the system worked well, though there were some anomalies. For example, the naval Commander-in-Chief at Plymouth had under his command few naval forces – some old destroyers and a few fast patrol boats. Yet he was Air Vice-Marshal Bromet's immediate superior at the headquarters directing the large force of aircraft now engaging U-boats crossing the Bay of Biscay.

The location of the air patrols was decided at the highest level. During the morning naval combined-staff conference, the RAF Group commanders received their directives over a specially secure telephone that linked the Admiralty submarine-tracking room at Whitehall, the Coastal Command operations room at Northwood, and the four Combined Area Headquarters. Commander Roger Winn, at the submarine-tracking room, would usually open the proceedings with a commentary on the known positions and expected movements of the U-boats. Then there would be a general discussion of the sightings and attacks made during the previous twenty-four hours. Next, the Admiralty would issue its list of convoys and 'Monsters' (large, fast, independently routed troopships, like the *Queen Mary* and the *Queen Elizabeth*) likely to be threatened and therefore requiring air cover. The provision of such air cover always had first priority: the Admiralty, through Coastal Command, required above all else the 'safe and timely arrival' of the ships. Air Vice-Marshal Slatter's No. 15 Group was responsible for providing air cover for the Atlantic convoys, and he could call on the other Groups for additional aircraft if he needed them. Since his main need was for aircraft with a very-long-range capability, however, the shorter-ranging aircraft used by the other Groups were rarely of use to him. Now the primary needs had been met, the remaining aircraft were allo-

Lieutenant Hugh Williamson (above right), a Royal Navy submarine officer who had learned to fly at his own expense, wrote the first tactical treatise on anti-submarine aircraft in 1912. *Fregatten Leutnant* Baron Otto von Klimburg (above left) was observer in one of the two Lohner flying boats (right) which caused fatal damage to the French submarine *Foucault* (below) on 15 September 1916 – the first submarine to be lost in open water as a result of an air attack.

The first aircraft designed from the beginning for the anti-submarine role was the British SS (Submarine Scout, above). The car was a cut-down fuselage from a BE 2 biplane; two 112-pound bombs may be seen under the rear. Some seventy small airships were in commission with the RAF by the end of World War I. Wing Commander John Porte (left) played a leading part in the introduction and development of the large flying boat for the Royal Naval Air Service. Typical of these was the Curtiss H-12 *Large America* (below) seen here taking off with a 230-pound bomb under the port wing.

ovations for 1918: the de Havilland 6 (top), judged unsuitable as a trainer, was pressed into ice against U-boats in the *Scarecrow* role. At the other end of the effectiveness scale was the ckburn Kangaroo (centre), here seen carrying two 230-pound flat-nosed anti-submarine nbs. A different approach was the Felixstowe F2A flying boat (bottom), with hydrophone ening equipment; in an actual search the boom would be swung to the vertical position.

The British 100, 250 (above) and 500-pound anti-submarine bombs in servic the beginning of World War II proved dangerous to the aircraft which release them and of only limited effect against boats. *U-46* (left, in dry dock) suffered direct hit from a 100-pounder but still reached port. More effective was the 4 pound naval depth charge, modified fo air use by the addition of simple nose ε tail fairings. One of these (below) is be loaded on to the wing rack of a Catalir flying boat.

The first airborne radar to enter squadron service, in early 1940, was the ASV Mark I; the picture at the top of a Hudson – actually engaged in air-to-surface rocket trials – shows the two unobtrusive ASV aerials mounted on the aircraft; the first one is well forward on the side of the nose, the second one can be seen just to the left of the port engine. Another important British anti-submarine type was the Short Sunderland flying boat (bottom picture); this one belonged to 210 Squadron. Right and centre: operating far from land, mechanical failure could be disastrous – here a Whitley of 502 Squadron is unable to maintain height on one engine and is ditched.

Admiral Karl Doenitz (above, third from left) pictured at his headquarters bunker near Lorient in France early in 1942. *Kapitanleutnant* Doublebsky von Eichhain, a staff officer, explains the current situation during a morning briefing. Less than two hundred miles to the north, in a concrete bunker near Plymouth, Air Vice Marshal Geoffrey Bromet (below, centre) the commander of 19 Group of Coastal Command, reviews the situation with his senior air staff officer, Group Captain Brackley.

The introduction of the Leigh Light in the summer of 1942 made routine night attacks on U-boats possible. The Wellington (above) was the first aircraft to carry it, mounted in a retractable 'dustbin' under the rear fuselage. This Wellington is also carrying the ASV Mark III – its scanner is in the blister under the aircraft's nose. Squadron Leader Humphrey de Verde Leigh (right) was the inventor of the airbourne searchlight. He was the operator during the first successful trial early on the morning of 4 May 1941 when he illuminated the British submarine *H-31* (below).

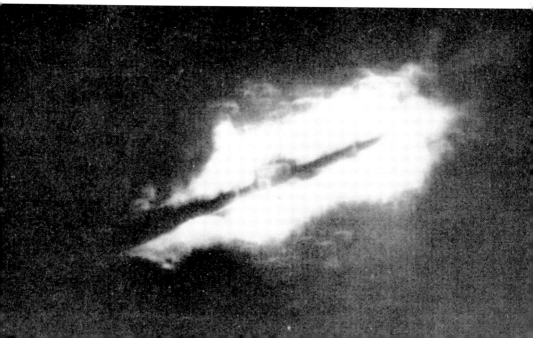

The very-long-range Liberator Mar
(above) provided air cover over the
mid-Atlantic during the winter of
1942. Note the under-fuselage pack
for four 20mm cannon; the ASV M
II radar's sideways-looking aerials o
the rear fuselage; and the homing
aerials on the nose and wings.
Squadron Leader Bulloch, DSO
(below) served with 120 Squadron
during the period; behind him is t
Liberator carrying his personal
emblem. Particularly devastating v
his attack on *U-597* (left). He
attacked along her length; one dep
charge is exploding under her ster
and more are about to go off.

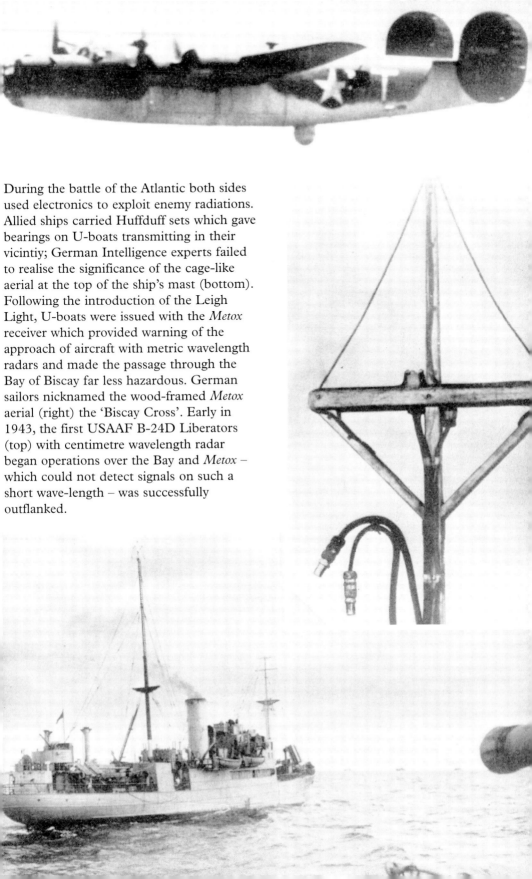

During the battle of the Atlantic both sides used electronics to exploit enemy radiations. Allied ships carried Huffduff sets which gave bearings on U-boats transmitting in their vicintiy; German Intelligence experts failed to realise the significance of the cage-like aerial at the top of the ship's mast (bottom). Following the introduction of the Leigh Light, U-boats were issued with the *Metox* receiver which provided warning of the approach of aircraft with metric wavelength radars and made the passage through the Bay of Biscay far less hazardous. German sailors nicknamed the wood-framed *Metox* aerial (right) the 'Biscay Cross'. Early in 1943, the first USAAF B-24D Liberators (top) with centimetre wavelength radar began operations over the Bay and *Metox* – which could not detect signals on such a short wave-length – was successfully outflanked.

The top-scoring aircraft captain during the Battle of the Bay was Wing Commander Oulton (bottom right) of 58 Squadron. He sank *U-463* (top right, straddled by his depth charges) and *U-663*, and shared in the destruction of *U-563*, all within 26 days. The last major action in the Bay was on 30 July 1943 when *U-461*, *U-462* and *U-504* (top left) attempted to fight their way through on the surface by day. The first attack was by two Halifaxes of 502 Squadron, releasing 600-pound anti-submarine bombs from altitudes of over 1500 feet; one of these landed close alongside the twisting *U-462* (below left), crippling her – she was later finished off by an RN escort group.

The German Navy fitted *U-441* (above) with an especially powerful armament as an 'aircraft trap'; she carried two quadruple-barrelled 20mm guns, a semi-automatic 37mm gun, additional armour and extra gunners. Following a pitched battle with aircraft, however, in which *U-441* suffered heavy casualties, the aircraft trap idea was dropped. Nevertheless during the latter half of 1943 there was a considerable strengthening of U-boat anti-aircraft armament; *U-745* (below right) carried one quadruple-barrelled and two double-barrelled 20mm guns. One British answer to the surfaced U-boat was the 6-pounder (57mm) anti-tank gun fitted into the lower nose section of the Mosquito (below left).

During the early months of 1944 US Navy Catalina flying boats of Squadron VP-63 (above), carrying magnetic detection equipment shared in the destruction of three U-boats attempting to pass submerged through the Straits of Gibraltar. The magnetic head was fitted at the extreme rear to reduce magnetic interference from ferrous metals in the aircraft itself (centre left). To make possible accurate attacks with the short-ranging magnetic detector the retro-bomb (bottom) was developed. When the rocket motors fire the bombs slid backwards of their rails and then, their forward speed cancelled, fell vertically. The twelve bombs are divided into four groups of three, each with the rails 'toed' out at a slightly greater angle than its inboard neighbour to produce the correct bomb pattern.

Carrier-borne anti-submarine aircraft: the robust American Grumman Avenger (top) shown here carrying eight rockets, a podded searchlight installation and centimetric wavelength radar fitted to the starboard wing. The underfuselage aerials are for the sonobuoy receiver. The slow but manoeuvrable Fairey Swordfish (centre) operated successfully even from small merchant aircraft carriers; it carries a typical anti-submarine armament comprising eight rockets and smoke-markers. The ASV Mark II radar aerials can be seen on the outer wing struts; the transmitter aerial is along the centre of the upper wing. The Japanese Navy operated the Nakajima B5N Kate, (at bottom) from escort carriers. The forward-looking radar aerials can be seen on the leading edge of the wing, inboard of the fold; the sideways-looking aerials are on the rear fuselage.

From the summer of 1943 the rocket was the primary Allied weapon for attacking surfaced U-boats. Top, a close-up of the stub-wing rocket installation fitted to some Liberators. The 3-inch rockets each carried a 25-pound solid head and the specially shaped nose caused the missile to pitch up once in the water and thus describe a gentle curve before breaking surface. By aiming the rockets to strike the surface just short of the U-boat, it was possible to inflict lethal underwater damage. *U-763* (left) was fortunate to survive this 'dry' rocket hit; the missile passed clean through her ballast tank and out the other side. Below, Mosquitoes launch salvo after salvo of rockets at U-boats on the surface of the Kattegat during their rampage of 9 April 1945.

Flying Officer Cruickshank (top left) was awarded the VC for pressing home his attack on a U-boat in spite of severe wounds. Flying Officer Trigg, RNZAF (above right) was awarded a posthumous VC for pressing home an attack on a U-boat with his blazing aircraft, on evidence from the German survivors. Flying Officer Moore, RCAF, (centre right) and his crew sank two U-boats in twenty minutes on the morning of 8 June 1944. Below, armourers are loading 250-pound depth charges, used in all the above attacks, into the bomb bay of a Liberator. Note the concave noses and thin metal breakaway tails of the weapons, designed to slow their rate of sinking.

The *Schnorkel* breathing tube (top left) gave the German submarine fleet a new lease of life with near-immunity from detection from the air. When the war ended, the formidable Type XXI submarine was being mass-produced and about to go into action. The large sections (bottom) could be moved to the assembly yards only by canal, and the Allied strategic bombing imposed severe delays on this. Top right, *U-3008*, a Type XXI boat, on her way to Britain after the war.

cated to other tasks – for example the Bay of Biscay air patrols.

Once the pattern for the day's operations had been decided, the Group commanders and their staffs were responsible for converting these instructions into operational orders, and passing these to the stations concerned.

Backing the British commanders was a highly efficient operational research team; moreover, through the medium of the 'Sunday Soviet' meetings held at the Telecommunications Research Establishment now situated at Malvern, they were able to keep in close touch with the latest technical developments. Their German counterparts, we shall observe shortly, were far less well served in these two important respects.

By the beginning of 1943, the pattern of the German U-boat Command was also well established. At this time *Grossadmiral* Dönitz had his operational headquarters in Paris, in a large requisitioned house in the Avenue Marechal Maunoury. His chief operational staff officer, *Konteradmiral* Godt, presided over a carefully chosen team of ex-U-boat commanders who had proved themselves in action. Sometimes with Dönitz himself, these men determined the course of the German side of the Atlantic battles. With the exception of Godt, who was forty-two, the average age of the team was in the early thirties. For that reason the U-boat staff was sometimes referred to as the staff without potbellies (*Stab ohne Bäuche*).

Acting on the best Intelligence information available on Allied shipping movements, the headquarters would direct ten or fifteen U-boats to form a group that would establish a patrol line in mid-ocean at right angles across the route the convoy was expected to take. In the Atlantic, a typical patrol line ran from north to south, with some ten miles between boats. During this phase of the action U-boats on or near the patrol line maintained strict radio silence, to prevent Allied shore direction-finding stations determining the positions of the boats waiting in ambush.

The first U-boat to sight the convoy immediately broke radio silence, and flashed details of the convoy's position, composition, heading, speed and the strength of the escorts, to the headquarters in Paris. The arrival of this report would sting Dönitz's operational staff into anthill-like activity. The officers hastened to the operations room, where a large wall-map studded with pins indicated the known or expected positions of boats. Now the aim was to pass orders to the remaining U-boats in the group, to bring them into contact with the convoy as quickly as possible and set up the devastating night surface attacks.

The U-boat making the initial sighting would maintain contact with the convoy, to report any heading change. Meanwhile, over the horizon, the German patrol line dissolved as each U-boat made for its ordered intercept point on the surface at its best possible speed. For the furthest-out U-boats in the line, which could be up to 140 miles from its prey, this might mean a run on the surface of about fifteen hours before they reached the convoy. Other boats would get there earlier, of course, and when a 'quorum' of three U-boats was in contact the attack could begin.

The German Naval High Command was fully aware of the dangers of an insecure cipher system, and it immediately followed up each and every hint that their own had been broken. Its signals experts noted, for example, that during the three-week period in January 1943 not one of the patrol lines laid out in mid-Atlantic had caught a convoy. During February few convoys were sighted, and in each case they had been reported by boats operating singly or by those at the ends of patrol lines. If the convoys were being routed round the patrol lines, how did the Allies know where these danger areas were?

One incident that aroused considerable suspicion had occurred on 12 January 1943. The submarine tanker *U-459* (*von Wilamowitz-Moellendorff*), having taken up its prearranged position deep in the south Atlantic to refuel the Italian boat *Kalvi*, ran into enemy destroyers close to the rendezvous point. She had been lucky to escape. If the meeting had been a coincidence it was a long one, for the rendezvous position was some 800 miles from the nearest Allied base and well clear of the convoy routes.

Grossadmiral Dönitz had his Director of Signals re-examine the cipher systems for security, and any sign that the information had leaked from that source. Bit by bit naval staff officers painstakingly built up a plausible picture of the U-boats' movements from the sort of information that would have been available to Allied Intelligence officers: sightings, radio bearings, radar locations and so on. Also, they expected the Allies to receive first-class information from spies at the French and Norwegian bases. On discovering one agent's transmitting station in France, the Gestapo had found documents giving the times of departure of the various boats with information on whether they were bound for the north or the south Atlantic. After weighing the available information, on 5 March Dönitz concluded in his War Diary:

With the exception of two or three doubtful cases, British conclusions are based on data regarding submarine positions that is readily available to them, on submarine positions and on their own plotting of the boats' movements, combined with a quite feasible process of logical deduction. The most important result that has emerged from this investigation is the all-but-certain proof that with the assistance of his airborne radar the enemy is able to discover submarine dispositions with sufficient accuracy to enable his convoys to take evasive action.

In assessing military Intelligence, when there is insufficient information available on the enemy it is usual to consider the 'worst likely case'. After the capture of the H2S equipment, the German naval staff knew that the Allied radar equipment was technically far superior to the German. The problem was, they had no way of knowing the extent by which it was superior. Dönitz based his assessment on Allied aircraft being fitted with a long-range radar able to detect U-boats on the surface at distances of more than twenty-five miles. In fact the best ASV radar in service at the beginning of 1943 could detect a U-boat at a range of ten miles only under optimum conditions. In truth, there was little chance of locating a submarine patrol line by airborne radar alone. But Dönitz had no way of knowing that. The shock of the capture of the H2S radar had eroded German technical judgements.

For both the Allies and the Germans, the circumstances of the cipher-cracking war held certain similarities. On both sides it was a case of the most brilliant minds patiently seeking and exploiting the mistakes of the overstrained, the undertrained or the under-brained in their opponent's signals organisation. Even a relatively small lapse in concentration or procedure could be sufficient to enable the experts to make a new inroad through the enemy cipher. Yet whoever made the mistake, the result was almost invariably the same: sooner or later men at the front had to pay for any indiscretion with their blood.

To return to the Paris headquarters: at this time the U-boat service fought its battles and learned its lessons almost entirely from within the immediate resources of the German Navy. There was no independently minded operational research section, such as that which kept a critical eye on Coastal Command's activities. Nor was there any of the easy-going contact between the fighting men, their commanders and the scientists, such as existed in

Britain during the 'Sunday Soviet' meetings. Almost until the end of 1943, the German Naval High Command would regard such things as unnecessary, and perhaps diverting, institutions. Could there be any matter concerning naval warfare that was all that far beyond the grasp of a trained and dedicated naval officer? Before it learned the answer to this question, the U-boat service was to sail perilously close to a metaphorical lee shore; that the 'rocks' it eventually struck were of its own making was only one of the resultant ironies. All of this would take time, yet there can be no doubting that the foundations of the failure, and the resulting crisis of confidence in the autumn of 1943, had been firmly laid by the beginning of the year.

At the close of January 1943 the German Navy had thirty-seven U-boats operating in the 'Atlantic Gap', beyond the reach of all but a few Allied patrol aircraft, patiently waiting for the next convoy to run the gauntlet. Their chance came early in February, with the appearance of the sixty-three merchant ships in the east-bound convoy SC 118. Twenty U-boats went into action against it, and they sank thirteen ships for the loss of three of their number. Towards the end of that month the westbound convoy ON 166 suffered a similarly rough handling, losing fourteen ships in exchange for only one U-boat destroyed. During February the U-boats sank sixty-three ships, totalling more than a third of a million tons.

The clear need was for air cover, any sort of air cover, in the dangerous mid-Atlantic area where the U-boats were wreaking havoc. Yet there was still only one squadron able to operate over these distant waters from shore bases: No. 120 Squadron of the RAF, which at this time possessed only seventeen very-long-range Liberators. Sir Philip Joubert had made continual requests for more of these aircraft, but the expanding strategic bomber forces received first priority. Moreover, the Liberators now coming off the production lines and becoming available to Coastal Command were all of the 'improved' Mark III (B-24D) version. These had many features intended to enhance their value as high-altitude bombers, able to fight through the enemy defences. As a result, an extensive process of demodification was necessary to prepare these Liberators for the very-long-range, low-altitude, anti-submarine role. The self-sealing liners to the fuel tanks and most of the armour plating were removed, as were the turbo-superchargers for the engines and the underneath gun turret. This weight pruning made it possible for the aircraft to take off carrying more than two thousand gallons of high octane fuel, plus an offensive load of eight 250 pound depth-charges. At this stage the very-long-range Liberators all carried the old ASV Mark II radar, whose emissions the German Metox receivers could detect. In mid-Atlantic this was not a great shortcoming, however, for the aircraft could achieve their primary aim – that of ensuring the 'safe and timely arrival' of the convoy – merely by forcing the U-boats to submerge and so lose contact with the convoy.

An alternative method of providing air cover in mid-Atlantic was by using shorter-ranging aircraft operating from escort carriers. During March the USS *Bogue* became, at last, the first of these ships to engage in anti-submarine convoy support operations in the north Atlantic, when her aircraft provided cover for HX 228. The Avengers sighted only one U-boat, but it is clear that by their very presence they had a stifling effect on the German attempts to intercept the ships. *Bogue* stayed with the convoy until it was south of Greenland, but then her covering destroyers began to run low on fuel and she had to return to Newfoundland. Then the U-boats pounced, and sank four ships before the convoy came within the range of the continuous patrols from Iceland-based aircraft.

That first use of an escort carrier to cover a north Atlantic convoy had been a tame affair. But *Bogue* was a new vessel, barely worked up for operations. As the German sailors would soon learn, the escort carrier was a deadly opponent and one to be feared.

There was no escort carrier available to protect the slow convoy SC 122, comprising sixty merchant ships, which left New York for Liverpool on 5 March. Nor was there one three days later when a second eastbound convoy, the slightly faster HX 229 with forty ships, set out behind it on a similar course. During the following week the two groups of ships plodded their way eastward, with the faster convoy gradually catching up with the slower one.

In the meantime, the German Navy had not been idle. On 13 March its cryptoanalysts had deciphered a British signal ordering a route change for SC 122. As a result, *Grossadmiral* Dönitz was able to position the eleven-strong U-boat pack *Raubgraf* in a line across the path of the convoys. To act as 'long-stops' for the *Raubgraf* boats, he laid out a further two patrol lines in mid-Atlantic: the eighteen-strong *Stürmer* pack and, somewhat to the south of it, the ten-strong *Dränger* pack.

These carefully laid German plans could not take into account the unexpectedly severe weather in the western Atlantic, however.

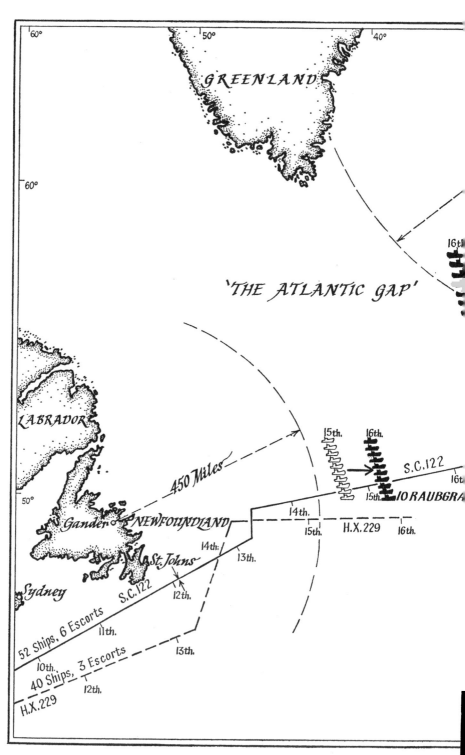

SC122/HX229 convoy action.

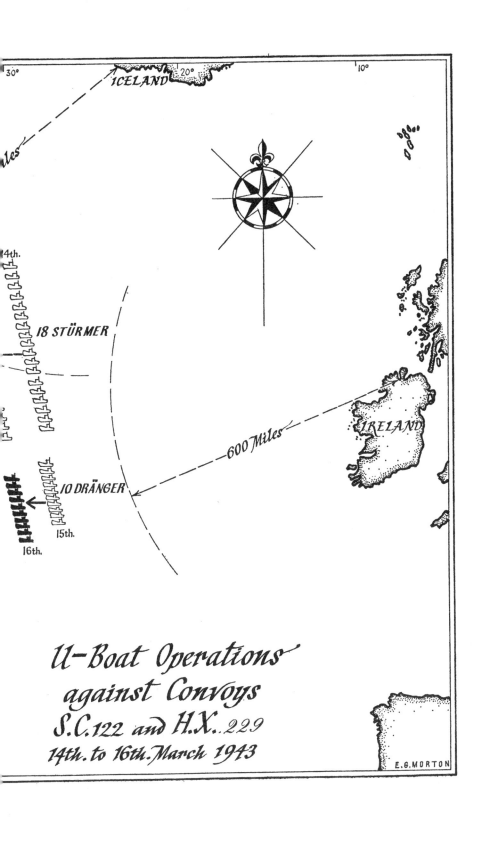

30°   20°   10°

ICELAND

14th.

18 STÜRMER

600 Miles

IRELAND

10 DRÄNGER

15th.

16th.

*U-Boat Operations
against Convoys
S.C.122 and H.X. 229
14th. to 16th. March 1943*

E.G.MORTON

Because of this the *Raubgraf* boats were late getting into position, and they missed the merchant ships altogether. But then the U-boat command had a stroke of luck: on the morning of the 16th, as *Kapitänleutnant* Feiler was nursing *U-653* home with engine trouble, he found himself sailing almost as part of a large convoy – HX 229. Feiler flashed the news to his headquarters, and soon the ether hummed with orders for U-boats in the area: the *Raubgraf* boats, together with eleven from the southern end of the *Stürmer* patrol line, were to converge on the convoy at their best possible speed. During the afternoon of the 16th and the early morning darkness of the 17th, eight *Raubgraf* boats made contact and went into action. They torpedoed eight ships, two of which sank almost immediately.

Meanwhile, about a hundred miles to the north-east, the U-boats from the *Stürmer* pack detached to engage HX 229 ran into SC 122; the latter convoy was more powerfully escorted, however, and the attackers found it difficult to close on their prey. Only *U-338* penetrated the screen of escorts, but *Kapitänleutnant* Manfred Kinzel made the most of his opportunity. He torpedoed four ships in rapid succession, two of which sank.

By the early morning of the 17th it was clear to *Grossadmiral* Dönitz and his staff that the U-boats had found two separate convoys. He ordered the remaining boats in the *Stürmer* group, and all of those in the *Dränger* group, to attack. More than forty U-boats were now closing on the two convoys. There can be little doubt that such a force would have swamped the defences and caused great execution, had not the 'US Cavalry', in the form of No. 120 Squadron's Liberators, arrived in a nick of time. During the day, three of these aircraft patrolled in the area; their crews sighted eleven U-boats and attacked six of them. As a result all the boats in contact with SC 122 except one had to dive and break contact. Only the redoubtable Kinzel in *U-338* kept up, and he sank the only ship the convoy lost that day. When night came the Liberators, lacking Leigh Lights, could do little to deter the U-boats from surfacing and closing on the slow merchant ships. During the darkness SC 122 lost two more ships. HX 229 also lost two ships during the 17th, and U-boats despatched five damaged ships that had become stragglers.

On the 18th the U-boat crews again had trouble with the patrolling aircraft: during the day five of 120 Squadron's Liberators spent time with the convoys. In the vicinity of SC 122 they sighted seven U-boats and attacked five; the convoy suffered no losses that day. HX 229, less well protected, lost two more ships.

Early on the morning of the 19th SC 122 lost one further ship, and later in the day a U-boat trailing HX 229 finished off a straggler. By now, however, the convoys were within 600 miles of the airfields in Iceland and Northern Ireland, and the shorter-ranging aircraft could also join in the battle. Notable among the covering operations flown that day was that of Flight Lieutenant Knowles, in a Fortress of No. 220 Squadron based at Ballykelly in Northern Ireland. Knowles arrived in the area of SC 122 during mid-morning, and received orders from the escort commander to circle the ships at a distance of twenty miles. Shortly afterwards the Fortress crew sighted a U-boat on the surface, which they attacked with four depth-charges as it was in the act of diving; nearly a minute later the submarine surfaced, her tanks gushing oil. Then she submerged slowly with no way on. As she was going down Knowles made a second attack with three depth-charges. It is possible this was Manfred Kinzel's boat, *U-338*, which suffered serious damage from an air attack that morning. Like Quaet-Faslem, who had fought such a hard battle with aircraft the previous winter, Kinzel was a qualified aircraft pilot; that might account for his success in the face of the air patrols. On this occasion, however, it would appear that he had taken one chance too many. *U-338* limped back to France.

The U-boats kept up their pressure throughout the 19th, but so did the RAF: that day six Liberators, seven Fortresses and three Sunderlands provided cover for the two convoys. Co-operation between the escorts and the aircraft was good, with the latter making frequent excursions to investigate Huffduff plots on U-boats' transmissions. For example, as the escort commander for SC 122 reported for that evening:

18.50 Aircraft told to investigate 287° 10 miles.

19.26 Aircraft reported he had attacked U-boat 280° 45 miles.

21.50 Aircraft told to investigate contact 224° 5 to 10 miles.

22.36 Aircraft reported that he had investigated and made two contacts that disappeared; also found a straggler, bearing 215° 45 miles.

23.36 After further bearings in the same area the aircraft told to search again 3 to 10 miles. Aircraft reported U-boat 240°

from convoy 9 miles. Attacked by aircraft with machine-gun
fire, bomb doors failing to open . . .

During the twenty-four hours ending at 08.00 hours on the 20th,
aircraft sighted twelve U-boats and attacked eight. From then on
relays of Fortresses flew close cover round each convoy, while
Sunderland flying boats swept the sea to either side, behind and in
front of the ships, to keep the U-boats submerged. Their continual
harassment successfully prevented the submarines from reaching
firing positions, and the two convoys suffered no further losses. It
was during this final part of the battle that a Sunderland of No.
201 Squadron sank the only U-boat lost in the entire action –
U-384 (von Rosenberg-Gruszczynski).

On the morning of the 20th, *Grossadmiral* Dönitz called off his
wolves. In spite of the throttling effect of the air patrols during the
closing stages of the action, it was clear that his men had won a
great victory. During the four-day action the U-boats had sunk
twenty-one merchant ships, totalling 141,000 tons. Almost all of
these ships had been torpedoed while moving in convoy, and
the escorted convoy was the Allies' chosen method of protecting
shipping.

It was beginning to look as though *Grossadmiral* Dönitz's Wolf
Pack tactic could indeed defeat the convoys. In Allied naval circles,
voices were raised questioning the value of continuing with the
convoys. Yet the only alternative, to route merchant ships
independently, hardly seemed likely to provide any relief. As a
British Admiralty report later acknowledged: 'The Germans never
came so near to disrupting communication between the New
World and the Old as in the first twenty days of March 1943'. All
that, for the loss of a single U-boat.

Even as the SC 122/HX 229 action was drawing to a close,
German Naval cryptoanalysts were preparing for the next battle.
On 20 March they laid bare a signal giving the time and position
of the rendezvous in mid-ocean between the main body of the westbound convoy ONS 1, and several ships scheduled to join it from
Iceland. Thus, once again, *Grossadmiral* Dönitz's staff officers had
a precise datum point on which to base their search. Acting on the
deciphered report, they established patrol line *Seeteufel*, with
seventeen U-boats, at right angles to the anticipated track of the
convoy. By 26 March patrol line *Seewolf*, with fifteen U-boats, was
in position to the south of *Seeteufel*. Together, the thirty-two
U-boats covered the long strip of ocean running south eastwards

from the southern tip of Greenland. There they waited in silent ambush for the oncoming merchant ships. Once again the north Atlantic was at its storm-tossed worst, however. The U-boats gained and then lost contact with the convoy ONS 1, but ended up chasing the eastbound convoys SC 123 and HX 230. Yet there was no repeat of the previous victory, for the storms made life hazardous for friend and foe alike. On 28 March *Kapitänleutnant* Purkhold, commanding the *Seeteufel* boat *U-260*, recorded in his log:

> 22.00 Pursuit broken off. While trying to run before the storm at full speed, the boat plunged twice. By blowing tanks, putting my helm hard over and reducing speed I managed to hold her reasonably well on the surface. To remain on the bridge was impossible. In just half an hour the captain and the watch were half-drowned. Within a short time five tons of water cascaded into the U-boat through the conning tower hatch, the voice pipe and the diesel air intake.

When the storm abated, the German sailors faced harassment from the air: the escort carrier *Bogue* stayed with convoy SC 123 until it was within range of normal air patrols from Iceland. Despite the appalling weather, the carrier had been able to operate her aircraft on four out of the six days she was with the convoy.

Between them, the weather and the aircraft wrecked the carefully laid ambush, and the actions against convoys ONS 1, SC 123 and HX 230 ended in failure for the U-boats. The combined force of more than thirty boats sank only one ship, a straggler. That cost two of their number, *U-169* (Bauer) and *U-469* (Claussen), both despatched by Fortresses of No. 206 Squadron based in Northern Ireland. Yet more important than the actual losses to either side was the fact that now, at last, the so-called 'Atlantic Gap' in the air cover was within sight of being plugged by the Liberators and aircraft operating from small escort carriers like the *Bogue*. The days of easy pickings for the U-boats in mid-Atlantic were fast drawing to a close.

While the bitter convoy battles were being fought to their conclusion, the fast independently routed liner *Empress of Scotland* was ploughing her own way across the Atlantic. In her hold she carried a precious cargo: the first of the highly secret 'Mark 24 Mine' homing torpedoes to be delivered to Britain. The custodian was

Acting Group Captain Jeaff Greswell, the man who made the first
Leigh Light attack and who was now returning from a liaison visit
to the USA. He later recalled the elaborate security precautions
that attended the move:

> The homing torpedo arrived at the quay at New York in a US
> Navy lorry escorted by armed guards; there seemed to be guns
> all over the place. The weapon was packed in three large
> boxes: one contained the nose, one the centre section and one
> the tail. These the sailors brought on to the ship, formally
> handed them over to me, and I signed for them. Then I
> witnessed the placing of the boxes in the captain's safe, and
> he gave me a receipt. At Liverpool it was the same thing in
> reverse. There we were met by an RAF lorry, again with
> armed guards. I received the boxes from the captain and
> signed for them, then I handed them over to the RAF officer
> and obtained his receipt. The demands of security had been
> observed to the letter. Now my part in the operation was over,
> so I went off for a few days' leave.
>
> I had been at home for a couple of days when I received a
> buff-coloured envelope with 'OHMS' across the top, by
> ordinary post. Inside was a letter from His Majesty's
> Customs; they wanted to know why I had imported into the
> United Kingdom 'packing cases containing what is believed
> to be some form of aerial homing torpedo for use against
> submarines.' Why had I failed to declare them?

Greswell immediately passed the letter to Air Chief Marshal
Joubert under a secret cover, with a frantic appeal, 'For heaven's
sake do something about this one.' He heard no more about it.

April 1943 proved to be a relatively quiet month for the Atlantic
convoys. The increasing use of escort carriers coupled with the
expansion in the force of very long range Liberators – now there
were about thirty – meant that it had become perceptibly more
difficult for U-boats to concentrate against convoys. And,
even when they reach a favourable position, the weather had cast
its wrath impartially upon both sides and made battle almost
impossible.

The lull was unlikely to continue, however. At the beginning of
May *Grossadmiral* Dönitz had more than ninety U-boats in the
North Atlantic. As the year advanced and the weather improved,

he looked forward to a repeat of the successful attacks on SC122 and HX 229. The German commander-in-chief's tactics of concentration had been tried and proved during scores of battles. His men were well trained, blooded and confident, and morale was high. In spite of the difficulties encountered during the first four months of 1943, the U-boats had torn serious gaps in the Allied merchant fleets: 264 ships sunk, totalling one and a half million tons.

In his news broadcasts, Dr Goebbels assured listeners again and again that nobody, not even the 'Anglo-Saxons', could continue to endure losses of shipping and war material on such a massive scale. Worried Allied naval planners had to agree that he was right.

During the first four months of 1943 the German and Italian Navies lost fifty-seven submarines in action. Of those, twenty-eight were destroyed by aircraft operating independently, and four by aircraft co-operating with ships. If the German grip on the trade routes was to be loosened, the Allies would have to do better than this.

Yet they were now about to do so. The very-long-range Liberator, able to provide cover for convoys in the dangerous mid-Atlantic area, was about to become available in greater numbers. So were the escort carriers to escort convoys. The 'genuine shallow-setting' depth-charge was in service, and so was the centimetric-wavelength ASV radar. The sonobuoy and the magnetic airborne detector were both ready for action. And the 'Mark 24 Mine' homing torpedo was being delivered to operational bases in Newfoundland, Iceland and Northern Ireland.

During the late spring of 1943, both sides looked forward to a hard but victorious fight that summer. The stage was set for the climax of the Battle of the Atlantic.

CHAPTER 7

The Wolves' Fangs are Drawn

May to August 1943

There can be no talk of a let-up in the U-boat war. The Atlantic is my first line of defence in the West. And even if I have to fight a defensive battle there, that is preferable to waiting to defend myself on the coast of Europe. The enemy forces tied down by our U-boats are tremendous, even though the losses inflicted by us are no longer great. I cannot afford to release these forces by discontinuing the U-boat war.

Adolf Hitler, 31 May 1943

The action that opened the decisive phase of the Battle of the Atlantic began, auspiciously enough for the German Navy, at the end of the first week in May 1943. On the 8th its experts stripped away the ciphering from two important British signals dealing with the routing of the fast eastbound convoy HX 237, and the associated slow convoy SC 129. Armed with this Intelligence, *Grossadmiral* Dönitz's headquarters broadcast orders to thirty-six U-boats to move into position to engage the convoys.

Two days later, as the submarines were nearing their assigned patrol lines, a further German deciphering success revealed the expected position of HX 237 on 11 May. This time there was no storm in the area to blunt the cutting edge of the attack. With such a concentration of U-boats, it seemed that all was set for a repeat of the triumphant action against SC 122/HX 229 less than two months earlier.

Since the March battle, however, the Allies had made potent additions to their forces. There was now a second very-long-range Liberator squadron, No. 86, able to reach the mid-Atlantic area. Moreover its aircraft, and those of No. 120 Squadron, now carried the deadly new 'Mark 24 Mine' homing torpedo. Alone, these aircraft were sufficient to give the U-boats a difficult time. Yet there was a further hazard in store for the German sailors: sailing with HX 237 was the escort carrier HMS *Biter*, carrying nine Swordfish and three Wildcat aircraft.

The battle opened on the afternoon of 10 May, when a Swordfish from *Biter* attacked *U-403* (Clausen), shadowing HX 237. The German sailors got the better of the encounter, for their return fire inflicted damage on the aircraft. But it was a hollow victory, for the U-boat was forced to dive and lost contact with the convoy. The Swordfish limped back to its carrier.

On the morning of the 12th one of *Biter*'s Swordfish took off to investigate a Huffduff bearing on a U-boat's transmissions. Soon afterwards the crew reported that they were attacking a submarine on the surface; during this radio conversation, listeners on *Biter* could hear the clatter of machine-gun fire in the background. In his book *Iron Coffins*, *Leutnant* Herbert Werner, executive officer of *U-230*, described what happened next:

It was too late to dive. The single-engined plane came in low in a straight line exactly over our wake. I fingered the trigger of my gun. Again the gun was jammed. I kicked its magazine, clearing the jam. Then I emptied the gun at the menace. The mate's machine-gun bellowed. Our boat veered to starboard, spoiling the plane's bomb run. The pilot revved up his engine, circled, then roared towards us from dead ahead. As the plane dived very low its engine spluttered, then stopped. Wing first, the plane crashed into the surging ocean, smashing its outer wing on our superstructure as we raced by. The pilot, thrown out of his cockpit, lifted his arm and waved for help, but then I saw him disintegrate in the explosion of the four bombs meant to destroy us. Four violent shocks kicked into our starboard side astern, but we left the horrible scene unharmed.

That afternoon the Swordfish avenged their dead comrades, when one of them guided a destroyer and a frigate to a U-boat seen to submerge ahead of the convoy; the subsequent attack put paid to the career of *U-89* (Lohmann).

While these actions were in progress, three of No. 86 Squadron's new Liberators arrived to add their considerable weight to the escort. Each aircraft carried two homing torpedoes, in addition to four normal depth-charges. If they found a U-boat and it submerged, the crew would attack it with homing torpedoes. If it remained on the surface, they would attack it with depth-charges. Due to the homing torpedo's vulnerability to enemy counter-measures, there were rigid rules concerning its use in action. Since one might conceivably run ashore and be captured, its use was forbidden in waters close to an enemy-held shore. Moreover, it was not to be used if its method of operation could be observed from the target or another enemy craft in the vicinity.

On that day, 12 May, Flight Lieutenant J. Wright had the distinction of scoring the first success with a homing torpedo (it was, incidentally, also the first-ever success for a self-homing guided missile of any type). As Wright approached *U-456* she obligingly dived, and he took his Liberator over the diving swirl and released the torpedo. The Liberator then circled the area for the next two minutes, while the crew's doubts grew regarding the new weapon's effectiveness. Then, about nine hundred yards from its point of entry, there was a small upheaval in the water. It looked as though a depth-charge had exploded with less than its normal force (at the time of the explosion both the U-boat and the torpedo were far beneath the surface, and the force of the explosion had spent itself in the deeper water).

The damage to the U-boat was serious, but it was not im-mediately lethal. *Kapitänleutnant* Teichert brought his crippled craft to the surface, still with enough fight to open accurate fire on the Liberator as it approached. By now the aircraft was nearing the limit of its endurance, however, and Wright had to leave the defiant submarine wallowing on the surface. Concerning the incident, *Grossadmiral* Dönitz noted in his War Diary:

> Between 12.00 and 13.30 hours *U-456* reported that she had been hit from the air, she is in no condition to dive and is in urgent need of assistance. Later she reported, several times, that she is leaking badly at the stern, presumably as a result of an aerial bomb hit [*Fliebotreffer*] . . .

Four U-boats attempted to reach *U-456*, without success. She survived the night, only to be relocated early the following morning by a Sunderland of the Canadian No. 423 Squadron. Teichert dived his boat for the last time, and soon afterwards two of the convoy's escorts arrived on the scene to put *U-456* out of her agony.

Fortunately for the Allies, the secret of the 'Mark 24 Mine' – which might easily have been betrayed during its very first attack

– remained secure. Teichert and his crew had no suspicions regarding the nature of the weapon that had exploded against their hull with such precision.

By mid-day on the 13th the two convoys were out of the mid-Atlantic danger area, and now enjoyed almost continuous air cover from land-based aircraft. Those U-boats remaining in contact now broke off the action. During the battle the two convoys had fought their way through a concentration of thirty-six U-boats for a loss of five ships, three of which had been straggling and alone at the time of being hit. The air and sea escorts had destroyed four U-boats and damaged others. And, more important, they had prevented a co-ordinated attack on the merchant ships.

HMS *Biter*'s aircraft had played an important part in neutralising the German pack tactics. After the operation the C-in-C Western Approaches, Admiral Sir Max Horton, himself a World War I submarine commander, commented on the operation: 'The value of carrier-borne aircraft in the protection of trade has been fully demonstrated.' The reader might consider that this point had already been 'fully demonstrated' a full eighteen months earlier, during HMS *Audacity*'s final cruise.

As the HX 237/SC 129 action was drawing to its close, on 14 May, Allied aircraft made two apparently lethal attacks with homing torpedoes. A Liberator of No. 86 Squadron and a Catalina of US Navy Patrol Squadron 84 launched their weapons at U-boats that had just dived. In each case there was a mushroom-like disturbance in the water some time afterwards, but there was no other immediate evidence to indicate that the weapon's 100 pound warhead had caused fatal damage. From German records, however, we know that *U-266* (Jessen) and *U-657* (Göllnitz) disappeared without trace in positions corresponding to the two attacks.

For the German Navy these losses, coupled with the failure to get to grips with the two convoys, had been bad enough. Yet worse was soon to follow. The following eastbound convoy, SC 130, had been duly located by the German cipher-breaking service on 18 May. *Grossadmiral* Dönitz ordered the seventeen U-boats of the *Donau* group to engage it. Convoy SC 130 lacked the support of an aircraft-carrier, but by the third week in May the force of very-long-range Liberators had expanded to fifty. Of those, an average of fifteen aircraft was available for operations at any one time. Moreover, part of the *Donau* patrol line extended into waters within range of the Iceland-based Hudsons of No. 269 Squadron, which promptly sank two of them – *U-646* (Wulff) on the 17th and *U-273* (Rossmann) on the 19th.

During 19 May relays of Liberators from Iceland combed the waters around the convoy; again and again they forced U-boats to submerge and thus lose contact with the plodding merchant ships. That day there were eighteen sightings of U-boats in the area around the convoy. The sole attack was by Flight Sergeant W. Stoves of No. 120 Squadron, who launched his two homing torpedoes at a U-boat that had just submerged. Half a minute later there were two small upheavals some seventy yards from the diving swirl, but yet again there was no immediate indication that either weapon had found its target. In that area and on that day, however, *U-964* (Loewe) vanished leaving no indication of her fate; for *Grossadmiral* Dönitz the loss was a terrible personal blow, for his son was serving as a junior officer in that boat.

The powerful air cover around SC 130 had hamstrung the efforts of the *Donau* U-boat group. As one German naval officer later noted:

> From the second day the convoy had continuous air cover, and repeated surprise air attacks through low cloud made it impossible to shadow or close in to the attack. The most surprising feature of the enemy's success was that, according to our radio Intelligence, there were never more than one or two aircraft in the air at the same time.

On the final day of the battle, 20 May, a Liberator of 120 Squadron depth-charged and sank *U-258* (Mässenhausen). With the two boats destroyed by the convoy's surface escort, this brought the German loss during the action to six U-boats. In return for this thrashing the German Navy had achieved nothing at all: not a single merchant ship had been hit. Ironically, at a time when the German Navy cipher-breakers were achieving some of their greatest successes in providing Intelligence on convoy movements, the U-boats were unable to exploit the information owing to the seemingly omnipresent air cover.

As the battle around SC 130 dissolved, another began around the westbound convoy ON 184. And accompanying this convoy was the escort carrier USS *Bogue*, now fully operational. During 21 and 22 May *Bogue*'s Avenger aircraft fought a series of inconclusive actions with U-boats in the area. So far no aircraft operating from an escort carrier had scored a 'kill' by itself, but that was about to change. On the afternoon of the 22nd Lieutenant W. Chamberlain sighted *U-569* in a shadowing position twenty miles to port of the convoy. He promptly ran in to attack and planted his four depth-charges accurately across the submerging boat, inflicting serious damage. *Oberleutnant* Johannsen was forced to resurface, but then found himself under attack from Lieutenant H. Roberts in a second Avenger. The boat up-ended and plunged to 350 feet before Johannsen regained the surface by blowing all tanks. There was barely time for part of the crew to abandon the craft before she sank for the last time. Meanwhile, convoy ON 184 passed through the danger zone without loss.

On the following day, 23 May, the escort carrier HMS *Archer* had her chance. She was part of the escort of the fast eastbound convoy HX 239, which was now passing through U-boat-infested waters. That morning she despatched a Swordfish and a Wildcat down a Huffduff bearing, towards a U-boat that was shadowing the convoy. Under its wings the Swordfish carried eight of the new rocket projectiles, making their debut as an anti-submarine weapon. Sighting his quarry about ten miles ahead, Sub-Lieutenant H. Horrocks turned his Swordfish into a convenient cloud, and headed for what he estimated to be a point abreast of the U-boat. He then turned to port and emerged from cloud to find the submarine about a mile away and slightly to port. Horrocks pushed down the nose of the aircraft and pointed his formidable battery at the U-boat, which by then had begun to dive. He fired his first pair of rockets from 800 yards, and these hit the water 150 yards short of the target; the second pair, from 400 yards, fell thirty yards short; the third pair, from 300 yards, struck the water ten yards short and the fourth pair, fired from 200 yards, struck the stern above the water line. It will be remembered that these rockets had been designed to strike the water a little short of the target, so that their curved underwater trajectories would strike the target *below* the water line. That was precisely what happened with at least one of the rockets in Horrock's third pair: it struck *U-752* on her No. 4 diving tank, then punched clean through her pressure hull. A wide jet of water cascaded uncontrollably through the wardroom. *Kapitänleutnant* Schroeter immediately counter-manded his order to dive, and the U-boat wallowed to the surface, discharging large quantities of oil.

The German sailors tumbled out of the conning tower to man their anti-aircraft guns, and Horrocks, his rockets expended, with-drew to a prudent distance. Now it was the turn of the Wildcat, whose pilot loosed off six hundred rounds of 0.5-inch ammunition during one long burst at the conning tower. The burst killed Schroeter, and wounded several of those in the conning tower with him. The survivors then scuttled their crippled boat, and were picked up by a convoy escort shortly afterwards.

Archer's aircraft successfully kept the U-boats down throughout the passage of HX 239, and that convoy suffered no loss.

The fortnight following the opening of the HX 237 action, on 10 May, had proved disastrous for the German cause in the North Atlantic. Although the U-boat crews had excellent Intelligence and handled their craft resolutely, they suffered serious losses and achieved virtually no sinkings. During those fourteen days no fewer than ten convoys, with some 370 merchant ships, passed through the mid-Atlantic danger area. Between them they lost only six ships, of which three had been stragglers. For this meagre return the German submarine service lost thirteen U-boats: seven to aircraft, two to aircraft working with naval escorts, and four to naval escorts operating alone. After coming near to defeat, the convoys had won a major victory, while it was the German Navy's 'Wolf Pack' tactics that were failing in their purpose.

On the day after the sinking of *U-752*, on 24 May, *Grossadmiral* Dönitz called a halt to the one-sided battle in mid-Atlantic. He ordered some of the U-boats to form a new group off the Azores, where the Allied defences were thought to be less strong; the remaining boats he recalled to France. On the final day in May he travelled to Berchtesgarden, to report directly to Hitler on the crisis in the war at sea. *Grossadmiral* Dönitz informed his Führer:

> Aircraft carriers are being used in conjunction with the North Atlantic convoys, so that all convoy routes are now under enemy air protection. However, the U-boat crisis has not resulted solely from the increase in the number of enemy aircraft. The determining factor is a new device, also used by surface vessels, by means of which aircraft are now able to locate U-boats . . . We do not even know on which wavelength the enemy locates our boats; neither do we know whether high-frequency or other location devices are being employed. Everything possible is being done to find out the cause.

The Germany Navy had suspected, correctly, that centimetric-wavelength radar was responsible for some of the surprise attacks on U-boats (although, in the continued absence of an operational Naxos-U receiver to detect such radar signals, even that was a matter of conjecture).

In fact, of course, the new radar was not the only method available to the Allies to locate U-boats. The cipher breakers at Bletchley Park were now reading almost the whole of the signals traffic between the U-boats and their headquarters, and with little delay. By the late spring of 1943 the information obtained from this source had become so reliable that the Allies were able to streamline their procedure for providing air cover over the Atlantic. Convoys known to be under immediate threat were code-named 'Stipple' convoys, and almost the entire available air cover was concentrated around these. Convoys without the 'Stipple' designation received little or no air cover. Thus the growing number of very-long-range Liberator aircraft could be employed to maximum effect

Moreover, while the Allied cipher breakers went from strength to strength, those of the German Navy received a severe setback. The Allies introduced a new and more effective naval cipher, which at a stroke cut off much of the Intelligence gained from the intercepted traffic.

Also at this time, the warships escorting convoys were making considerable use of their Huffduff equipment to locate U-boats transmitting in the vicinity of convoys. If an aircraft or an escorting ship was available, it was sent to attack the shadowing boat or force it to submerge and lose contact. To complicate the task of the direction finders, U-boats' radio operators made regular frequency changes as dictated by their headquarters. Provided the U-boats kept their transmission short, the Allied radio operators had insufficient time to find the frequency and tune in their direction finders before the transmission ended. For that reason, the German Navy did not take seriously the possibility that Allied warships employed short-range direction finders to exploit the U-boats' transmissions. Yet the signals ordering the latters' frequency changes were being read at Bletchley Park, and that information was immediately passed to the convoy escorts. That meant the Huffduff operators already had their direction finders tuned to the frequency of the U-boat transmissions, even before the latter began.

The failure to appreciate the importance of Huffduff was a major Intelligence failure by the German Navy. Moreover, as in the case of the earlier failure to detect centimetric-wavelength radar signals,

German Intelligence officers might have learned of the existence of the device had they but opened their minds to that possibility. In truth everything they needed lay buried, securely guarded, in the German Naval Intelligence files.

When convoy escorts took bearings on a transmitting U-boat, each ship transmitted its finding to the escort designated as Huffduff collator, which plotted the bearings to get a 'fix' on the U-boat. That ship-to-ship chit-chat carried a long way, however, and German monitoring stations in France often picked it up. Sometimes the German cipher experts were able to read the messages. Yet, having done so much that was difficult, the German Navy failed to clear what might have been the simplest hurdle of all: they did not realise the significance of the device, even when they knew its name.

Top-secret *X-B-Bericht* (cryptoanalysis service report) No. 16/43 dated 22 April 1943, whose distribution list included the U-boat operational and signals staffs, would have revealed to anyone who got as far as Page 24 that:

A radio conversation on 9.4 mentioned that the Coastguard cutter *Spencer*, operating with Task Unit 24,1,9 attached to Convoy ON 175, is equipped with a high-frequency direction finder [*Kurzwellenpeiler*] . . .

Yet such pointers, and there were others, were ignored. When captains of returning U-boats voiced the suspicion that enemy ships or aircraft might have homed onto their transmissions, this was dismissed as 'unlikely'. Almost certainly, the Intelligence officers repeated, the detection had been made with radar. As we observed earlier, that presupposed an Allied ship-borne or airborne radar able to detect U-boats at twenty miles or more – a performance beyond the finest centimetric-wavelength radars then in existence. Yet how could the German Navy judge this? Following the shock of the discovery of the 'Rotterdam' equipment, how could they safely set a limit to their enemy's radar capability?

There was further evidence that the German Navy ignored, and that might have provided a signpost to the correct road. From vantage points in the Spanish port of Algeciras, German agents frequently took long-range photographs of Allied warships lying off Gibraltar. On some of these pictures the Huffduff aerials were clearly visible. To an Intelligence officer lacking detailed knowledge of electronics, it was easy to dismiss the cage-like structure as the aerial of some rather ancient radar set; and that was precisely what happened. To compound the irony, some of the Algeciras photographs were included in the ship recognition books issued to all U-boats. Yet to conceal the source in case one of the books fell into Allied hands, the Gibraltarian background had to be carefully painted out – and in this 'tidying-up' process the Huffduff aerials were deleted as well.

With hindsight, of course, it is a simple matter to sort through the conflicting pieces of information on Allied location systems available to the German Navy, and separate the wheat from the chaff. Had that service enjoyed the support of an operational research section like those supporting the Allied efforts, things might have been different. Had operational U-boat crews been able to air their suspicions before top scientists at meetings like the 'Sunday Soviets', things might have been different. But now the lack of an effective line of communication between German scientists and the fighting men was having a serious effect on the course of the conflict.

For the reasons outlined above, during the conference on German naval affairs on 31 May 1943 Adolf Hitler learned relatively little of the Allies' U-boat location methods. *Grossadmiral* Dönitz outlined his hopes for the immediate future, which centred on two new weapons soon to be introduced, which he hoped would give U-boats a better chance against attacking warships and aircraft. The first was the *Zaunkönig*, an acoustic homing torpedo (similar in operation to the 'Mark 24 Mine', though he had no inkling of the Allied work in this area). The second weapon was the new quadruple-barrelled 20 mm anti-aircraft gun, which had a high rate of fire and promised to be lethal against aircraft closing in to short range to deliver their attacks.

The *Grossadmiral* concluded with his summing up of the situation following the U-boats' defeat in the mid-Atlantic: 'Losses are too high. We must conserve our strength, otherwise we shall play into the hands of the enemy.' It was vitally important, he said, to keep the U-boat force in being. Even if Allied shipping losses were low, very large forces of ships and aircraft were tied down to maintain this state of affairs. Hitler expressed himself in complete agreement. He said the Atlantic was his first line of defence in the West; even having to fight a losing battle there was better than having to await an attack on the coast of Europe. Moreover, he could not afford to allow the Allies to release their powerful anti-submarine naval and air forces for other mischief.

The Führer's final statement demonstrated a firm grasp of this particular situation. By the summer of 1943 more than eleven hundred Allied aircraft were engaged in anti-submarine operations over the Atlantic. Supporting these were equivalently large training and supply organisations. On the naval side there was a veritable armada of small warships – far more numerous and costly to maintain than Dönitz's U-boat force – committed to the anti-submarine task. Certainly there were tough times ahead for the German sailors. But there seemed no reasonable alternative to maintaining the pressure until, with the introduction of an advanced new type of U-boat in the planning stage (and of which more later) the German Navy could again threaten the Allied shipping routes across the north Atlantic.

No decrypted enemy transmission, no radar or Huffduff device, could by itself cause the destruction of a U-boat, or even force one to withdraw from a convoy. To achieve supremacy it was necessary to have sufficient aircraft in position to threaten, and possibly destroy, any U-boats attempting to concentrate around convoys and press home attacks. The lack of such aircraft had made possible the German victory in March 1943. When the necessary air cover became available, later that spring, the U-boat offensive collapsed.

Could such air cover have been made available earlier? Technically the answer has to be 'Yes', for both the very-long-range modified aircraft and the escort carrier had been proved in action by the beginning of 1942. We have observed that the reason for the delay in the supply of very-long-range aircraft was the prior demands of the strategic bomber forces. The view that the diversion of sufficient heavy bombers to the anti-submarine role would have had a debilitating effect on the bomber offensive scarcely stands examination. As No. 120 Squadron demonstrated time and again, a single aircraft in the vicinity of a threatened convoy was often sufficient to throw an entire Wolf Pack attack into disarray. An additional three very-long-range squadrons, comprising about forty aircraft, would have gone – and later did go – a considerable way towards nullifying the threat to convoys in mid-Atlantic. During the winter of 1942–3 RAF Bomber Command frequently lost half that number of four-engined bombers during a single attack on Germany.

During the early months of 1943 the Allied strategic bomber forces, on naval insistence, were directed to attack the U-boat bases on the west coast of France. The German Navy had foreseen this possibility, however, and had constructed massive bunkers to house the U-boats and repair shops. The sixteen-foot-thick reinforced-concrete roofs were proof against any bomb then in use, and although the attacks caused substantial damage to the ports they did not seriously affect U-boat operations. Indeed, from German records we know that no submarine's cruise was delayed as a direct result of these attacks. In the summer of 1943 *Grossadmiral* Dönitz commented:

> The Anglo-Saxon attempt to strike down our U-boat arm is being undertaken with all the means at their disposal. You know that the towns of St Nazaire and Lorient have been rubbed out as main submarine bases. Not a dog, not a cat is left in these towns. Nothing remains – but the U-boat shelters. The Todt Organisation built them on the farsighted orders of the Führer, and the submarines are repaired in them.

Between January and May 1943, the Allied bomber forces had lost more than a hundred heavy bombers during attacks on the U-boat bases. Apart from some useful operational training for newly formed American units, the raids produced little else of direct value to the Allied cause.

After the war there was a lively debate between senior air force and naval officers concerning the delay in providing very-long-range air cover for the Atlantic convoys. Yet had they employed their own resources more effectively, the naval staffs could have done much to relieve the situation. HMS *Audacity* had shown a way to provide air cover for convoys in mid-Atlantic, before she was sunk at the end of 1941; yet nearly eighteen months elapsed before the small aircraft-carrier became a regular feature of the convoy escorts. Much of the delay was due to the need to cure faults that became evident when these ships were used to operate high-performance fighter aircraft. But the naval staffs displayed less than Nelsonian vigour in pushing the conversion of simpler escort carriers to provide anti-submarine cover.

The eventual answer was the merchant aircraft-carrier, or MAC-ship: fast grain ships or oil tankers, fitted with a flight deck some 400 feet long and 60 feet wide. These vessels operated three or four

Swordfish aircraft, but retained the ability to transport about four-fifths of their normal cargo. The conversion work took about five months, with a further two months needed to work-up the vessel for operations. The first MAC-ship to become operational, the 8,000 ton *Empire MacAlpine*, sailed with a convoy at the end of May 1943.

The MAC-ship proved to be the simplest and cheapest answer to the problem of providing continuous air cover for convoys. Admittedly, under marginal flying conditions when the wind was too light or the sea too rough, these ships became difficult landing platforms. As a result several Swordfish were wrecked in crashes. Yet these accidents were seldom fatal, and an aircraft costing a few thousand pounds was a fair object to risk if it meant increasing the survival chances of loaded merchant ships each worth several million pounds.

Yet as the spring of 1943 gave way to the summer, it became clear that the Allies had indeed won a great victory. When Convoy HX 240 arrived at Liverpool on 4 June, it was the seventh successive convoy to cross the North Atlantic without loss.

Squeezed out of the North Atlantic at the end of May, *Grossadmiral* Dönitz decided to shift his attack to the south, against shipping in the Central Atlantic area. There the sea routes were teeming with targets, as the American forces moved vast quantities of men and materials to the Mediterranean area for the forthcoming invasions of Sicily and Italy. For the Allies the position regarding land bases for air cover was even worse than over the North Atlantic: there was no airfield available between Bermuda and the coast of North Africa, some three thousand miles away (the Allies did not gain Portuguese government permission for use of an airfield on the Azores until the autumn). The German naval C-in-C had good reason to hope that his sailors would find a new 'Atlantic Gap', in which they could once more grapple with the convoys.

The first large-scale engagement in the new area opened early in June, around the westbound convoy GUS 7A. On the German side were seventeen U-boats of the *Trutz* group, strung out in a line to the south of the Azores. Unfortunately for the attackers, however, GUS 7A was no harmless fly about to blunder helplessly into their web to be butchered at leisure; she was a wasp with a deadly sting in her tail – the escort carrier *Bogue*. The battle opened on the 4th, when Avengers made unsuccessful attacks on three U-boats in the German group. On the following day a two-aircraft team from

Bogue found *U-217* (Reichenbach-Klinke), and carried out a well co-ordinated attack. First the Wildcat fighter strafed the U-boat and forced her to dive, then while she was still visible Lieutenant McAuslan in the accompanying Avenger straddled her with a stick of four depth-charges. Her pressure hull slit, the boat plunged to the bottom.

U-217 had been on the southernmost fringe of the *Trutz* patrol line, and as a result the merchant ships were able to pass to the south of the line without being seen. Once convoy GUS 7A was safely clear of the danger, *Bogue* moved to shepherd an eastbound convoy. Again, it prevented the U-boats from making contact. Their primary task of safeguarding the convoys completed, *Bogue* and her four attendant destroyers headed back to the *Trutz* area, looking for trouble. The prying Avengers soon found it. On the afternoon of 8 June a searching aircraft came upon *U-758*; she was one of the first U-boats fitted with the new quadruple-barrelled 20 mm anti-aircraft gun. The unexpectedly hot reception forced the first attacking pilot to release his depth-charges too early; the second, summoned by radio and arriving shortly afterwards, attacked but suffered several hits and limped back to *Bogue* with a wounded crewman. His U-boat still undamaged, *Kapitänleutnant* Manseck remained defiantly on the surface: engaging aircraft with the new armament was a fine sport. Next on the scene were a couple of Wildcat fighters, but initially their pilots, too, found the hail of defensive fire disconcerting. Finally Lieutenant Perabo pushed his Wildcat through the barrage and his rounds smashed into *U-758*'s conning tower, wounding eleven gunners and knocking-out two of the gun's four barrels. This time things had gone too far, and Manseck decided to dive. As he did so a further Avenger attacked with depth-charges, but the U-boat made good its escape.

On the following day *Bogue*'s aircraft took their revenge on the submarine tanker *U-118* (Czygan). She was not so well armed as *U-758*, and a total of seven aircraft took part in her destruction. The hunting group scoured the waters for a couple of days longer, but found no sign of the U-boats, which had pulled out of the area, having sunk nothing.

During the following two months, July and August, the American escort carriers enjoyed their own 'happy time' in the waters round the Azores. *Bogue*, and her sister ships *Card*, *Core* and *Santee*, which arrived shortly afterwards, accounted for no fewer than thirteen U-boats. *Santee* introduced the 'Mark 24 Mine' homing torpedo to the area in July, sending her aircraft out in pairs, one to force the U-boat to dive, the other to plant the homing torpedo just ahead of the diving swirl. These tactics accounted for *U-160* (Pommer-Esche) on the 14th, *U-509* (Witte) on the 15th and *U-43* (Schwantke) on the 15th. The last-named U-boat was literally 'hoist by her own petard', when the homing torpedo detonated the mines she was carrying.

The fact that the escort carriers so often seemed to be in the right place at the right time was, of course, no coincidence. This more-direct use of the information from the decrypted German signals was hotly disputed in some quarters, for it was argued that if there were too many such 'coincidences' the German Navy would be certain to suspect the truth. Those who wished to make greater use of the information argued, with equal force, that to gain such Intelligence was purposeless unless it was used. And who could say that the Germans might not discover the truth anyway, or change to a more secure system as a matter of course? If the latter came about, much valuable Intelligence information would have been wasted.

At the end of August *Grossadmiral* Dönitz pulled his depleted forces back from the Central Atlantic; it was clear that there were no easy pickings to be found there. What should have been a happy hunting ground for his men turned out, for many, to be their grave-yard. The only military value he could claim, for a cost of fifteen U-boats, was the tying down of substantial Allied anti-submarine forces.

Concurrent with the unsuccessful attempts to strike at convoys off the Azores, U-boats operating singly had enjoyed somewhat greater success against ships sailing independently in the distant waters off Brazil, the West Indies, and off the west and south-east coasts of Africa. During the first nine days of July they disposed of twenty-one ships in these waters without loss to themselves; but then the shore-based aircraft hit back.

Between 9 July and the end of August aircraft, almost all of them US Navy planes, destroyed fourteen U-boats. Usually the aircraft made short work of the submarines once they had found them, though on three occasions this was far from being the case.

On the evening of 18 July there was a unique fight to the death between a US Navy blimp and a U-boat off the southern tip of Florida. By the summer of 1943 the US Navy operated some thirty non-rigid airships to patrol the waters off the east coast of the Americas. The most numerous type was the 'K' Class, 251 feet long and powered by two 425-horsepower engines that gave it a cruising speed of 55 mph. The ten-man crew had radar, a magnetic airborne detector and sonobuoys to assist them to find U-boats, and four 375 pound depth-charges with which to attack them. The value of these craft against submarines was a matter of some debate. After the war the official US Navy historian wrote:

> An important if relatively ineffective component of the naval air arm was the lighter-than-air dirigible, the so-called blimp. Most naval officers, in view of the rapid development of planes, were very sceptical of these handsome sausage-shaped airships. But they had advocates who had been trained in their operation; the company that manufactured them was influential; and at a time when the U-boats looked like winners the Navy dared reject nothing that might contribute to the final victory . . . But most naval officers regarded them as inferior to planes for area patrol and worse than useless in convoy coverage, because they could be sighted by a U-boat even further away than the most smoke-careless freighter.

Scathing though these comments were, those who operated the blimps could truthfully point out that of the eighty-nine thousand ships they escorted during World War II, not one was lost to submarine attack.

The blimps were far better at deterrence than destruction, however. During the action on 18 July Lieutenant N. Grills, commanding the blimp K-34, attempted to press home an attack on *U-134*, which was cruising on the surface. Long before the airship got anywhere near the boat, *Kapitänleutnant* Brosin's gunners had found the range and were pumping cannon shells into her. The rounds passed through the envelope without exploding, but in the process they slashed holes in the fabric, allowing the vital lifting helium to escape. K-34 slowly lost altitude, but her onward momentum carried her over the U-boat; then, by a twist of irony, the release gear failed and the depth-charges remained in their racks. As the dying blimp collapsed on the water, Brosin submerged and left the area. He radioed brief details of the encounter to his headquarters, but otherwise he would not be able to savour his unique victory: on the way home *U-134* fell foul of British air patrols over the Bay of Biscay, and was sunk with all hands.

In neither world war did an airship, unaided, sink a submarine.

Yet if one accepts the dictum that 'a saved ship with its cargo is of more value to the Allied cause than a destroyed enemy submarine', the operations by these craft cannot be judged ineffective.

The smaller and faster aeroplanes made much more difficult and dangerous targets, but early in August a U-boat put up a remarkably plucky fight against no fewer than nine of them. The boat was *U-615* and her commander was *Kapitänleutnant* Ralph Kapitzky, who had earlier served as a pilot in the air arm. On the evening of 5 August, a Trinidad-based US Navy Mariner flying-boat found *U-615* on the surface off the coast of Venezuela. The depth-charges caused no damage, but by the following morning the hounds were in full cry in the area. Lieutenant A. Matuski, flying a similar aircraft of the same squadron (VP-205), relocated the U-boat, and his first attack caused considerable damage; his radio operator signalled the headquarters at Port of Spain, 'Sub damaged with bow out of water making only two knots, no casualties to plane or personnel'. Matuski then ran in to finish off the U-boat, but Kapitzky's gunners were ready and they scored several hits on the flying-boat. The latter's next – and final – message was more dramatic: 'Damaged – damaged – fire.' The aircraft then crashed into the sea, leaving no survivor.

For the German sailors it was a Pyrrhic victory, for their boat was severely damaged and could no longer dive. They were, moreover, in the position of poachers who had killed the policeman sent to apprehend them: from all over the area, aircraft converged on the scene. Another Mariner flying-boat regained contact with the crippled submarine, and delivered its attack in the face of heavy return fire that scored hits on the starboard wing. The US crew then orbited the defiant U-boat, summoning assistance. This arrived shortly afterwards in the form of a twin-engined Ventura bomber, whose stick of depth-charges caused further damage to the U-boat. The two aircraft, their bomb racks empty, then orbited the submarine until they were joined by yet another Mariner. The three aircraft then attacked together, but the move did little to draw the German fire away from the main target: the pilot of the latest Mariner to arrive received fatal injuries, and his crew released the depth-charges prematurely. The flying-boat then limped out of the area. In its place came yet another Mariner, the fifth aircraft of this type to take part in the action; its bombing and strafing attack resulted in the death of some of the German gunners and injuries to others. Still Kapitzky refused to admit defeat: while there was life there was hope, for night would soon fall and there was a chance he might escape to one of the small islands that dotted those waters and effect repairs.

Yet there was to be no relief for the battered submarine and her doughty crew. During the early evening a Mariner dropped flares to illuminate the boat, and then a US Army B-18 Bolo delivered its attack. The U-boat's charmed life continued, and she survived that engagement also. Soon after midnight a seventh Mariner illuminated *U-615* with flares but, uncertain of the identity of the craft, did not attack.

Only after first light, with the arrival on the horizon of a US Navy destroyer, did Kapitzky give up the grossly unequal struggle: he ordered his crew to abandon the boat, then scuttled the U-boat and went down with her. During this remarkable action *U-615* had come under attack by nine aircraft, of which one was shot down and two were damaged.

As has been said, the greater part of the air patrols in the 'distant waters' were mounted by US Navy planes, and aircraft from that service achieved the majority of the successes. One notable exception, however, was in the waters off West Africa, where RAF Coastal Command was active. On 11 August Flying Officer L. Trigg, piloting a Liberator of No. 200 Squadron, came upon a U-boat on the surface some 240 miles south-west of Dakar. He raced in to attack but the German sailors replied with heavy and accurate cannon fire. His aircraft burning fiercely, the pilot held his course and released his stick of depth-charges across the target before crashing into the sea. The explosions ruptured the pressure hull of *U-468*, and within a short time she followed the aircraft to the bottom. The only survivors of the action, the U-boat's commander, *Oberleutnant* Schamong, and seven of his men, managed to scramble aboard an inflated rubber dinghy that broke clear of the Liberator when it sank. Three days later, a British warship rescued them.

There was a remarkable sequel to this action some four months afterwards when, on the sole evidence of the German survivors, Trigg received a posthumous award of the Victoria Cross. He was the first airman engaged on anti-submarine operations to receive Britain's highest decoration.

The German Navy's attempts of June, July and August 1943 to regain the initiative in the battle against the convoys, which had slipped from their fingers in May, had in each case ended in failure. No matter where *Grossadmiral* Dönitz directed his attack, in the

North, the Central or the South Atlantic, the Allies seemed to have overwhelming forces available to defeat him.

Moreover, as we shall observe in the next chapter, at a time when the U-boats were proving unable to disrupt their enemy's transit routes, the patrolling aircraft were causing carnage along those routes the German sailors had to use. For during this same period, the U-boat service also suffered a major defeat in the Bay of Biscay.

CHAPTER 8

Climax in the Bay

May to August 1943

The Bay is the trunk of the Atlantic U-boat menace, the roots being in the Biscay ports and the branches spreading far and wide, to the North Atlantic convoys, to the Caribbean, to the eastern seaboard of North America . . .

Air Marshal Sir John Slessor, C-in-C Coastal Command, writing in a memorandum to the Combined Chiefs of Staff in April 1943

The Bay of Biscay is the strip of water bounded on its east by the coast of France, and on its south by the coast of Spain. The Bay is not wide: its east–west axis – the important one in this story because it points straight into the Atlantic – is some 800 miles wide. This was the stretch of sea that three out of every four U-boats had to cross to get to and from their operational areas, the stretch of water that Sir John Slessor termed 'the trunk of the U-boat menace'. Since the summer of 1941, No. 19 Group of Coastal Command had been nibbling at this trunk, though for almost two years there was relatively little to show for its unremitting labour. Then, in the spring of 1943, the Group suddenly emerged into a keen-toothed, sharp-clawed beaver-like creature, which gnawed vigorously at the trunk that had resisted it for so long. It swiftly slashed through the protective bark, to gouge deeply into the sap-carrying, living wood underneath. No. 19 Group was making its bid to sever the U-boats' most important transit route.

We had left the struggle in the Bay of Biscay at the end of April 1943. Then the German Naval High Command was becoming increasingly concerned at the number of U-boats returning from operations, whose captains complained of night attacks by aircraft with no prior warning from the Metox receiver. There were also a disconcerting, though still small, number of U-boats that disappeared in those waters leaving no clue as to their fate.

From the beginning the German Navy had suspected, correctly, that some form of centimetric-wavelength radar might be at the root of the trouble. There was, however, little direct evidence to support this notion. Until the new Naxos-U receiver came into service, designed to give U-boat crews warning of the approach of Allied aircraft carrying the new radar, *Grossadmiral* Dönitz had told his sailors to remain submerged while crossing the Bay during the night. They were to surface to recharge their batteries only during the daytime, when the patrolling aircraft could be seen and the submarines could usually dive before an attack could develop. If there was no time to dive, the German sailors were to engage the aircraft with their new armament and either shoot them down or drive them away.

The fact that the U-boat crews had changed their tactics was immediately apparent at Air Vice-Marshal Bromet's headquarters at Plymouth: during the first week in May his crews sighted U-boats on seventy-one occasions during the daytime, and delivered attacks on forty-three. They sank three outgoing submarines, and damaged three more to such an extent that they had to abandon their patrols and return to base. Moreover, aircrews reported that on seventeen separate occasions U-boats had remained on the surface and tried to defend themselves with anti-aircraft fire.

When Sir John Slessor heard of the new 'fight back' tactics he was keen to take up the German gauntlet. He saw clearly that the scales were weighted heavily in favour of his Command: an aircraft, even a large and expensive one like the Liberator, cost £60,000 and carried a crew of ten. A U-boat, on the other hand, cost upwards of £200,000 and carried a crew of more than fifty. The Air Marshal wrote to his crews:

> The habit of fighting back may cost us a few more aircraft lost; but if persisted in (which is at least open to doubt), it will undoubtedly mean more U-boats killed. It is up to us to take the fullest advantage of the good opportunities offered, before the buzz goes round in the Bay ports that fighting back is an expensive and unprofitable pastime.

To exploit the opportunity to the full, Air Vice-Marshal Bromet concentrated the whole of No. 19 Group against U-boats crossing the Bay by day; he even abandoned the night patrols, so that his

Leigh Light squadrons could assist in this task. During May the Group sank six U-boats in the Bay, and inflicted severe damage to a similar number. The 'fight back' tactics claimed six attacking aircraft.

The top-scoring anti-U-boat crew in May was that of Wing Commander Wilfred Oulton, commander of the Halifax-equipped No. 58 Squadron. His crew opened their tally on the 5th, with the sinking of *U-663* (Schmid). Ten days later they carefully stalked the submarine tanker *U-463* (Wolfbauer) from up-sun. In the attack that followed, Oulton's accurate stick of depth-charges exploded almost immediately underneath the boat; she sank by the stern until only her bow pointed vertically out of the water, then that too sank. On the 31st Oulton and his crew rounded off their private war on U-boats with numbers ending '63', when they shared in the destruction of *U-563*.

Realising that his earlier 'fight back' tactics had failed, in June *Grossadmiral* Dönitz ordered a change: U-boats were to cross the Bay of Biscay in convoy. They were to leave their bases on the surface in daylight, and form into groups. On the approach of Allied aircraft they were under strict orders to remain on the surface and use their combined fire power to drive them away or shoot them down. At night the U-boats were to submerge and maintain prescribed speeds; at dawn they were to surface, re-form into their group and continue as before until they were clear of the Bay. It was a striking reversal of previous tactics, for previously the U-boats had always tried to avoid fighting against aircraft if they possibly could. Now the new tactics would make such fights inevitable.

At first the U-boats' convoy tactics worked well. A pair of U-boats returning from the Atlantic crossed the Bay together safely and arrived at Brest on 7 June, as did a second pair on the 11th. Then on the 12th a patrolling aircraft sighted the first of the large outgoing group to run the gauntlet – five U-boats running on the surface about ninety miles north of Cape Ortegal. Night fell before reinforcing aircraft arrived on the scene, and, as ordered, the U-boats cruised submerged during the hours of darkness. The following evening a lone Sunderland of No. 228 Squadron, captained by Flying Officer L. Lee, regained contact with the group, which was now some 250 miles west of Cape Finisterre. Undeterred by the hail of return fire, Lee pressed home his attack. His depth-charges straddled *U-564*, before the mortally wounded flying-boat crashed into the sea with its crew.

Oberleutnant Fiedler pulled his seriously damaged U-boat out of the group and headed back to Brest escorted by *U-185* (Maus). Soon after midday on the following day, 14 June, a Whitley of No. 10 Operational Training Unit – a training unit that RAF Bomber Command had lent to Coastal Command – sighted the two returning submarines. After orbiting for two hours in a vain wait for reinforcements, its captain, Sergeant A. Benson, decided to attack alone. His depth-charges finished off *U-564*, but the Whitley suffered heavily too: first it radioed that it was returning with damage, then that German fighters were attacking it. Nothing more was seen of the bomber or its crew. *U-185* continued back to Brest, carrying nineteen survivors of *U-564*. Of the five U-boats that had attempted to fight their way across the Bay, one had been lost and one had to return early. Even allowing that two attacking planes had been shot down, that could scarcely be considered a victory for the German Navy.

The two U-boat groups that followed had varying fortunes. Both set out on 12 June. The first group, comprising three boats from La Pallice, crossed the Bay without loss and the U-boats' return fire inflicted damage on two attacking aircraft. The second group comprised five boats from the Brest and Lorient flotillas. On the 14th a patrol of four Mosquito fighters of the Polish No. 307 Squadron found them off Cape Finisterre. Squadron Leader Szablowski ordered his aircraft into line astern and led them down to strafe the U-boats with their cannon. Return fire wrecked one of Szablowski's engines, and he flew 500 miles on his remaining one before he crash-landed at his base in Cornwall. Yet the submariners did not get off scot-free either: the Mosquitoes' cannon shells caused so many casualties aboard *U-68* (Lauzemis) and *U-155* (Piening) that both had to return to base. The remaining three U-boats successfully entered the Atlantic.

After two weeks of these daylight-surfaced group sailing tactics, *Grossadmiral* Dönitz could see that such prolonged coat trailing was hazardous for the U-boats. Moreover, it was unnecessary. The object of the new tactics was not to shoot down aircraft, but to get U-boats safely across the Bay. Accordingly, on 17 June, he revised his tactics. U-boats were to stay in groups and surface by day, but only for the minimum time necessary to recharge batteries – about four hours in every twenty-four. At first it seemed that the new tactics were an answer to the Bay of Biscay air patrols. The reduction in the time U-boats spent on the surface, exposed to air attack, made it more difficult for Coastal Command to find, concentrate aircraft and attack the groups. As a result, during the final two weeks of June, only one U-boat was damaged in the Bay from air attack.

If there was to be 'coat trailing', Dönitz felt it should be done by U-boats specially armed for this purpose – the so-called 'submarine-aircraft-traps' (*Unterseebootflugzeugfalle*). The first boat so converted was *U-441*. She lost her 88 mm deck gun and in its place received two armoured 'bandstands', one forward and one aft of the conning tower. On these were mounted two quadruple-barrelled 20 mm guns, and a single-barrelled 37 mm gun – by any standard a formidable anti-aircraft armament. Commanded by *Kapitänleutnant* Götz von Hartmann, *U-441* carried a sixty-seven-man crew – sixteen more than usual for such a Type VII boat. The extras included a doctor, two scientists to operate equipment to investigate the Allied submarine detection methods, and a specially trained team to man the guns. Von Hartmann's orders were unequivocal: 'The aircraft are not to be driven away. They are to be shot down.'

U-441's first cruise in her new role, at the end of May 1943, ended inconclusively. After a day spent running invitingly on the surface at the western edge of the Bay of Biscay, a Sunderland took the bait. During the subsequent action the German sailors found that a weld on the after 20 mm gun mounting had failed, and the weapon was unusable. *U-441* had therefore to face her first major test lacking a major proportion of her firepower. The remaining guns caused serious damage to the attacking aircraft, but the pilot bravely continued his attack. He dropped his depth-charges close alongside the U-boat before the aircraft crashed into the sea with its crew. For her part *U-441* had suffered a severe shaking, damage to her steering gear and an uncomfortable leak; she hobbled back to Brest for repairs.

By the first week in July *U-441* was ready for her second 'aircraft-trap' operation. The damage suffered during her first had been repaired, as had the disconcerting fault to the after 20 mm gun mounting. Now, von Hartmann had little reason to doubt, his powerfully armed U-boat would have a proper chance to prove herself in action. If his gunners could shoot down three or four enemy planes, and perhaps inflict damage to a couple more, it might cause Allied aircrews to be rather less enthusiastic about attacking U-boats in the Bay.

On 8 July the 'wolf in sheep's clothing' set out from Brest again, and for the next four days she cruised enticingly up and down the

Bay on the surface and in the sunshine. It almost seemed as if the Allied aircraft knew her business, for none attempted to molest her. Then, on the afternoon of the 12th, a patrol of three Beaufighters of No. 248 Squadron spotted her. The British fighters were out looking for Junkers 88s that had been active in the area; but U-boats were fair game, too. Flight Lieutenant C. Schofield led his formation in a diving turn towards the unexpected prey. Thus, instead of the lumbering under-gunned bomber the German sailors had expected, they now faced three nimble fighters with a combined firepower of twelve 20 mm cannon and eighteen machine-guns.

Von Hartmann's wisest course would have been to take his U-boat down out of harm's way, and stay there until the Beaufighters had gone. But he was confident in his weapons, and the idea of running away from the first serious fight did not appeal to him. As the distance between the two adversaries closed, each side pumped explosive shells at the other, the twinkling lines of tracer rounds crossing and recrossing each other. The Beaufighter pilots noted that the U-boat's bridge and deck 'were crammed with men serving the many guns'. Schofield had 'something about the size of a cricket ball' – almost certainly a 37 mm shell – flash past his cockpit.

Yet the German sailors also had difficulties, for the swell made accurate fire difficult and 'the aircraft, obviously well controlled by radio, attacked alternately and without pause from all sides.' In an action such as this a single accurate burst from either side could decide the issue, and one such fusillade struck the boat during the planes' second strafing runs. Cannon shells thudded into the conning tower and gun positions, reducing them to a shambles and scything down her captain, officers and gunners. Ten sailors were killed, thirteen more were wounded. From his vantage point Schofield observed: 'All fire from the U-boat stopped, and the Beaufighters were now able to press home their attacks to a much lower level.'

On *U-441* the only officer still uninjured was the surgeon, Dr Pfaffinger. While the Beaufighters made three more firing runs on the now-defenceless submarine, he directed the recovery of the wounded sailors below decks. The surgeon's coolness is all the more remarkable if one considers that he could not know the aircraft carried no depth-charges, and the next attack might not end with such a lethal salvo. Finally, having delivered the living to safety, Pfaffinger initiated the diving manoeuvre and took *U-441* home. For his courage he later received the *Deutsche Kreuz*, a major decoration.

Remarkably, when *U-441* reached Brest, there was no shortage of volunteers willing to partake in her next cruise. That was indicative of the continuing high morale in the U-boat service, despite the vicious blows it had suffered. To *Grossadmiral* Dönitz the lessons of the two 'aircraft-trap' cruises were clear enough, however; later he wrote:

> So far as the U-boat Command was concerned . . . this action showed clearly that a submarine was a poor weapon with which to fight aircraft, and all further modification work on U-boats as 'aircraft-traps' was abandoned.

In future, U-boats were to fight it out with aircraft only when there was no alternative, or if they were in convoy and could bring their concentrated firepower to bear. *U-441* was modified back into a commerce raider, though she retained a large part of her anti-aircraft armament. The Royal Air Force would settle its score with this boat, but later.

The failure of the 'submarine-aircraft-trap' experiment was not one of *Grossadmiral* Dönitz's major concerns regarding July's events in the Bay of Biscay, however. It will be remembered that in mid-June he had ordered U-boat groups to run on the surface during the day to recharge their batteries. Otherwise boats were to cruise submerged.

Coastal Command had rapidly taken the measure of the new sailing tactics, and its response soon took lethal effect. Sir John Slessor saw that the obvious answer to group-sailing U-boats was group-attacking aircraft. Accordingly he had his tactical planners devise a scheme to enable No. 19 Group aircraft to spread out while combing their designated area for submarines, then concentrate speedily once a U-boat group had been found. The system, which came into use during the latter part of June, bore a striking resemblance to Dönitz's own 'Wolf Pack' tactics for locating and attacking convoys. Three times each day a force of seven aircraft flew on parallel tracks through two areas – code-named Musketry and Seaslug – which lay astride the U-boat's transit routes. If an aircraft sighted a group of enemy submarines, it was to orbit them and radio details to its headquarters. The latter would then direct the other machines in the 'pack' to the scene.

Each of the patrol areas extended more than 115 miles in their east–west dimension, the maximum distance a U-boat would cover in a day if it spent four hours on the surface and the remaining twenty cruising submerged. There was a good chance, therefore, that at least one of the three daily air patrols would find a U-boat group if there was one was running through the area.

With the almost unnatural languor round the North Atlantic convoys at this time, Coastal Command could afford to detach aircraft from its other groups to strengthen No. 19 Group for the Musketry and Seaslug patrols. Even so, during their first two weeks of operations the air patrols did little to ruffle German confidence. Then, on 2 July, a Liberator of No. 224 Squadron inflicted damage on the outbound submarine tanker *U-462* (Vowe) and forced her to return to Bordeaux. That action opened the score for what was to be a most successful month for No. 19 Group, in which it sank eleven U-boats and damaged three more, for a cost of six planes lost to the U-boats' return fire.

To describe every single action would risk swamping the reader in a mass of detail, for each was unique in itself and none was truly typical. However, there were three clashes that deserve particular mention.

Although the U-boats usually endeavoured to stay together in groups when crossing the Bay, the aerial harassment frequently caused boats to lose contact with each other. That was why *U-514* (Auffermann) came to be passing Cape Finisterre on the surface, heading west alone, on the afternoon of 8 July. There she was sighted by Flying Officer C. Campbell, manning the port waist-gun position of a Liberator of No. 224 Squadron. Even at this early stage in the engagement the U-boat's chances survival were slim, for the captain of the Liberator was the top-scoring anti-submarine pilot, Squadron Leader Terrence Bulloch. He was now back on operations after a rest tour lasting seven months. Bulloch was always interested in innovation, and he brought with him the most formidable array of anti-submarine weapons yet carried aboard a single aircraft. The Liberator was laden with eight 3 inch rockets, eight 250 pound depth-charges and a 'Mark 24 Mine' homing torpedo.

Seemingly oblivious to its peril, the U-boat remained fully surfaced. At a range of 800 yards Bulloch fired his first pair of rockets. One and a half seconds later, at range of 600 yards, he fired a second pair. Three-quarters of a second after that and at a range of 500 yards, he loosed off his remaining four rockets in a salvo. As Bulloch hauled on the control column to level out the

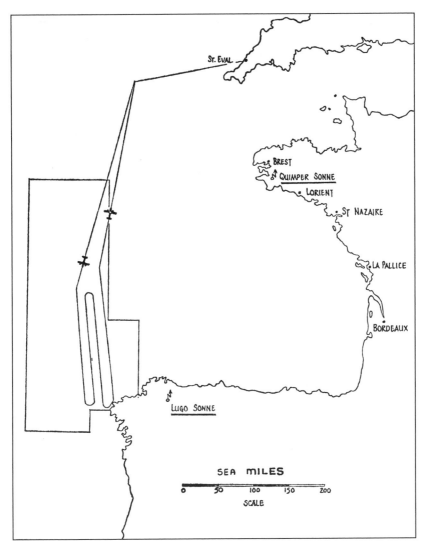

This is the track that was flown by a Liberator of No. 224 Squadron on 14 July 1943 during a Musketry patrol; the flight time was 13 hours 15 minutes. Also marked are the combined Musketry and Seaslug areas, and the *Sonne* transmitting stations at Quimper and Lugo.

Liberator, one of his gunners observed a rocket emerge from the water on the far side of the U-boat; almost certainly it had punched its way clean through the hull below the waterline. As the submarine plunged beneath the waves, Bulloch pulled the Liberator across its diving swirl and put down a stick of eight depth-charges, followed, immediately after their detonation, by the homing torpedo. When the rampage ended and the turbulent waters settled, the only sign of U-514 was a large patch of oil punctuated with pieces of flotsam.

Just over a fortnight later, on the 24th, a Leigh Light Wellington of No. 172 Squadron engaged on a day patrol came upon the submarine tanker U-459, in the Musketry patrol area. During the subsequent exchange of fire the Wellington suffered heavily, but its pilot, Flying Officer W. Jennings, pressed on with the attack. Then followed what Sergeant A. Turner, the rear gunner and sole survivor from the aircraft, later remembered as 'a loud explosion' before he found himself struggling in the water. The bomber had struck the U-boat on its starboard side, carrying away the single- and quadruple-barrelled 20 mm guns and the ratings serving them. The wings, tail and engines continued on into the sea, leaving parts of the fuselage draped across the rear part of the conning tower. The sailors cut away the twisted remains of the Wellington and heaved them over the side. Only then did they discover that two of the plane's depth-charges were lying on the deck. Korvettenkapitän von Wilamowitz-Moellendorff, the boat's commander, decided to get rid of them in the same way a destroyer would: he took his boat up to maximum speed and ordered his sailors to roll the weapons off the after-deck into the water. It was a neat plan, and had these been ordinary ship's depth-charges it would have worked. But von Wilamowitz-Moellendorff had no inkling of the effort the Royal Air Force had devoted to producing a depth-charge that would explode close to the surface. The first one over the side functioned exactly according to specification: at twenty-five feet, and almost directly underneath the stern of the U-boat, it went off. The explosion wrecked U-459's steering gear, jolted her diesel motors off their mountings and caused a fire in the electric motor room. She was still blundering round in circles when a second aircraft, a Halifax of No. 547 Squadron, arrived on the scene. U-459 was now in a hopeless position: with most of her armament out of action she could not defend herself, and she was too badly damaged to submerge.

Von Wilamowitz-Moellendorff ordered his men to abandon the craft, then set the scuttling charges and went down with her. Ten hours later a British warship reached the area and picked up Turner and the forty-four German survivors.

No. 19 Group's final action during the hard-fought month of July 1943 illustrates how effective its new 'Wolf Pack' tactics could be against a convoy of U-boats. Early on the 30th the crew of Liberator of No. 53 Squadron sighted a trio of submarines running through the Musketry area on the surface: the submarine tankers *U-461* and *U-462*, with *U-504* in company, trying to break out into the Atlantic. At the controls of the Liberator, Flying Officer W. Irving orbited the boats while his radio operator tapped out details of the find to the headquarters at Plymouth. The call summoned no fewer than six more aircraft to the scene: a Liberator, two Halifaxes, two Sunderlands and a Catalina. First to attack was Flight Lieutenant Jenson, piloting a Halifax of No. 502 Squadron. His aircraft carried three of the new 600 pound anti-submarine bombs, weapons that functioned in the same way as an ordinary depth-charge but had strengthened and more streamlined cases to suit them for higher-altitude release. Yet even at his attack altitude of 1,600 feet – comparatively high for an attack on a U-boat – the German gunners scored hits on the Halifax. Jenson's bombs fell wide, and he headed for base in his damaged aircraft. Next, Flying Officer Hensow, piloting a Halifax of the same squadron, made three deliberate bombing runs on the U-boats from 3,000 feet, releasing a 600 pound weapon on each. One bomb fell close alongside *U-462* (Vowe) and knocked out her propulsion system. The U -boat slowly lost way and slid to a stop.

That was the cue for the main charge to begin. Irving's Liberator took the lead, accompanied by a Liberator of No. 19 Squadron US Army Air Force. Bringing up the rear was a Sunderland flying-boat of No. 461 Squadron Royal Australian Air Force. With their superior speed the Liberators steadily outpaced the flying-boat, and both felt the kick of exploding cannon shells as the sailors concentrated their fire on them. But in the confusion Flight Lieutenant D. Marrows, at the controls of the Australian Sunderland, commenced his attack run on *U-461* almost unnoticed. Only at the last moment did *Kapitänleutnant* Stiebler's gunners begin to traverse their weapons onto the flying boat, and by then the Sunderland's nose gunner had found the range and a long accurate burst silenced the U-boat's armament. Freed from that distraction, the pilot laid his stick of seven depth-charges across the submarine. When they exploded, *U-461* appeared to break in two and she sank almost immediately.

Seeing one of his comrades sunk and the other immobilised, *Kapitänleutnant* Luis in *U-504* decided the time had come to dive and dive deep. That prudent move availed him little, however. While the other aircraft had been engaging the U-boats, the

Catalina flying-boat summoned to the area a submarine-hunting group of five Royal Navy warships patrolling nearby. An observer on board the sloop HMS *Woodpecker* later wrote:

> The Senior Naval Officer in *Kite* made the signal 'General Chase'. Off we went at full speed, line abreast – a grand sight – smooth blue sea and blue sky – all ratings and officers at action stations. Soon we saw the aircraft circling low and diving to drop depth-charges. Two of the U-boats were visible by this time, and the Sunderland dropped a couple of depth-charges plumb on either side of the conning tower of one of them. That broke the U-boat's back and she disappeared pretty quickly, leaving some survivors and a raft in the water. Simultaneously, all our ships opened fire with 4-inch [guns] on the second U-boat.

The 'second U-boat', *U-462*, floundered under this cannonade and joined her sister on the bottom. That left only *U-504*. The sloops quickly located her with Asdic, and under the thunder of deep-set depth-charges she too succumbed.

Afterwards the sloops picked up some seventy German survivors. When details of the action were assembled they revealed a remarkable coincidence. The attacking Sunderland, Aircraft 'U' of No. 461 Squadron, had sunk *U-461*.

During the first two days of August the Bay air patrols continued in their triumphant vein, sinking four more U-boats. But then the German C-in-C called a halt: enough was enough. On 2 August Dönitz bent before the storm: he ordered those U-boat groups already in the outer Bay to split up and proceed alone, surfacing to recharge their batteries only at night. He recalled the six U-boats that had just set out, and directed the four boats returning from the Atlantic to hug the Spanish coast closely without regard for territorial waters.

Thus the Battle of the Bay reached its climax. During the three hundred days up to 26 April 1943, Allied aircraft combing this stretch of water had sunk eight U-boats and damaged sixteen, an average of one sinking per thirty-seven days. Between 27 April and 2 August 1943, a period of only ninety-seven days, aircraft destroyed twenty-six U-boats and damaged seventeen: an average of one sinking every 3.7 days.

The unprofitable early period is explained by the introduction of Metox, and the deficiencies in Allied equipment up to the spring of 1943. On 27 April *Grossadmiral* Dönitz had raised the stakes and told his crews to surface in that area only during the day, and if Allied aircraft approached they were to fight back. On 3 August he recognised these tactics to be at fault, and ordered his crews to surface only at night. We may conclude, therefore, that the slaughter of the U-boats in the Bay of Biscay during the summer of 1943 was due, at least in part, to a serious tactical error on the part of the German High Command. Had the U-boats continued to surface only at night, and perhaps stayed close to the coast of Spain, where the shoreline made radar detection difficult, that slaughter could have been avoided.

This, however, in no way lessens the triumph of Air Vice-Marshal Bromet and his crews. An old adage assures us that 'Chance does nothing that has not been prepared beforehand.' Beforehand, No. 19 Group of Coastal Command had indeed prepared well. By then its equipment and weaponry were effective and its air and ground crews were proficient in their work. When its opportunity came, the force was able to wring the last ounce of advantage from it.

One question that neither High Command could have answered with certainty, before the battle, regarded the effect of the U-boats' increased firepower and their convoy tactics. Would these deter the Allied crews from delivering accurate low-level attacks on the U-boats? Now they had their answer: 'No'. It was 'No' because the aircrews' training was good enough, and their morale was high enough. And there was one other factor that few could have foreseen. In the words of one who flew on these operations:

It is difficult to describe the intense boredom of the sorties we undertook: hour after hour after hour with nothing to look at but sea. I am sure that when they found U-boats many crews pressed home their attacks regardless of what was being thrown at them, merely because it was a welcome relief from the boredom.

Thus, when the U-boats offered to trade blow for blow with the attacking aircraft, they unquestionably got the worst of it. During the ninety-seven days of pitched battle, the German sailors shot down about a dozen Allied aircraft over the Bay of Biscay; for each of those, a fraction over two U-boats were sunk. For the Allies that rate of exchange was extremely profitable. There were, of course, occasions when the U-boats' guns dissuaded aircraft and there was no loss to either side. But it is clear that this happened rarely, and overall the U-boats' 'fight back' tactics failed dismally.

With the admitted benefit of hindsight we can see that in the spring of 1943 *Grossadmiral* Dönitz had overreacted to the bogey of the unheralded night attack, just as he had overreacted to it ten months earlier when the Leigh Light made its debut. And once again, although the German C-in-C had no way of knowing it, only a small part of No. 19 Group was responsible for the rumpus. In April 1943, out of about a dozen anti-submarine squadrons in the Group, only two carried both the Leigh Light and centimetric-wavelength radar; and moreover, because of its novelty, serviceability of the latter was often poor.

In war the correct tactics are those that achieve the aim with the minimum cost in men and materials; during the Battle of the Bay Dönitz's aim was merely to run his U-boats through that stretch of water with minimum losses. Had he ordered his crews to come to the surface to recharge their batteries only at night, and accepted the loss of a few boats to air attack without warning, his force would certainly have suffered substantially fewer losses than it did. Since the Leigh Light aircraft could and did join in the day battle, the decision to surface only during the day multiplied Air Vice-Marshal Bromet's effective force by a factor of six.

Having seen that the German Navy made a disastrous mistake, it is important to realise the difficulty of charting a correct course considering its ignorance regarding the capabilities of the Allied submarine-location systems. Since they had scarcely any oppor-tunities to examine actual hardware, German Intelligence officers had to place their trust in more fallible sources: reports from agents and returning crews, interrogations of the few Allied prisoners who knew anything about this subject, and by deduction from decrypted signals. Given such a ragbag of Intelligence, truth, half-truth and fiction became almost impossible to disentangle. Already this ignorance had been instrumental in concealing the danger of the Huffduff equipment, as well setting the conditions for defeat in the Battle of the Bay. At the beginning of August 1943 came the most bizarre result of all, leading to the demise of the inoffensive Metox receiver.

Throughout the Battle of the Bay one question continued to exer-cise the German High Command: how did the Allied aircraft locate U-boats with such precision, without emitting radiations that could be detected by the Metox receiver? At first the Intelligence officers thought, correctly, that some sort of centimetric-wavelength radar was responsible. In May 1943 the long-awaited Naxos-U warning receiver began operational trials; these should have cleared up the mystery of the Allied night attacks once and for all. But instead, the device merely deepened the German bewilderment.

In truth the early Naxos U receiver was an insensitive device. If it was in good condition and properly set up, it could warn of signals from the British ASV Mark III radar at a maximum range of about five miles. That left little margin for safety if the set was not working at its best. Like the earlier Metox, the Naxos-U had a portable aerial that clipped onto the conning tower. A long coaxial cable, running through the open conning tower hatch, connected the aerial to the receiver in the radio room. That coaxial cable was to prove a weak link in the system: a size 9 boot landing on the cable during the rush to get below for an emergency dive could crush or kink the cable. Such damage would not always be obvious on casual examination, but could cause a sharp deterioration in the device's already inadequate performance. The net result was that the Naxos-U missed rather more signals than it detected. And the U-boat Command continued to receive complaints of night attacks without prior warning. So the question remained: just how were the Allied aircraft locating the U-boats in the Bay of Biscay?

The failure of Naxos-U to provide the expected answer led the German Navy to reconsider the threat. Could it be that the aircraft used a method altogether different from radar, to locate the U-boats? In the mid-summer of 1943 suspicion turned to the Metox receiver. For the signals service had discovered that the Metox, a super-heterodyne-type receiver, radiated from its local oscillator stage.

Could it be that Allied aircraft were homing on to those Metox radiations? Many signals experts scorned the idea; the radiations were feeble and they felt, correctly, that radar was a much more efficient system. Yet the German electronics experts had been proved wrong before: indeed, who in Germany could say what was, and what was not, possible to an enemy known to be technically more advanced in this area? The shock of the discovery of the British centimetric-wavelength radar, earlier in the year, still haunted German thinking.

During July and August 1943 the German Navy conducted a series of flight trials, using an especially sensitive receiver to pick up the radiations from Metox. The trials revealed that these radiations could be detected out to a distance of thirty miles. So it was possible to home on to a U-boat by this means!

Thus began 'the great radiation scare'. On 3 August Dönitz sent a top-priority signal, ordering U-boat crews to cease using Metox immediately. The Naxos-U programme slid into the background as the German electronics industry set about the major (and, the reader will note, quite unnecessary) task of mass-producing a new radiation-free metric-wavelength warning receiver.

Just over a week later the already-bizarre tale took another twist. On 12 August *Grossadmiral* Dönitz grimly noted in his War Diary:

> As a result of the interrogation of a prisoner, it is *confirmed* [author's italics] that the English have been using the radia- tions from our search receivers to locate and attack our U-boats. The order is going out to all boats that the Metox device is no longer to be switched on.

On the following day, the talkative prisoner allegedly told his captors more, and this was included in an amplifying signal sent to all operational U-boat bases on 18 August:

> The prisoner stated during an interrogation on 13 August that the ASV set was scarcely used because a run-in on the U-boat's own radiations was possible. It was alleged that the radiations could be detected from ranges of up to ninety miles at a height of 3,000 feet. The prisoner's statement is accepted as true, though the range is improbably long and could be obtained only with a particularly sensitive receiver. *It must, however, be assumed that the enemy has the best possible equip- ment . . .* [author's italics].

The German C-in-C assured his men that the situation was now in hand: the new search receiver being built was virtually free of radiation and would shortly be fitted to all U-boats.

Who had serenaded the modern German sailors with the Lorelei strain that was to lead them onto rocks of their own making? In this writer's opinion there are three possibilities, given here in ascending order of likelihood.

The first possibility is that a Coastal Command crewman with considerable technical knowledge had been taken prisoner, and on his own initiative he had fabricated the cock-and-bull story. He produced it at just the right time to match German fears, and stuck to the story throughout what would have been a detailed and rigorous interrogation.

The second possibility is a variation of the first, that a specially primed man had allowed himself to be captured under plausible circumstance, so that he could pass on the story.

In spite of extensive inquiries among Intelligence and service ex-officers during the research for this book, this writer found no evidence to support or disprove either notion.

There remains a third possibility, that there was no prisoner at all. It is known that the British Intelligence service had an elaborate system for using double agents, or turned enemy agents, to pass misleading reports to the enemy. Using this system as a conduit, it would have been a relatively simple business to pass on the canard of a special receiver that enabled aircraft to home on the Metox radiations.

In the absence of hard evidence either way, this author is inclined to support the third of those possibilities as the 'least unlikely'. The other two possibilities would have involved a high degree of risk for the individual involved, and therefore an increased chance of failure. German reports attributing the information to 'a prisoner' should not be taken as confirming that this necessarily was the case. Intelligence officers are always conscious of the need to protect sensitive sources, and a seemingly well-placed agent in the enemy camp would certainly have been one of these.

In some respects, picking through military Intelligence reports is rather like studying the Bible: if one searches diligently enough, it is possible to find passages that will support almost any notion. Thus when *Grossadmiral* Dönitz called on Hitler at the 'Wolf's Lair' in East Prussia on 19 August to report on the latest develop-ments, he could link the Metox radiations to some previously unsolved mysteries. For example, the German C-in-C knew that aircraft were locating and sinking most U-boats during the transit and lying-in-wait stages of the operational sortie, rather than at the actual convoys. Yet when boats reached the convoy area their wire-less operators invariably switched off Metox and dismounted its clumsy 'Biscay Cross' aerial, so that the boat could dive quickly in an emergency. By linking those two facts, which were in fact unre-lated, Dönitz presented them as plausible evidence of the Allied exploitation of the Metox radiations. Moreover, it was known that Wellington aircraft were responsible for several of the unheralded night attacks, and the German Navy believed (erroneously) that the twin-engined bomber was too small to carry a centimetric-wavelength radar. The notion of homings on Metox seemed neatly to explain away that mystery as well.

The Führer listened with sympathy, and agreed that Dönitz's explanation seemed to explain some of the baffling things that had happened in the past. With this discovery, Hitler said, 'A great step forward has been taken.' The audience ended on a note of cautious optimism: since the order to cease using Metox, in the Bay of Biscay there had been no U-boat losses for sixteen days.

In fact, as the reader has seen, the sudden lack of success by the Bay air patrols was due in part to the greatly reduced U-boat traffic through the area. Another factor was the order that U-boats should surface only by night and should keep close to the Spanish coast, where the radar clutter made detection difficult. The new-found release had nothing whatsoever to do with the juggling with the warning receivers.

If the German leaders derived comfort from this excursion into Cloud-cuckoo-land, the painful reality of the U-boats' defeat was only too clear. Between the beginning of May 1943 and the middle of August the German and Italian Navies had lost no fewer than 118 submarines to enemy action – seventy-eight to aircraft operating alone, six shared between aircraft and ships and thirty-four to ships operating alone. Most of the boat's crews were killed or captured. For their part the Axis submarines had sunk just over 600,000 tons of merchant shipping. It was not an inconsiderable total, yet it was one the bustling Allied shipyards could replace from current production.

In the next chapter we shall observe the strenuous efforts the German Navy made to redress this discomforting state of affairs.

CHAPTER 9

Slipway No. 5 at Danzig

September 1943 to May 1944

The apparent slackness of the submarine war was due to a single technical invention of the enemy's. We are busy neutralising it, and we are convinced that we shall succeed within a very short time.

Adolf Hitler's New Year's Day speech, January 1944

The enemy has succeeded in gaining the advantage in submarine defence. We shall catch up with the enemy. The day will come when I shall offer Churchill a first-rate submarine war. The U-boat arm has not been broken by the setbacks of 1943. On the contrary it has become stronger. In 1944, which will be a successful but hard year, we shall smash Britain's supplies with a new weapon.

Grossadmiral Karl Dönitz, 20 January 1944

During the spring and summer of 1943 the Allied anti-submarine forces had indeed won a great victory. Between the third week in May and the middle of September, not a single ship had been lost to U-boat attack on the important North Atlantic route. This *Grossadmiral* Dönitz conceded, and this he felt certain to change with the new group of U-boats now putting out into the Atlantic. He was confident that the next time a Wolf Pack battled against a convoy the Allies would recognise that although they had won a battle, they had not won the war.

During the final days of August and the first week in September, twenty-two U-boats and a U-tanker nosed out of the French Biscay ports. Six more boats set out from bases in Norway and Germany, to join them in the Atlantic. These boats had all been recently modified, with increased conning tower armour and quadruple 20 mm guns for protection against aircraft. Each U-boat carried two of the new *Zaunkönig* acoustic homing torpedoes for use against the convoy escorts. Also (though it would not, of course, make any difference), each boat carried the new *W.Anz* search receiver, which radiated scarcely at all. *Grossadmiral* Dönitz informed his crews: 'All the essentials for a successful campaign are to hand . . .'

By hugging the Spanish coast, and surfacing only briefly and then only at night, at first the boats from the Biscay ports avoided the attentions of the searching aircraft altogether. Dönitz, believing that the absence of Metox radiations was the reason for this new-found immunity from attack, was understandably elated. On 3 September he noted that the enemy was still 'searching feverishly'.

On the following day there came a report that rekindled the old doubts: a U-boat radioed that it had come under attack at night from a Leigh Light aircraft, and the *W.Anz* receiver had provided no warning. This proved to be an isolated event, however, and the German C-in-C cautiously recorded: 'Only further observation will enable us to say whether this was a chance sighting, or whether the aircraft radar was working on a centimetric wavelength . . .' Only later did it become clear that a similar surprise night attack had accounted for *U-669* (Köhl) off the coast of Spain, during the early morning darkness of 7 September. Yet before Dönitz received that news, he knew that the other twenty-seven U-boats had successfully infiltrated their way past the thicket of air patrols, and had entered the Atlantic.

The German Navy had jumped its first hurdle with surprisingly little effort. It remained to be seen whether the U-boats, with their new homing torpedoes, would enjoy a similar success against the convoy escorts. By the evening of 16 September the *Leuthen* submarine group was in position in mid-Atlantic, its twenty U-boats strung out in the familiar north–south line astride the convoy routes. In a mood reminiscent of happier times in the past, *Grossadmiral* Dönitz sent a rousing signal to his crews:

The Führer is watching every phase of your struggle. Attack. Follow-up. Sink.

By the afternoon of 18 September two westbound convoys were nearing the concentration of U-boats: the slow convoy ONS 18 and, about 120 miles behind it, the faster ON 202. Sailing as part of the former was one of the new merchant aircraft-carriers, the *Empire MacAlpine*. The action began with an inconclusive skirmish round the slow convoy, which ended without loss on either side.

On the following day, the 19th, the first blood went to the Allies: a very-long-range Liberator of the newly re-equipped Canadian No. 10 Squadron, operating from Newfoundland, sank *U-341* (Epp) to the north of ON 202.

In the meantime, several U-boats had made contact with the fast convoy ON 202, and there the battle began on the morning of the 20th. The first to feel the sting of the new German homing torpedo was the frigate HMS *Lagan*, as she investigated a Huffduff bearing on a shadowing U-boat. The *Zaunkönig* smashed into her engine room, blowing off the stern and killing twenty-nine of her crew. *Kapitänleutnant* Hepp in *U-238* made the most of the confusion, and penetrated the escorting screen to torpedo two merchantmen.

While this was happening *U-338* made contact with the convoy, signalling, 'I am remaining on the surface, to attack.' The boat's commander was *Kapitänleutnant* Manfred Kinzel, the man who had handled her so well in the face of the air patrols during the SC 122 battle the previous March. When an Iceland-based Liberator of No. 120 Squadron came into view and curved round to attack the boat, the German crew stood their ground and fought back. By combining evasive turns with accurate return fire, Kinzel caused the first stick of depth-charges to fall harmlessly clear of his boat.

Following this truculent reception, the Liberator pilot, Flying Officer J. Moffat, contented himself with circling his enemy and loosing off the occasional burst of machine-gun fire at it. He knew he could afford to be patient. In the end Kinzel decided to make a break, and judging the Liberator to be poorly placed for an immediate attack, he took his U-boat down. Unknown to the German skipper, however, this was precisely what Moffat wanted him to do. The British pilot thundered down on the fading swirl of the now-submerged boat, and planted a single 'Mark 24 Mine' homing torpedo. The weapon exploded against *U-338* and she sank with her entire crew. So Manfred Kinzel met his end, because he did not allow for the fact that his enemy might be carrying weapons as advanced as some of those in his own torpedo tubes.

That night the fast convoy joined up with the slow one, and the combined mass of sixty-six ships plodded on protected by fifteen escorts. With the coming of darkness, however, the patrolling aircraft left the area. Once again the stalking *Leuthen* U-boats closed in. They used their deadly *Zaunkönig* torpedoes to sink two more escorts, before a swirling sea fog forced them to lose contact with the convoy. Throughout the following day the convoys rumbled on through the banks of fog, and the ineffectual game of hide and seek continued.

Not until the afternoon of 22 September did the fog start to lift, and as visibility improved the U-boats again began to concentrate around their prey. The temporarily clear skies made life easier for the air patrols, too, and Newfoundland-based Liberators inflicted serious damage on *U-270* (Otto) and *U-377* (Kluth). Also on that day *Empire MacAlpine*'s Swordfish made unsuccessful rocket and depth-charge attacks, which nevertheless forced down some of the U-boats. Yet in spite of this air cover, sufficient U-boats remained in contact when night fell, and the *Leuthen* submarines sank another escort and four merchantmen.

Dawn on 23 September brought clear blue skies, and the Liberators and Swordfish soon cleared the surface of U-boats. As the latter fell far behind they lost contact, and *Grossadmiral* Dönitz ordered his crews to break off the action. To the German C-in-C it appeared that the *Leuthen* group had achieved a magnificent victory, for the U-boats reported having sunk nine merchantmen and twelve escorts. Although made in good faith, the claim was exaggerated: the Germans crews had yet to learn that the *Zaunkönig* homing torpedo often exploded either prematurely or in the wake of the target ship. Each explosion had been counted as a hit; for in the heat of battle there could be no question of a U-boat closing on its victim to confirm the result of an attack. In fact the Allied losses amounted to six merchantmen and three escorts, all of which had been torpedoed at night when no air cover was available. Only three U-boats had been sunk, so the German Navy had won the action 'on points'.

To the German High Command, the *Leuthen* group's action gave a welcome fillip to morale, and seemed to confirm the correctness of the various measures taken since the beginning of August. Following a long process of trial and error, the German Navy had stumbled upon the correct tactics to get U-boats through the Bay of Biscay without suffering swingeing losses. At the convoy, poor weather had enabled the submarines to defy the odds and snatch a brief victory that became inflated in the telling. The new *W.Anz* receiver had emerged from its first operational test with its reputation largely intact. There had been only two suspicious night attacks in the Bay of Biscay, and none at all in the Atlantic. The reasons for this were not as simple as they appeared to the German Intelligence officers, however. The cause of the former was the difficulty of detecting on radar U-boats running close inshore, while the latter was simply owing to the lack of searchlights or illuminating flares on the Liberators and Swordfish that had taken part in the action.

Grossadmiral Dönitz confidently re-formed the *Leuthen* group in readiness for another battle, but the next three convoys across the North Atlantic skirted neatly round the German patrol line. Moreover, patrolling aircraft sank three of the U-boats that had been waiting in vain.

Not until 7 October did the U-boats make successful contact with a North Atlantic convoy: the eastbound SC 143, whose escort included the merchant aircraft-carrier *Rapana*. And this time the weather did not favour the German sailors. Early on the morning of the 8th a U-boat sank an escort with a homing torpedo. But with the coming of the dawn and clear skies *Rapana*'s Swordfish, together with the Iceland-based Liberators of Nos 86 and 120 Squadrons, steamrollered all attempts by the U-boat to close on the merchant ships. Two boats, *U-419* (Giersberg) and *U-643* (Speidel), either did not see or did not fear the approaching Liberators, and failed to dive in time. They paid the supreme price for their error. During the early evening a Sunderland of the Canadian No. 423 Squadron put in a brief but adequate appearance, and sank *U-610* (Baron von Freyberg-Eisenberg-Allmendingen). Nor did dusk bring the German sailors relief from the aerial harassment: that night, for the first time in mid-Atlantic, a very-long-range Liberator fitted with a Leigh Light kept the ships company. There was, however, a brief hiatus between the limit of the Liberator's endurance and dawn. One U-boat exploited this opportunity and moved in and sank a single merchantman. After daybreak on 9 October the convoy came within range of the medium-range air patrols, and the U-boats were forced to break off the action. The success that *Grossadmiral* Dönitz had so confidently expected had eluded him. His boats had sunk only one merchantman and one escort, for the loss of three of their number.

If the German Commander-in-Chief entertained any thoughts that the SC 143 failure might have resulted from an unfortunate piece of luck for the Allies, he was soon brought back to stark reality. One week later the *Schlieffen* group intercepted the westbound convoy ON 206, but lost four boats to air attack and two to the surface escorts, in return for only one merchant ship sunk.

It now was clear to *Grossadmiral* Dönitz that his earlier problems in mid-Atlantic had still not been solved. Moreover, the news from U-boats operating in other waters was equally depressing. In mid-

September the Italian government sued for peace, and the German C-in-C ordered seven U-boats to pass through the Straits of Gibraltar to reinforce his flotilla in the Mediterranean. By hugging the coast of neutral Spain as they ran at night on the surface, the U-boats had previously been able to avoid the attentions of the Bay of Biscay air patrols. Yet this was more difficult in the complex sea currents that are a feature of the waters in the Straits of Gibraltar. Moreover the Leigh Light Wellingtons of No. 179 Squadron, based at Gibraltar, were alert and ready. Its aircraft carried the ASV Mark III radar, whose centimetric-wavelength emissions would not register on the German *W.Anz* receivers.

The first U-boat to brave the powerful defences was *U-223* (Wächter), during the final week of September. Although she was twice surprised on the surface at night and attacked, the U-boat reached the Mediterranean unscathed. Less successful was *Kapitänleutnant* Schroeteler's boat *U-667*, which came under air attack on five separate occasions and suffered such a shaking that it had to return to St Nazaire. On learning of the aggressiveness of the air patrols round Gibraltar, *Grossadmiral* Dönitz postponed his attempt to push more boats into the Mediterranean.

The news of his boats' rough handling was serious enough for the German C-in-C, but the spate of reports of surprise night attacks from the air was even more disconcerting. The new *W.Anz* receiver should have put an end to that complaint, at least. Since the Allied aircraft could not possibly home on radiations from the new receiver, it seemed that centimetric-wavelength radar might be to blame (it was). Accordingly *Grossadmiral* Dönitz ordered that for the next attempt to pass reinforcements through the Straits, at the end of October, all the U-boats would carry the Naxos-U warning receiver.

Readers will remember the shortcomings of the insensitive Naxos-U receiver, however, and will not be surprised to learn that the device afforded U-boat crews little protection. No. 179 Squadron, of course, knew nothing of the German difficulties. To its crews this seemed merely to be a sudden and welcome increase in U-boat activity in their area. With great promptitude one of the unit's Wellingtons despatched the leading boat, *U-566* (Hornhohl), on the night of 23 October.

There followed almost a week of quiet, before *Oberleutnant* Böhme attempted to run the gauntlet in *U-450*. The skirmish that followed is significant only because a particularly vivid account has been written of the action. On the evening of 29 October,

Squadron Leader Hodkinson of No. 179 Squadron lifted his Leigh Light Wellington off the runway at Gibraltar for an anti-submarine patrol. The aircraft carried a passenger, an army officer who had never previously flown, going along 'for the ride'. The passenger was unschooled in the technicalities of anti-submarine warfare, yet because of this the account he wrote afterwards conveys with rare precision the 'feel' of such an engagement:

There is no moon, but the stars are bright and if you look down you can see occasional white patches on the water. In the distance a few lighthouses glow at regular intervals. Except for the roar of the motors – which you don't notice, and the infrequent remarks on the 'intercom' – which you don't understand, everything is still and silent. The pilot is lying on his belly in the nose of the machine and the second pilot is at the controls. I am standing in the nose, with one foot on the step leading from the wireless room and the other on the bracket sticking out of the pilot's platform. The luminous dials on the instrument board give off a faint light. We have been out about four hours and a half and I am wondering when they will unpack the coffee.

The little Scotsman speaks over the 'intercom' but I don't get it. The first pilot starts to crawl back and I squeeze myself up against the door behind me in order to let him slide in under the controls while the second pilot is worming himself out. The second pilot goes into the nose and lies flat on his belly. The first pilot checks over the instruments with the aid of the tiny beam from his flash lamp. I make a mental note to bring a torch on my next trip. It's been arranged that if we go into action I will man the front gun, but I hesitate to go in now because I don't want to appear too dramatic. Perhaps it's just a routine changeover, but the second pilot is pulling at my leg so I crawl forward and take up my position behind the gun. I am crouching with one foot on either side of him, both hands are in the grips and my thumbs are on the button. I can't see a thing ahead, but a lighthouse is flashing way off to the right. We are gathering speed and I wonder what we are after.

How will I know whether or not to shoot ? I don't want to speak over the 'intercom' as they may need it for more important things, so I lean down, pull the earphone away from the second pilot's left ear and shout as loud as I can 'Hit my leg when you want me to shoot.' I try this twice, but he keeps looking straight ahead, so I give up and get back to my gun. We seem to be gaining more speed, and I peer out trying to see beyond the black wall in front. What are we going to meet? A sailing boat? A plane? Whatever it is I am sure it will be friendly, but how am I going to know? Next time I will fix this up before we take off.

What the Hell?! I suppose they have turned on the search-light: we are in a thick white fog and all I see is the rivets holding together the glass stuff in the nose. Damn it! I can't see a bloody thing outside! Yes I can. It's a submarine. Probably British. Someone is yelling in the 'intercom', so I press my thumbs and a line of red golf balls sails down towards it. I should have got this signal business worked out before. Somebody will get Hell for this; probably me. We keep on the dive and the first few golf balls are now the size of ciga-rette ends. They take a long time to get there. We are going faster than ever now, and I can see quite a few cigarette ends to the right of the tower. Now there are some to the left. They are all mixed up with mine. They seem to get bigger, and dull red tennis balls start to float past us. They're shooting at us! It's a U-boat! Thank God! I press my thumbs as hard as I can and try to follow the course of my golf balls. Those tennis balls are going to come right into the nose. No. They go over. We are in a sort of a funnel of slow moving red tennis balls. I never thought it would be like this. I wish mine were a different colour, I can't follow them. We're going to hit the conning tower. I hope we knock it off. No. We're over it. The light has gone out. I look down to the left and can see only stars.

On the right there is a flashing in the sky. Another plane? No. It's a lighthouse. The pilot is hollering in the 'intercom', 'We got the bastards. We got the bastards.' There seems to be a lot of fresh air around, and a slight smell of oil. The pilot calls out each man's name. 'Bill! Are you all right Bill?' 'Yes, sir.' 'Wilson, are you there Wilson?' 'Yes, sir, but the light has been shot out.' 'Tommy, are you OK?' 'Yes, sir.' 'Scotty?' He calls Scotty three times, each time with more urgency in his voice. Then Scotty answers. We are all all right.

The second pilot has crawled out from between my legs and is poking around under the pilot's platform. He has a little light and I look over his shoulder. There is a tangle of bright pipes with oil oozing out of some and squirting out of others. There is a hole in the side of the aircraft you could put your hand through. After a bit we start for our base.

In fact Hodkinson's depth-charges had not straddled the U-boat, as he had thought, and *U-450* reached the Mediterranean without damage. The wounded Wellington limped back to Gibraltar carrying a somewhat more knowledgeable army officer.

Although *U-450* had passed through the Straits unscathed, the next two U-boats to make the attempt were less fortunate. Naval forces destroyed *U-732* (Carlsen) on the night of 31 October. On the following night Wellingtons of 179 Squadron co-operated with surface ships to hunt *U-340* to exhaustion. *Oberleutnant* Klaus shook off the pursuing warships with a high-speed underwater run, but in doing so he used almost all the charge in his batteries. With the hunters likely to regain the scent at any moment, Klaus took his boat to the surface and scuttled her. Spanish fishing boats took off the U-boat's crew, but the German sailors were still standing on deck in their distinctive lifejackets when the sloop HMS *Fleetwood* arrived on the scene. There followed an incident that may bring the reader to smirk or scowl, depending upon one's nationality or regard for international law. Tongue firmly in cheek, a contemporary Royal Navy chronicler noted:

> To the Captain of *Fleetwood* the dictates of humanity were clear and strong; the medical officer, who was called into the conference, felt exactly the same: it was their duty to take off the exhausted men and give them all the care and attention their ship could provide. The Germans did not see things in the same light, but there was no resisting *Fleetwood*'s humanitarian principles when they really got going.

During the rumpus round *U-340*, *Kapitänleutnant* Brünning sneaked *U-642* through the narrows unseen. Thus, out of the five U-boats that attempted to penetrate the defences, three had been sunk and only two succeeded.

It had been a small-scale action, but no less disastrous to the German Navy for that. Moreover, the evidence seemed now to impugn the tentative theories regarding the Allied U-boat detection methods. The *W.Anz* and Naxos receivers should have detected radar emissions in the part of the wavelength spectrum each one covered. And thorough tests had shown that neither device gave off radiations that might betray its presence.

Were the Allies perhaps using some completely different method of U-boat detection? As we know, they were not. The German setback resulted from the use of aircraft fitted with centimetric-wavelength radar, acting in concert with a powerful concentration of warships to sterilise a narrow strip of water. Yet again, we observe the intractable maze through which the German Intelligence officers sought to trace a coherent path.

Nor did the news from the more distant waters do anything to raise the cloud of despondency that had settled over *Grossadmiral* Dönitz's operational headquarters that October. For the renewed attempt to strike at the convoys passing through the waters round the Azores had met a similar rebuff. On the morning of the 4th a patrolling Avenger aircraft from the escort carrier USS *Card* 'accidentally' came across a German refuelling operation actually in progress: the submarine tanker *U-460* had just finished suckling *U-264*, while *U-422* and *U-455* awaited their turn. Made in the face of a concerted defence from the boats' gunners, the Avenger's depth-charge attack was ineffective. So, having radioed for reinforcements, Lieutenant R. Stearns patiently orbited the force, staying outside the range of the U-boats' guns. He would wait until somebody or something persuaded the German crews to submerge; then he could plant the homing torpedo remaining in his bomb bay. Soon afterwards *Kapitänleutnant* Scheibe prudently dived *U-465* to safety, but the possibility that the highly secret 'Mark 24 Mine' might be seen from one of the three boats on the surface prevented an immediate attack.

Card despatched a striking force of two Wildcats and an Avenger, which duly arrived on the scene. But then, again, the boats' anti-aircraft fire broke up their attack. The German sailors then took their U-boats down, but for one of the crews it would be for the last time. That was the chance for which Stearns had waited, and he planted his homing torpedo in front of the swirl left by the largest U-boat. A couple of minutes later a small hump of water rose up, then oil and debris from *U-460* (Schnoor) began floating to the surface. Later that day *Oberleutnant* Poeschel inexplicably brought *U-422* to the surface, only three miles from the morning action. For this effrontery the U-boat came under almost immediate air attack, and when she dived a homing torpedo sent her to the bottom.

Just over a week later, on the 12th, one of *Card*'s aircraft spotted the nucleus of another refuelling operation. The tanker *U-488*

(Studt) fought a spirited action with four Avengers that lasted over an hour. And when it dived, the now-usual homing torpedo was in pursuit. Yet on this occasion fortune favoured the brave, for the weapon appears to have detonated prematurely. Studt nursed his damaged boat back to Bordeaux.

On the following morning *U-402* (von Forstner) sought out her refueller but instead found only *Card*'s aircraft. A 'Mark 24 Mine' sniffed her out and destroyed that boat also.

On the same day, 13 October, there was a tussle that highlighted the vulnerability of carrier-borne aircraft to battle damage. Following an inconclusive fight with a U-boat, Lieutenant Fryatt returned to *Card* in his Avenger with a damaged hydraulic system and a starboard undercarriage leg that refused to extend. He orbited the carrier for nearly an hour while she recovered her other aircraft; in the meantime darkness had fallen and the sea had become rougher. Finally, with only his port undercarriage leg locked down, Fryatt made his approach. Then, at the last moment, his Gods looked the other way. The Avenger's hook missed the arrester wires and she bounced off the deck and sailed clean over the crash barrier. Crumpling her starboard wing when it hit the bridge in passing, the maverick aircraft then smashed down onto the foredeck. She came to a halt after cannoning another aircraft, which had been parked near the bow, into the sea. Fryatt and his crew were indeed lucky to emerge unscathed from their wrecked aircraft.

During the second half of October, the escort carrier USS *Core* moved into the waters to the north of the Azores. Her aircraft sank one U-boat and damaged another, before she left the area at the end of the month.

As October drew to its close, the cautious German optimism of early September had been firmly squashed: during these two months thirty-three U-boats had been lost in action (twenty-four to aircraft and two shared with warships). On the other hand the submarines had sunk some forty merchant ships totalling some 200,000 tons during this period, not a negligible total. Moreover, the U-boat arm continued in its secondary aim of holding down substantial Allied forces. For the future there was ample room for confidence on the German side, for *Grossadmiral* Dönitz still had some aces up his sleeve.

By the summer of 1943, the aircraft had established itself as the U-boats' most deadly foe. Yet the boats were vulnerable only when they were on – or had just been on – the surface, usually in order to recharge batteries or move rapidly into position to intercept a convoy. If these periods of enforced exposure on the surface could be reduced, or even rendered unnecessary, U-boat operations would be less at the mercy of the air patrols. The answer, as Dönitz had known all along, was a craft much closer to the 'true' submarine – a boat able to run submerged at higher speeds and for considerably longer periods than the boats currently in service.

The first urgent need was for some means to allow submarines already in service to continue to operate, without the need to come to the surface so often to recharge their batteries. The answer was the *Schnorkel* (nose), which consisted of an air pipe that could be extended above the surface when the boat was at periscope depth. At the top of the pipe was a simple ball-cock (similar in operation to that fitted to a lavatory cistern), to close the pipe and prevent water flooding into the boat when a wave washed over the inlet. With a supply of air entering the boat in this way, a submarine could run almost entirely submerged indefinitely on its diesel engines, without needing to expend precious current from its batteries.

During the summer and autumn of 1943 a trial installation of the *Schnorkel* underwent testing. After some improvements to the design, the German Navy felt sufficiently confident with the device to initiate a large-scale modification programme to fit it to all operational U-boats. Yet even this, the short-term answer to the German submariners' problem, would take several months to introduce into service in the numbers needed. This relatively simple device could, of course, have been introduced in the U-boat Service much earlier in the war; but until the air threat became serious there had been no need for the German Navy to pursue it.

It must be stressed that the introduction of the *Schnorkel* was purely a defensive measure, brought about by the need to make boats less vulnerable to detection from the air. The device had its limitations. It could not be used when a submarine attacked a convoy, for the noise from the diesel engines would betray the boat's position to the enemy while preventing its crew using their own listening equipment. When running on the *Schnorkel* the Type VII U-boat's maximum speed was about 6 knots. That meant its mobility was much reduced, compared with that possible when the boat ran on the surface. Moreover if the seas were rough or depth-keeping was poor, from time to time a wave would wash over the air tube. If that happened the ball-cock slammed shut, leading to a period of considerable discomfort for the boat's crew. The diesel motors continued to gulp in air, which was now drawn from the limited supply inside the boat. It took a few seconds to shut down the diesel motors and clear the valve. During that time the air pressure inside the boat fell markedly, leaving the crew gasping with popping ears and bulging eyes.

Despite those limitations, for the German Navy the *Schnorkel* represented a large step in the right direction. To be sure, the air pipe extending above the surface could still be seen from the air both visually and on radar. But its detection range was very much less than for a fully surfaced U-boat.

For the longer term, *Grossadmiral* Dönitz had German submarine designers prepare plans for a completely new type of ocean-going U-boat, which would have the best possible underwater performance commensurate with the use of proved techniques. It would have a hull shape optimised to give the best possible underwater performance, and its battery capacity was increased be a factor of three compared with earlier boats. During the summer of 1943, the German Navy's ideas began to crystallise along these lines. The 'vital statistics' for the new U-boat, designated the Type XXI, were finalised: maximum speed fully submerged on the electric motors, 18 knots able to be maintained for one and a half hours. Or it could run submerged at 12 to 14 knots for ten hours. Cruising speed on electric motors, 6 knots for up to 48 hours – giving the craft a range of nearly 300 miles completely submerged. Using a *Schnorkel* of improved design, the boat could run partially submerged on its diesel engines at speeds up to 12 knots. The vastly increased battery capacity meant that the Type XXI boat was somewhat larger than previous commerce raiding boats, with a surface displacement of about 1,600 tons (compared with 770 tons for the earlier Type VII boats). The offensive armament of the new boat comprised six torpedo tubes, with twenty-three torpedoes; for anti-aircraft defence it was planned to fit four 30 mm cannon in two remotely controlled turrets. The crew would number 57.

Like the *Schnorkel* itself, the new high-performance U-boat would have been technically feasible somewhat earlier in the war. But until the spring of 1943 it had seemed that the earlier types of boat were quite capable of strangling the Allied trade routes.

By mid-1943 almost the entire German shipbuilding capacity was devoted to the construction of U-boats. *Direktor* Cords, previously the principal naval architect at the Germania works at Kiel, undertook the detailed design of the new boat.

The German Navy placed an order for 290 Type XXI submarines, all to be delivered by the end of February 1945. To meet that challenging deadline, *Reichsminister* Albert Speer appointed Otto Merker to head the production programme. Earlier, as general director of the Magirus company, Merker had made a name for himself overseeing the mass-production of vehicles for the German Army. Although he had never been involved with warship construction, he would introduce several novel and clever ideas in the new programme.

Using normal methods, the gestation time for the Type XXI submarine, from the advancement of the tactical requirement to the delivery of the first production model, would have been about two and a half years. That is to say, the prototype would begin trials early in 1946. With Germany now locked into a life-and-death struggle, that timescale was clearly unacceptable. Regardless of effort, regardless of cost, that gestation period had to be telescoped.

The first step was the most obvious. The craft was to be ordered off the drawing board, and mass-production would be well advanced before the prototype entered the water. With the previous methods of submarine construction, the major bottleneck was the time each boat spent on the slipway prior to launch: anything between thirty-six and fifty weeks for the Type VII boats. Merker slashed this period by dividing the new boat into eight sections, which were to be prefabricated in factories all over Germany. The various components, including the motors and the batteries, were to be delivered to yards dotted about the country that would assemble the sections. Upon completion, the sections were to be moved to three large final assembly yards at Hamburg, Danzig and Bremen. The use of canals to move the completed sections was vital to the scheme, on account of their size. For example the No. 3 section, complete with the two diesel motors, weighed 150 tons. It was about 27 feet long and 25 feet high, about the size of a two-storey suburban house. Once they reached the final assembly points, the sections were to be pushed together and welded in place. Then the various air, oil, water and fuel systems would be connected up, the remaining items of equipment installed, and the U-boat launched.

Using these means, it was proposed to cut the time each boat spent on the slipway to only twelve weeks. The widespread dispersal of work throughout the country would make the programme less vulnerable to interference by air attack. The method promised great man-hour economies, since the cylindrical sections of the boat could be worked on from either end, in full daylight, with heavy lifting gear readily available.

Just as the design of the new submarine had to take into account the effectiveness of the Allied anti-submarine patrol aircraft, so Merker's plans for the production of the boat had to take into account the increasing potency of the Allied strategic bomber attacks on Germany. As if to underline that new-found effectiveness, exactly on cue RAF and US Army Air Force bombers had carried out six highly destructive attacks on Hamburg during the last week in July and the first week in August 1943. These razed whole sections of the city and caused extensive damage to the Blohm & Voss submarine construction yards. The yards lost an estimated four to six weeks' production: one U-boat was sunk, two unfinished ones had to be scrapped, and fifteen or so were lost due to general production delays.

To ensure that similar attacks on the final assembly yards would not disrupt the Type XXI programme, Otto Merker had plans drawn up for a vast bombproof submarine assembly factory at Farge near Bremen. The Germans were artists without peer in ferro-concrete, but the size of this creation would test even their abilities to the utmost. The exterior of the structure would be 1,350 feet long and 320 feet wide, covering an area about twice that of the Houses of Parliament in London. The walls would be ten to fifteen feet thick and the inside headroom would be 60 feet, topped off with a reinforced concrete roof 22 feet thick. To enable a Type XXI boat to test its *Schnorkel* while inside the bunker, the water level at the outer end was to be dredged to sixty feet. Men of the Todt Organisation began work on the assembly bunker soon after the start of the Type XXI programme, and Merker hoped that by August 1945 production at the yard would be running at fourteen boats per month.

In parallel with the Type XXI programme, the German Navy initiated a less ambitious scheme to produce a smaller submarine with an equally high underwater performance. Designated the Type XXIII, this craft was to have a surface displacement of only 232 tons and would be built in four sections. Its armament comprised two torpedoes already in the tubes – there were no reloads. Intended for operations relatively close to its base, this boat had a maximum range of some 1,300 sea miles. It carried a crew of fourteen. The German Navy ordered one hundred and forty Type XXIII boats, the first to be ready in February 1944.

So much for the German hopes for the future. For the present, there were the perennial worries regarding the Allied U-boat detection methods. But now, for a change, chance played into the hands of the German electronics experts. On 10 November a Leigh Light Wellington, short of fuel and unable to land at its base in Cornwall because of fog, was pointed out to sea and abandoned by its crew. Its tanks could not have been nearly as dry as supposed, however, for the aircraft droned across the English Channel and crashed in northern France. On 30 November *Luftwaffe* Colonel Dietrich Schwenke discussed the latest news on enemy equipment, during a conference in Berlin:

> A Wellington has been shot down [sic] which, for the first time [on this type] carries the Rotterdam device [centimetric-wavelength radar]. It had a depth-charge on board, which proves beyond doubt that Rotterdam is being used against U-boats.

Nor was that the only windfall to drop into the German lap. During 1943 Allied scientists had developed a family of new airborne radar sets working on the even shorter wavelength of 3 centimetres (compared with 10 cm wavelength for ASV Mark III and its contemporaries). The first production models of the new radar became available at the end of the year, and in the Allied camp there was an animated discussion that closely paralleled that of a year earlier: should the first of the new sets go to the strategic bomber force or to the maritime patrol units?

The C-in-C Coastal Command, Sir John Slessor, wrote to the Air Ministry regarding the threat posed by the German Naxos radar-warning receiver, which he feared would neutralise the ASV Mark III radar (he did not know the limitations of Naxos; these were still not obvious even to the German Navy). Slessor pointed out that ASV III had operated without hindrance from an enemy warning receiver for more than nine months, but now a replacement was 'a matter of immediate practical importance, after a period of grace considerably longer than we had any right to expect . . .' He therefore asked for the 3 cm radar to be made available first to his force, since it operated outside the frequency coverage of Naxos.

The old arguments, regarding the priority allocation of such equipment to the strategic bomber units, again prevailed. The anti-submarine aircraft would have to wait until the initial needs of the former had been met. The parallel with events the previous year continued, for in February 1944 *Luftwaffe* technicians salvaged an example of the new radar from a shot-down US bomber.

During the interval between these two important acquisitions, moreover, the German Navy had taken a major step towards putting its scientific house in order. At the end of 1943 *Grossadmiral* Dönitz, disenchanted by the conflicting advice and continual failures on the part of technical advisers from his own service, ordered the formation of a Naval Scientific Operations Staff (*Wissenschaftlicher Führungsstab*). Its duties corresponded loosely to those of the Allied operational research teams, which had played a major part in the development of Allied weapons and tactics for more than two years. It also introduced meetings along the lines of the British 'Sunday Soviets'. The German C-in-C informed his men:

> For some months past the enemy has rendered the U-boat war nugatory. He has achieved this objective not through superior tactics or strategy, but through his superiority in the field of science; this finds its expression in the modern battle weapon – detection. By this means he has torn from our hands our sole offensive weapon against the Anglo-Saxons. It is essential to victory that we make good our scientific disparity and thereby restore to the U-boat its fighting qualities. I have therefore ordered the creation of a Naval Scientific Operations Staff with its headquarters in Berlin . . . I have nominated Professor Küpfmüller as the head of this staff, subordinated directly to myself. Professor Küpfmüller is invested by me with all necessary authority for the execution of his duties. All naval authorities are ordered to give every assistance to the head of the Naval Scientific Operations Staff, his staff and subordinates.

This infusion of new blood quickly took effect. On his taking office, one of Küpfmüller's first actions was to increase the effective sensitivity of the Naxos receiver, by fitting it with a directional (as distinct from an all-round-looking) aerial. That gave the receiver increased sensitivity in the direction-of-look of the aerial, though the latter had to be rotated slowly lest an aircraft should approach from the 'blind' side. Almost immediately, there was a reduction in the number of surprise attacks at night reported by U-boat crews. Yet, strangely, this did not expose the mare's nest regarding the suspected Allied use of the Metox radiations: to the German Navy it seemed that the Allies had introduced the centimetric-wavelength radar into their anti-submarine aircraft only after the Metox receiver had been withdrawn from service.

Thus, by a small modification, Küpfmüller lanced an abscess that had tormented the U-boat service since the middle of 1943. And he did not stop there: he initiated design work on a modified Naxos equipment that would detect signals from the newly discovered Allied radar operating in the 3-centimetre-wavelength band. The new receiver was tested in the spring of 1944, and it actually entered service before Allied aircraft carrying the new radar began operating against U-boats. For the first time, the German Navy was ahead of events in the electronic battle. Yet it was to prove a hollow victory, for the months of uncertainty had left U-boat crews with a deeply entrenched mistrust of their radar warning receivers. The same reaction greeted the air-search radar *Hohentwiel*, fitted to several U-boats during the latter half of 1943. Schooled in the dangers of emitting any radiation onto which the enemy might home, German sailors usually left the radar switched off.

Küpfmüller was unwilling to depend on the random harvest of captured Allied equipment to tell him what his enemy was up to. He persuaded *Grossadmiral* Dönitz to fit out a U-boat with the necessary equipment to make a comprehensive search of the radar spectrum. *U-406* (Dieterich) was selected for this important task, and she set out from St Nazaire early in the New Year. In addition to her normal complement of torpedoes, the boat carried equipment to record radar signals in the band 3.75 metres to 3 centimetres (80 to 10,000 megacycles). She also carried an infrared receiver to detect whether such emissions were being used to illuminate U-boats (in fact the Allies had no such system). To operate this specialised collection of 'black boxes', the boat carried an electronics expert, *Kapitänleutnant* Dr Karl Greven, and two assistants.

That was a move on the right lines, but it failed in its purpose. On 18 February a Royal Navy frigate apprehended *U-406* as she was prowling near a convoy in the north Atlantic, and despatched her with depth-charges and gunfire. Dr Greven was among those taken prisoner, having added nothing to the sum of German knowledge of Allied detection methods.

One further German radar countermeasure deserves mention at this stage: the 'Aphrodite' radar decoy. This device comprised a hydrogen-filled balloon three feet in diameter, connected to a sea anchor by 180 feet of wire from which streamed three lengths of aluminium foil, each thirteen feet long. The idea was that Aphrodite would produce on an airborne radar a blip similar to that from a U-boat. If several of these decoys were set loose in the Bay of Biscay, the Allied air patrols could amuse themselves chasing them while the real U-boats moved through the area un-detected. The device achieved little, however, as one U-boat officer explained:

Riedel, in charge of the scheme, filled a balloon with hydrogen gas stored in bottles affixed to the railing. Then he attached a string of aluminium foils to the balloon, and its loose end to a float, and tossed the arrangement overboard. The float came to rest on the surface while the balloon rose and stretched the wire with the foils until it stood like a full-sized Christmas tree. The decoy rapidly disappeared astern in the ominous darkness. Five minutes later Riedel repeated the drop, and a second 'tree' floated erect over the waters of the Bay. These aluminium 'trees' were supposed to create an image like a U-boat's conning tower on the enemy's radar screens, allowing us to escape in the woods of our own making. Unfortunately, two more balloons became entangled in the railing and three others exploded while being filled with gas; in the commotion, the snarled foils made our position amply evident on the enemy radar screens. But our luck stayed with us. While Riedel fought with the foils and the balloons, we infiltrated a large French fishing fleet, which gave us more protection than the decoys and the guns. In fact, we discarded the aluminium 'trees' and never used them again. They were more a hazard than a help.

Other U-boat crews had more luck with Aphrodite, but the device had little success in seducing Allied aircraft. Indeed, it appeared on their radars only when the foil strips were seen side on; if the wind blew the streamers towards or away from the aircraft, their echoing area was too small to register on the radar.

Finally, if the warning and deception aids all failed, the U-boat was likely to be caught on the surface. Throughout the latter part of 1943 several crews submitted reports indicating that even the quadruple-barrelled 20 mm gun was not powerful enough to knock down attacking aircraft with any degree of certainty. For example, after one of the autumn convoy battles *Oberleutnant* von Witzendorff of *U-267* complained:

> The fuselage of the attacking aircraft was hit by the whole contents of a magazine, but without effect. The bridge watch claim to have seen 2 cm shells ricocheting off the cockpit repeatedly.

The implication was that the attacking aircraft carried extensive armour plating. Yet this was not so: anti-submarine machines had most of it removed to allow them to carry more fuel. Almost certainly von Witzendorff's men scored far fewer hits on the aircraft than they thought. Nevertheless, *Grossadmiral* Dönitz ordered a further strengthening of his U-boats' anti-aircraft batteries. During the closing months of the year a new weapon appeared: the 3.7 cm Flak 43, able to fire 1 pound shells at a rate of one hundred per minute. Although it remained German Navy policy not to invite stand-up fights with aircraft, if a U-boat was caught on the surface it could hit back hard.

With the heavier gun came improved protection for the gunners, box-like structures of armour plating on either side of the conning tower that were proof against enemy rounds of up to 20 mm calibre. The German Navy orders on combating air attack advised:

> During air attacks the bridge personnel should take cover at the critical moment, by kneeling behind the armour plating. This should also be done by the captain and officers of the watch. Remaining in the open during an attack has already cost many lives that might otherwise have been saved; this is not a sign of courage, but rather of thoughtlessness . . .

The additional armour proved a mixed blessing, however. The extra superstructure weight made the Type VII boat less stable, and in rough weather roll angles of up to thirty degrees to either side were not uncommon. That placed a considerable strain on the crews, especially the newer members.

Of all the weapons arrayed against them, the German sailors found the salvoes of air-launched rockets the most fearful to behold. On this subject the German Navy orders stated:

Rockets can be fired at distances of 2,000 down to 150 metres, the best distance being 500 metres. Low-level rocket attacks may be carried out at altitudes of between 10 and 20 metres. The aircraft are very manoeuvrable and can fire rockets when banking [though if they did, accuracy suffered]. Where there is no defensive fire the accuracy is very good, but where the defences are strong it is unsatisfactory. Good results are obtained by firing the rockets in salvoes; the rocket discharge is easily recognisable by a red glow under the wings, and smoke trails mark the rockets' trajectories . . . The morale effect of a rocket attack on young and inexperienced men is very powerful. It must be overcome by rigorous discipline.

To supplement its rocket-firing aircraft as a means of dealing with recalcitrant U-boats that remained on the surface and fought back, Coastal Command introduced the Mosquito Mark XVIII. This aircraft carried a 6-pounder (57 mm) anti-tank gun, which fired armour-piercing shot at a muzzle velocity of 2,800 feet per second. A clever automatic loading system allowed the weapon to fire at a rate of forty rounds per minute. Complete with loader, recoil mechanism and ammunition, the installation weighed just over three-quarters of a ton. The 6-pounder had an effective range of well over a mile, and thus it outranged the 37 mm gun being fitted to some German submarines. It could not pierce a U-boat's pressure hull at distances greater than 1,000 yards, however.

The first two Mark XVIII Mosquitoes were issued to No. 248 Squadron at Predannack in Cornwall, in October 1943. They began operations almost immediately. Previously patrols by Junkers 88 long-range fighters had provided a degree of safety for U-boats in the waters close to their French bases. But the fast and nimble gun-fitted Mosquitoes soon put a stop to that. The new weapon drew first blood on 7 November, when Flying Officer A. Bonnet, RCAF, surprised the returning *U-123* (von Schroeter) as she ran on the surface almost within sight of her base at Lorient. The Canadian pilot's rounds smashed into the conning tower, killing a petty officer and wounding two sailors. One round punched a hole 7 inches long by 2 inches wide through the superstructure. That rendered the U-boat temporarily incapable of diving, but she regained her base without further incident.

Because of the shortage of Mosquitoes and the specialised nature of the modifications, there were seldom more than two aircraft with 6-pounder guns available for operations. Most of their successes were against surface ships, though early in 1944 they sank one U-boat. On 25 March *U-976* was within forty miles of her base at St Nazaire, returning from a cruise in the Atlantic. *Oberleutnant* Tiesler and his crew had good reason to feel secure, for two heavily armed converted merchant ships were guarding them during this final part of the voyage. All the greater, then, was the surprise when a pair of Mosquitoes swept down out of the sun with guns barking. Between them the pilots made five separate attacking runs on the U-boat, and observed their rounds striking her. Her pressure hull pierced, *U-976* sank, leaving a large patch of oil. The warships that should have protected her from such an ending saved several of the crew, including Tiesler.

There were other innovations. To assist Allied aircraft patrolling the waters off the north and west coasts of Spain to navigate accurately, an important radio aid became available during 1943. The Allied name for the system was 'Consol', its German name was *Sonne* (sun), though the German-manned and installed ground transmitters were the same in either case. This unusual story began in February 1943, when British radio monitors noted unusual signals on a frequency of 316 kilocycles. Their source was tracked down to a transmitter near Brest, and reconnaissance photographs revealed an aerial array of giant proportions employing three towers 150 feet high, set out in a line with two miles between each. During April 1943 Allied monitoring stations heard the distinctive *Sonne* signals emanating from transmitters at Petten in Holland and Stavanger in Norway as well.

As the Allies learnt more about the system they discovered that it provided accurate bearings out to a maximum range of about 1,000 miles. The aid, employed by German ships, U-boats and aircraft, was extremely simple to use. The radio operator tuned his communications receiver to the selected *Sonne* transmitter, counted the trains of dots and dashes he heard in his earphones, then read off his bearing by referring that count to a special map. The cross of two or more such bearings gave him a 'fix' on his position.

In May 1943, interest in the German navigation aid reached the ears of the British war cabinet: a new *Sonne* transmitter had begun transmitting from a point near the town of Lugo in north-west Spain. The initial Whitehall reaction was a proposal to send a strong diplomatic protest to the Spanish government, to get the station shut down. Dr R.V. Jones, head of the scientific Intelligence department at the Air Ministry, questioned such a move. Might not the *Sonne* transmissions be useful to Allied aircraft and ships also?

That question arrived on the desk of Group Captain Dick Richardson, chief navigation officer at the Coastal Command headquarters at Northwood. His answer was not long in coming. With the dead reckoning methods currently in use, crews flying in this area could easily be as much as thirty miles out in their navigation. Using *Sonne*, that error might be reduced to five miles. Such an improvement in navigation could spell the difference between the success or failure of an anti-U-boat operation, and it was clear that *Sonne* was of considerable potential value to the Allied cause. So, in classic accordance with the dictum 'If you can't beat 'em, join 'em', the Lugo station was allowed to continue radiating without a whiff of protest. Allied radio monitoring aircraft carefully plotted the *Sonne* lobe patterns. Then a British printing company received an order for some special maps, which bore a distinct resemblance to those carried in German maritime patrol aircraft.

Dick Richardson came up with a cover-name for the pirated German navigational aid. *Sonne* was the German word for 'sun', and Allied aircrews were going to fix their position 'with sun'; in Spanish that was *con sol*, and 'Consol' it became. Allied crews used the system for the remainder of the war. Later in 1943 a second Spanish *Sonne* station went on the air near Seville in the southwest. It also proved very useful to Allied aircraft. After that there were tongue-in-cheek suggestions that the Allied governments should offer to share in the cost of any future *Sonne* stations the *Luftwaffe* might care to erect! (After the war the *Sonne* stations at Brest, Stavanger, Lugo and Seville remained in operation, and a captured transmitter was erected at Bushmills in Northern Ireland. These remained in operation for three decades after the war. Such longevity is proof of the soundness of the original *Sonne* concept. By an ironic twist the post-war transmitters were all known as Consol stations; the original German name had long since passed out of use.)

At the beginning of 1944 US Navy Patrol Squadron VP-63 was about to bring its own particular pressure to bear on the U-boats passing through the Straits of Gibraltar. For that unit's Catalina flying-boats were fitted with the magnetic airborne detector, MAD, and the special retro-bombs for use against submarines.

The German Navy had suspected the existence of such a system, though there was no evidence of its use by the Allies. Those suspicions were aired at a conference held on 10 March 1944, when the head of the development section of the German Navy's Technical Signals Department (*Amptgruppe Technisches Nachrichtenswesen*), *Kapitän zur See* Helmuth Giessler, informed the assembled officers:

> While we employ only acoustic location devices [to find submerged submarines] there is a suspicion, which we are examining carefully, that perhaps the enemy is using magnetic-field-change methods as well. The range of such magnetic locators, from ships or from aircraft, is now being examined; from aircraft, a range of between 200 and 400 metres would appear to be theoretically attainable.

Giessler's statement illustrates, yet again, the paucity of German Intelligence on the Allied anti-submarine measures. By that time the US Navy had had such a magnetic detection device in service for over a year, and only a fortnight earlier it had played an important part in the destruction of a U-boat.

For the crews of VP-63, 1943 had been a frustrating year. The unit had received its MAD-fitted Catalinas – nicknamed 'Madcats' – at the close of 1942. Early in 1943 the squadron began operating off the east coast of the USA and, later, off Iceland. But on each occasion the arrival of VP-63 seemed to coincide with a reduction in U-boat activity in those areas. In July the unit moved to Pembroke Dock in Wales to take part in the Battle of the Bay. But while the special detector and the retro-bombs were effective against U-boats cruising underwater, the slow flying-boats were vulnerable if a submarine stayed on the surface and fought back.

Early in 1944 the squadron moved to Port Lyautey in Morocco, to reinforce the units covering the Straits of Gibraltar. Since the October disaster the German Navy had been successful in sending U-boats through the Straits: one made the passage in November, two in December and four in January – all the boats attempting the passage got safely through.

By their geography, the Straits of Gibraltar are probably the best place in the world in which to conduct MAD searches for submarines. The waters are narrow: at its narrowest point the deep-water sleeve is only some four miles wide. The waters are deep: the 'sleeve' is rarely less than 600 feet deep except close to the shore, so there is little magnetic interference from wrecks lying on the bottom. The currents that flow through the Strait are complex and subject to fluctuations. But as a rough generalisation, down to the first 100 to 150 feet the water flows eastwards into the Mediterranean, while the deeper water flows westwards into the Atlantic. At its strongest, the deep westward-flowing current reaches 4½ knots – sufficient to prevent a deep passage by a U-boat entering the Mediterranean. That eastbound-running boats were unlikely to be deeper than 150 feet was important to the crews of the Madcats, for their equipment would not register a U-boat more than 400 feet away. Moreover the optimum German tactics, to approach the Straits charging the batteries during the night and then pass run those waters submerged during the day, also suited the Madcat crews: they had to fly their patrols at very low altitude, and this was possible only by day.

Before VP-63 began patrolling the Straits, MAD had been considered mainly as a follow-up device, to relocate boats previously seen on radar but which had submerged. Such were the limitations imposed on submarine navigation by the geography of the Straits, however, that the device could be used there as a *primary detection system.* The US Operational Research Group devised the tactics that were soon to be employed to good effect. The aircraft were to fly a 'barrier patrol' round an oblong four miles long and one mile wide, lying astride the narrowest point in the deep-water channel. Two Madcats, maintaining position opposite each other on the oblong, were to fly round it at 115 mph. Thus an aircraft passed any given point on the oblong once every three minutes. Against a 200-foot long submarine, moving at two knots and assisted by a favourable current of two knots, that gave a good chance of the boat registering on the MAD equipment twice as it passed through the barrier.

The Madcats of VP-63 established their barrier across the Straits during February 1944. Every morning, all morning, two aircraft flew up and down the oblong, completing one orbit every six minutes. Each noon, a second pair took over and repeated the performance during the afternoon. To get the best possible detection range on underwater objects, the Madcats had to fly at an altitude of 100 feet above the surface. This took away some of the monotony of this type of flying: as one American pilot later recalled: 'It was fun to take a relatively clumsy aircraft like the Catalina, and perform turns and wing-overs close to the water. It was even legal!'

The first U-boat to come up against the Madcat barrier was *U-761* (Geider). She had put out from Brest on 12 February, and began her passage through the Straits twelve days later. On the afternoon of the 24th, Aircraft Radioman J. Cunningham, operating the MAD equipment in a Catalina, excitedly saw the recording pen suddenly zigzag across the paper trace: the aircraft had passed over a magnetic disturbance. The pilot, Lieutenant T. Wooley, pulled the Madcat into a wide 'tracking circle' centred on the point of initial contact. Soon afterwards the second Madcat, piloted by Lieutenant H. Baker, joined in. The first thing to establish was whether the magnetic disturbance was moving. Repeated runs over the area, with a smoke marker released on each MAD indication, produced a line of markers on an underwater ferrous metallic object moving eastwards at about two knots: there could be no doubt this was a U-boat.

At this stage the destroyer HMS *Anthony*, also patrolling the Straits, attempted to engage. She made a brief contact with the boat on her Asdic, but conditions were poor and she soon lost it. However, her presence forced the Catalinas to climb to avoid colliding with her, with the result that they lost MAD contact too.

The Madcats restarted their search, circling the point where they had lost contact. Half an hour later the pen recorder in Wooley's aircraft again zigzagged. Again Wooley and Baker went into their tracking procedure, and laid out a line of ten smoke markers to indicate the submarine's course and speed. They also radioed a pointed request to the destroyers, to please keep clear of the smoke floats for the time being.

Finally Wooley judged the time ripe to attack the craft with his retro-bombs. When the MAD indicated 'overhead', he pressed the button to fire the bombs. One bomb failed to ignite, but the remaining twenty-three roared backwards off their rails, fell vertically and splashed into the water in a rectangular pattern.

Until now the crew of *U-761* had been moving underwater at a depth of 50 metres, oblivious to the commotion above. The layers of water at different densities, which had made Asdic conditions so difficult for the operators in *Anthony*, also made it difficult for the U-boat to remain at a predetermined depth. Then, without warning, came four loud detonations against her hull. The German sailors could only speculate on their cause. As the reports from the various sections of the boat reached *Oberleutnant* Geider, it became clear that the boat had suffered no appreciable damage. But one thing was clear beyond doubt: somehow their attempt to sneak through the Straits had been discovered. The feelings of those on the boat were rather like those of a burglar creeping through a darkened house, who suddenly feels a stone bounce off his shoulder.

Two minutes later, in the second aircraft, Baker delivered an attack with his complement of retro-bombs. Then *Anthony* put down a pattern of ten depth-charges across the head of the smoke markers. Those attacks left *U-761* in serious trouble. She reared up to the surface out of control, stern down and with little way on, then sank stern first. The destroyer HMS *Wishart* made contact and laid a pattern of depth-charges, to be followed shortly afterwards by another from *Anthony*.

The catalogue of damage to the U-boat at this stage makes grim

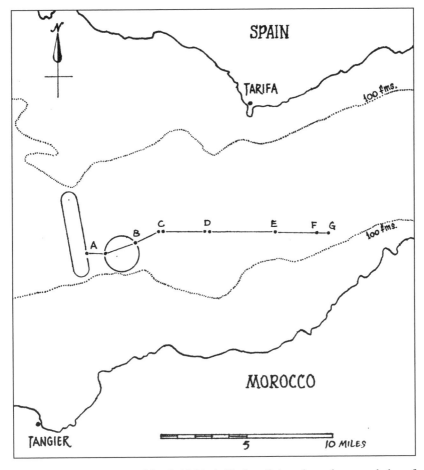

Action against *U-392*, 16 March 1944. A Madcat flying along the easterly leg of the patrol pattern makes contact at A. Shortly afterwards the two aircraft lose contact; begin flying a 'trapping circle' round the U-boat and regain contact at B. The U-boat's path established, the two aircraft attack in succession at C. The aircraft break off contact, D, to allow *Vanoc* to attack. *Affleck* makes a brief contact but loses it at E, regains contact at F and finishes off *U-392* at G.

reading. All her electrical installations, including the batteries and the motors, were damaged and out of action. The main electrical control panel lay broken in pieces on the floor plates. The hydrophones and all radio equipment were smashed. The compressors had wrenched loose from their straps. Water had entered the boat through a loose valve in the drain pump. The clutch between the diesel engines and the electric motors was jammed. Some high-pressure air lines had been ruptured, and all lighting except for the emergency lights was out. To crown it all, there were alarming signs of the presence of poisonous chlorine gas inside the hull. Geider ordered the boat to surface for the last time, but even as she did so she came under attack from an RAF Catalina and a US Navy Ventura. The sailors struggled clear of the sinking craft and the destroyers picked up forty-one of them.

The next U-boat to attempt to run the Straits was *U-618* (Baberg). Her commander found the defences too strong, and returned to France. *Oberleutnant* Schümann in *U-392* made a more determined attempt on 16 March. The Madcat 'sentries' were vigilantly at their posts and the U-boat was detected almost immediately. Moreover the lessons of the previous operation had been well learnt, and this time the co-operation between ships and aircraft was exemplary. The destroyers held clear while the Madcats tracked the U-boat with smoke markers. They then attacked it with retro-bombs, each scoring three hits. The senior aircraft commander then called in HMS *Vanoc*, which made an unsuccessful attack with her anti-submarine mortar; *Affleck* then finished off the still-submerged *U-392* with three hits from her mortar.

During the remainder of March three U-boats successfully passed through the Straits, in each case by sticking to the shallower water on the southern side. But on 5 May the Madcats located *U-731* (Keller), and the subsequent action was almost a repeat of that that had seen the end of *U-392*. Only one more U-boat attempted the dangerous Straits passage, and she cleared the defences successfully on 17 May. After that, events in northern France would force the German Navy to concentrate its attentions elsewhere.

Passing from the Straits of Gibraltar into the enclosed waters of the Mediterranean was, for the U-boat crews, like jumping out of the fire into the only marginally more comfortable haven of the frying-pan. The latter part of 1943 had seen a considerable increase in Allied anti-submarine forces in this area. Moreover the convoys were always routed within easy reach of ground-based air cover, and flying conditions were usually excellent. As a result aircraft and warships could employ the descriptively named 'Swamp' hunting technique, against any U-boat imprudent enough to reveal its presence by attacking a convoy. The craft immediately drew upon itself a massive air-sea hunt that lasted until, with her batteries or air supply exhausted, she had to rise to the surface and accept her inevitable fate.

Between December 1943 and the end of May 1944, Swamp operations in the Mediterranean accounted for five U-boats. In each case lavish effort was brought to bear. For example, the forty-hour-long hunt for *U-960* (Heinrich) during 18 and 19 May, involved a total of 458 flying hours. In general terms that meant about seventy-five sorties with an average duration about six hours. Such expenditure of effort against a single U-boat was possible only because the German submarine strength in the area was so low – only fifteen boats were in the Mediterranean at the end of April 1944. Following the loss of *U-960*, U-boat activity in the area came to a virtual end. Most of the remaining boats were destroyed during strategic bombing attacks on their bases at Toulon and Salamis, which lacked concrete shelters.

Shortly after mid-day on 19 April 1944, a lone reconnaissance Mosquito of No. 540 Squadron sped high over the German Baltic ports of Hela, Elbing and Danzig, photographing each in turn. In the days that followed the prints were examined keenly at the sprawling photographic interpretation centre at Medmenham in Berkshire. One of the Danzig photographs caused a particular stir, for debris in the water drew attention to a newly launched U-boat in the Schichau basin. Comparison with earlier photographs of the Schichau shipbuilding yard revealed an interesting sequence. On 8 March, Slipway No. 5 had been empty; on 14 April, a U-boat had been seen on the slip in an advanced state of construction; now, on 19 April, Slipway No. 5 was again clear and the U-boat had just been launched. Allied Intelligence officers reported:

From laying down to launching, not more than six weeks had elapsed, and it is clear that such speed in completion could only have been accomplished by the use of prefabricated sections. Further proof of this was provided by activity on an adjacent slip. Another U-boat of the same type was seen with the stern section separate, and obviously ready to be moved up to complete the hull.

The sequence of photographs solved a riddle that had furrowed Allied brows for some months past. In June 1943 aerial photographs of the various U-boat construction yards had revealed a total of 271 boats under construction. But since then there had been a steady decline in the number of U-boats on the slipways, until by March 1944 there were only 160. As completed U-boats were launched, at most yards no new ones were laid down to take their place. Yet the German propaganda machine was making continuous references to a new and more powerful U-boat offensive in the offing. What was happening? Now the answer was clear: U-boats of a new and more advanced type were being prefabricated in sections, and only the final assembly took place on the slipways.

In fact the newly launched U-boat photographed at Danzig was *U-3501*, first of the new Type XXI boats; her final assembly had begun as recently as 20 March. The thirty-one-day period separating her laying down and launching was somewhat shorter than that planned for the assembly of a Type XXI U-boat. But the shipwrights had cut many corners to get her into the water on time: on 20 April Adolf Hitler celebrated his 55th birthday, and the report of the successful launching was one of his most welcome presents.

What Hitler was not told – and what Allied Intelligence officers never discovered – was that *U-3601* was little more than a floating hulk. For already, the highly ambitious production schedules for the Type XXI and Type XXIII U-boats had run into serious difficulties. Rudolf Blohm, a partner in the Blohm & Voss shipbuilding concern, was unremitting in his opposition to Otto Merker's scheme to prefabricate U-boats. Soon after *U-3601* was launched, Blohm wrote a scathing report on the project:

Many designs have had to be changed because they are either not practical, or else entirely useless. For example, the steering mechanism was a total failure, and the first boats completed by the assembly yards could not be steered . . . The mistakes resulting from haste in the design, and the modifications found desirable during the testing of the first boats, have made assembly work more difficult; the Navy has demanded a hundred changes so far . . .

Moreover, the British and American strategic bombing attacks on German industrial targets superimposed further delays on the programme. During a conference with Hitler, *Grossadmiral* Dönitz reported delays of one month in the Type XXI schedule, and two months in that for the Type XXIII boats. The factory producing the all-important electric motors had suffered severe damage in an air attack, and until these motors were installed the completed rear-hull sections could not be welded up. Too few construction workers were available to repair the bomb damage. Hitler made sympathetic noises, then delivered a monologue on the need to give priority to the repair of the factories building fighter aircraft, 'otherwise industry might suffer yet more destruction, and U-boat production might be halted completely.'

The initial plan, to have the first Type XXI U-boats operational during the late summer or early autumn of 1944, was beginning to slide out of Dönitz's grasp. In the meantime the U-boat war had been simmering away, with scores of minor battles. During the seven-month period between the beginning of November 1943 and the end of May 1944, U-boats sank just over half a million tons of Allied merchant shipping – an unimpressive average of about 80,000 tons per month. Their main aims, now, were to continue to tie down the massive Allied anti-submarine forces, and keep the U-boat service ticking over until the formidable new submarines were ready to go into action. Yet in return for even those moderate returns the German Navy had to pay a high price in blood: during that same period 117 U-boats had been lost, an average of seventeen per month. Forty-three U-boats had been sunk by anti-submarine aircraft; five were destroyed during air attacks on their bases; fourteen had been shared between warships and aircraft; fifty-one had been sunk by warships and four had come to grief after detonating mines.

During May 1944 there was a marked decrease in naval activity in the Battle of the Atlantic. This was the lull before the storm. Along the English Channel both sides made feverish preparations as the time approached for the invasion of France, the battle that would decide the course of the war in the West. In the next chapter we shall observe in detail the massive anti-submarine operation set in train to block the path of U-boats trying to reach the huge concentrations of shipping lying off the landing beaches.

CHAPTER 10

Final Battles of the European War

May 1944 to May 1945

When men are equally inured and disciplined in war 'tis, without a miracle, number that gains the victory.
                                   Admiral Sir Cloudesley Shovell

No operation during World War II was so carefully planned as the invasion of the north coast of France. No operation compared with it in the lavishness with which men and equipment were put at risk. No other single operation could have so decisive an effect on the course of the war in the West. Should the invasion fail, Allied losses would be so great that Adolf Hitler need not fear for a threat in the West for a year, or perhaps two. That would give time to bring into service the new types of submarine, the jet fighters and bombers, and the robot weapons of bombardment on which the German leaders pinned their hopes. If the invasion succeeded, however, Germany's armed forces would be embroiled in a full-scale land war on a second major front – their recurring nightmare. With such issues at stake, *Grossadmiral* Dönitz was prepared to risk his entire submarine fleet, provided there was a chance of inflicting severe damage on the invaders.

Admiral Theodor Krancke, the commander Naval Forces West, was directly responsible for directing the German naval effort to counter the invasion. His plan was for the submarines to wait out the preparatory bombardment at their bases along the French Biscay coast. Sitting under the thick reinforced-concrete roofs of their pens, they would be safe from air attack. Once the invasion began the boats were to put out *en masse* and head for the landing area, fighting their way through the Allied defences and accepting heavy losses if necessary. The distances were not great: from Brest to what the Germans considered the most likely invasion area – the

Pas de Calais – was less than 300 miles. A U-boat with a determined crew could cover nearly half that distance on the surface in a single night. Krancke had every reason to believe that a good proportion of his boats would get past the defences and set about their work of destruction among the concentrations of vulnerable merchant shipping.

For the Allied planners charged with blunting such an attack, the task was far from simple: they knew that the invasion would take place on the coast of Normandy, within 200 miles of the nearest U-boat base. In January 1944 Air Chief Marshal Sir Sholto Douglas had replaced Sir John Slessor at the head of Coastal Command. Almost from the beginning of his tenure, Douglas and his staff were deeply committed to preparing to support the invasion.

The Allies' 'worst case' Intelligence estimate credited the German Navy with the ability to send 130 U-boats against the invading forces almost immediately, followed by seventy more within two weeks. The Straits of Dover are shallow and it was planned to block the seaway with minefields, to prevent the ingress of boats from that end. The main threat came from the western end of the Channel. Could aircraft erect a 'barricade' over that stretch of water?

Air Vice-Marshal Brian Baker's No. 19 Group of Coastal Command – he had taken over from AVM Bromet the previous autumn – was to provide the anti-submarine air patrols to support the invasion. His directive called for a Swamp-type operation across an area far greater than any previously attempted. The plan called for his aircraft to patrol intensively and continually, by day and by night, a stretch of water about 20,000 square miles in extent. It ran from the north-west coast of France to the south coast of Ireland, and extended eastwards into the English Channel as far as the Cherbourg Peninsula. The requirement was that a U-boat on the surface anywhere in that area would be seen on radar at least once every thirty minutes, and would come under immediate attack.

To meet this difficult requirement, Baker's Group was reinforced to twenty-five squadrons. His force now comprised some three hundred and fifty Sunderlands, Wellingtons and Liberators, Halifaxes, Mosquitoes, Beaufighters and Swordfish. Of that total, only about thirty planes were to be on patrol over the western end of the English Channel at any one time. At first sight that proportion of the total force might appear unambitious; but those patrols would have to be maintained twenty-four hours a day and seven days a week, for an indefinite period. The usual squadron establishment of fifteen aircraft meant between eight and twelve machines serviceable at any one time. So it would have been unrealistic for a squadron to attempt to maintain more than two aircraft continuously airborne. Certainly the squadrons could have mounted a greater effort in a short burst; but now the emphasis was on the long term, and the operation had to be planned accordingly. Moreover, there had to be reserve aircraft kept ready, to replace those on patrol that went unserviceable, expended their weapons or were shot down. Four squadrons, from the Royal Navy, were equipped with Swordfish and were suitable only for patrols close to the shores of England. Two more squadrons, equipped with Mosquitoes and Beaufighters, were unsuitable for normal anti-submarine patrol work.

How could the available thirty aircraft be used to maximum effect over the patrol area? It fell to Group Captain Dick Richardson and his navigation staff at Coastal Command headquarters to devise a means of systematically overseeing every part of that 20,000 square mile expanse of water, once every thirty minutes. After much discussion one of Richardson's staff officers, Flight Lieutenant James Perry, devised the best solution. It was a clever plan, and like most clever plans it was essentially a simple one. On a map of the area to be covered, Perry drew a series of twelve oblong boxes, each tailored to the capability of one type of patrol aircraft. The circumference of each box equalled the distance that type of aircraft would fly in either thirty or sixty minutes; if the latter, two aircraft were to follow each other round the circumference at thirty-minute intervals. The width of each oblong, and the distance between it and its neighbour, was twice the range at which the particular type of ASV radar would detect a U-boat on the surface. In that way Perry solved the problem of co-ordinating the patrols by several different types of aircraft, with differing cruising speeds and radars of varying performance.

The stretch of water under scrutiny could be regarded as an enormous cork that would act as a stopper in the English Channel; and Perry's oblongs immediately became known as 'Cork' patrols. With all thirty aircraft flying simultaneously round the circumference of each oblong, their radar operators would collectively examine every part of the area once every thirty minutes. Any U-boat that chose to submerge whenever it detected radar signals would soon exhaust its batteries and its supply of compressed air.

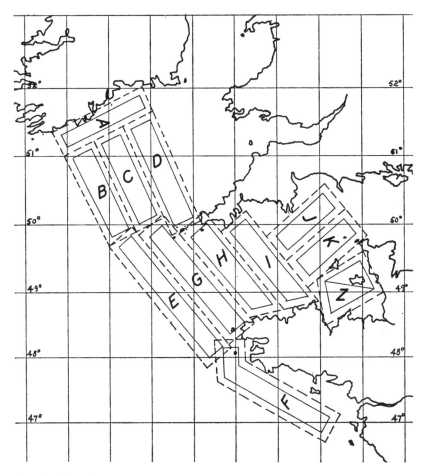

The Cork Patrols.

In some Cork patrols, aircraft would be required to fly within a few miles of German-held France. To guard against any *Luftwaffe* attempt to interfere with the lumbering anti-submarine planes, Allied fighters would be allocated to escort them during the daylight hours.

Even the best-laid scheme would be doomed to failure if aircrews lacked the training to accomplish it. During the preceding year the pace of operations had been such that crews had little time to become proficient with their new items of equipment. Moreover, early in 1944, two squadrons of Halifaxes and one of Sunderlands were converting for night operations, using the new high-intensity flares. Sir Sholto Douglas made good use of the general lull that spring, to release squadrons from the front line in turn to undergo intensive retraining.

To test the effectiveness of the Cork patrols, in April 1944 No. 19 Group ran a realistic full-scale trial in the Irish Sea. The submarine HMS *Viking* acted the part of a U-boat. Her skipper was told to move as fast as he could, surfaced or submerged, over a ninety-mile-long course intensively patrolled by aircraft. He was to do his utmost to avoid air 'attack', but at the same time he needed to ensured that *Viking* arrived at her goal in a condition fit to go into action.

The trials began as planned on 6 April, but initially there were no aircraft: fog over their bases prevented the first machines taking-off. As a result *Viking* was able to cruise on the surface undisturbed for an hour and a half. But then the belated arrival of the first plane forced her to dive. And from that time life became a misery for the sailors. During the next twenty-eight hours the submarine spent barely two hours on the surface, made up of nine periods averaging about thirteen minutes each. None of these periods was long enough for her crew to add any useful charge to the batteries, or add much to their dwindling supply of compressed air (though they did ventilate the boat). Finally, five miles from his goal, *Viking*'s commander decided to throw in the towel: his batteries were depleted to a point where the boat could go no faster than two or three knots. So the boat would have little chance of escape after delivering a torpedo attack. Moreover, there was sufficient high-pressure air to blow the ballast tanks only once more. The 'defeated' *Viking* surfaced, and, unable to dive, continued on the surface towards the finishing line. When the next aircraft appeared on Viking's radar, however, the submarine commander avoided detection by turning stem-on to the hunter. This, coupled with a poor radar watch in the aircraft, prevented detection and allowed the submarine to complete the course without being 'sunk' (though she was in no state to press home an attack on an escorted convoy).

The trial had been gruelling enough for *Viking*'s crew, though for them it was merely a game. For German sailors trying to move up the English Channel the psychological strain would be far more severe: they had more than a ninety-mile course to cover, and any aircraft that located them would not withhold its depth-charges. After the trial *Viking*'s commander wrote:

Further progress on the afternoon and night of the 7 April would have been very uncomfortable, and a U-boat meeting such opposition would have found it exhausting and demoralising . . .

All the more remarkable, then, was the fact that the crews of only two out of the nineteen aircraft taking part actually saw *Viking* on radar; and on neither occasion could they 'attack' her before she dived to safety. Throughout the war the question had frequently been asked: 'What good are aircraft doing flying over the sea day and night without seeing anything?' Here was the answer: nineteen aircraft had taken part in the trial and only two of their crews had seen the submarine on radar. Yet at the end of the trial *Viking* was barely effective as a fighting unit, and in a real action she would have been concerned more with her survival than with inflicting damage upon an enemy.

All of this was, of course, true only for those boats that lacked the *Schnorkel* breathing tube. As Allied Intelligence officers had discovered, this device was to be fitted to all operational German U-boats. Yet in spite of strenuous efforts on the part of the dock-yard personnel, the programme had slipped badly. At the beginning of June 1944, only nine of the forty-nine U-boats of the *Landwirt* group, allocated to the counter-invasion task, carried this modification. Many of the conversion kits would remain in their packing crates, trapped in goods yards by the systematic Allied aerial bombardment of the French railway system. And any U-boat that got through the web of aerial patrols would still have to run the gauntlet of some three hundred destroyers, frigates, sloops, corvettes and anti-submarine trawlers.

On 6th June 1944, the longest day dawned: at 05.13 hours head-quarters German Naval Forces West flashed an order to all boats of the *Landwirt* group to come to immediate readiness. The invasion had begun. In an order to his men *Grossadmiral* Dönitz had written:

Every [Allied] vessel taking part in the landing, even if it has but a handful of men or a solitary tank aboard, is a target of the utmost importance, which must be attacked regardless of risk. Every effort will be made to close the enemy invasion fleet regardless of danger from shallow water, possible mine-fields or anything else.

Every man and weapon destroyed before reaching the beaches lessens the enemy's chances of ultimate success.

Every boat that inflicts losses on the enemy while landing has fulfilled its primary purpose even though it perishes in so doing.

The die was cast. The greatest aircraft-submarine battle of all time was about to begin.

On the evening following the invasion the boats of the *Landwirt* group streamed out of their bases in France and headed north. Brest was the U-boat base nearest to the invasion area, and of the fifteen boats that left the port seven carried the *Schnorkel* device. The latter now cruised toward the target area submerged, relatively immune from air attack. The remaining eight boats lacked the breathing tube and intended to run at high speed on the surface – they needed to keep their batteries fully charged, ready to begin their underwater runs when dawn broke. We shall follow the fortunes of those eight boats: *U-256, U-373, U-413, U-415, U-441, U-629, U-740* and *U-821*.

The boats made their way into the darkness in single file, with about 300 yards between each; they did not have to wait long for the excitement to begin. The log of *Oberleutnant* Werner's boat, *U-415*, conveys a vivid picture of what followed:

01.40 Bright moonlight, good visibility. Left the escort off Brest. Course 270°, full speed.

01.45 The boat astern, *U-256*, is attacked by aircraft. We also open fire. *U-256* shoots down a plane. There are radar impulses coming from all round us, strength 3–4.

02.20 Radar impulses increasing in strength, from the starboard. A Sunderland appears, and attacks from 40° to starboard. I open fire. He drops four bombs ahead of me . . .

In his autobiography, Herbert Werner continued the story:

An instant later, four detonations amidships. Four savage eruptions heaved *U-415* out of the water and threw our men flat on the deck plates. Then she fell back, and four collapsing geysers showered us with tons of water and sent cascades through the hatch. This was the end. Both diesels stopped, the rudder jammed hard-a-starboard. *U-415* swerved in an arc, gradually losing speed . . . a target to be finished off with ease.

Before the expected deathblow came, however, Werner's engineers were able to restart the motors. The battered U-boat limped back to Brest in company with the similarly shaken *U-256* (Brauel). In fact the 'Sunderland' that had attacked him was a Wellington of No. 179 Squadron, attacking without its Leigh Light because the night was so clear and bright.

During the night of 6/7 June Allied aircrews sighted U-boats on twenty-two occasions and made seven attacks. In addition to *U-256* and *U-415* mentioned above, they sank *U-955* (Baden) and *U-970* (Ketels) and damaged two other boats.

With the coming of dawn the battle faded, as one by one the submarines dived to safety. *Kapitänleutnant* Vogler in *U-212* left his dive a bit late, and came under attack from two 6-pounder-gun Mosquitoes; the latter scored hits on the port diving tank and the port compensating tank. With six tons of negative buoyancy, *U-212* staggered back to La Pallice.

During all of this the anti-submarine aircraft saw nothing of the *Luftwaffe*. Indeed, that service's sole contribution to the U-boats' life-and-death struggle was to keep its *Sonne* transmitters running – a move that greatly assisted those Allied aircraft assigned to the more southerly Cork patrols.

The first night had gone well for No. 19 Group, but five-sixths of the counter-invasion U-boat force was still intact – forty-two boats. As darkness fell on 7 June the thirty-six boats without a *Schnorkel* rose to the surface, and resumed their eastward passage at full speed.

By now the leading U-boats were on the point of entering the western end of the English Channel. The Cork patrols were ready for them. Flying Officer Kenneth Moore was 'pacing his beat' in a Leigh Light Liberator of No. 224 Squadron during the early hours of 8 June, when his radar operator reported a contact twelve miles ahead. The Canadian pilot side-stepped his aircraft to position the contact between the bright moon and himself, then turned towards it. After a few minutes the navigator in the nose position caught sight of the U-boat against the shimmering line of the moon on the water: 'It was a perfect silhouette, as if it were painted on white paper. I could see the conning tower quite clearly.' Moore ordered the radar operator to cease the transmissions, which might have alerted the enemy, and prepared to attack. Passing only forty feet over the boat, he released six depth-charges; three fell to starboard of the boat and three to port – a perfect straddle. As they exploded

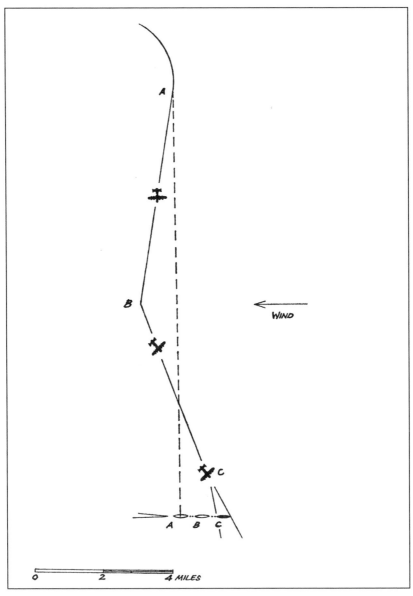

A Leigh Light attack, showing the tactics in use during the early part of 1944. The aircraft makes radar contact with the U-boat and turns until it is dead ahead (A). The wind speed is not accurately known, nor the U-boat's course or speed. The aircraft holds the heading established at A until B, halfway between A and the contact; now the drift angle is measured. At B the aircraft turns onto a new heading, allowing twice the established angle of drift. The Leigh Light, still off, is trained to one drift angle downwind of the track. At C the light is switched on, the beam is brought up along the angle of train and the U-boat is exposed.

the rear gunner excitedly shouted: 'Oh God, we've blown her clean out of the water.' Returning to the scene, the crew could make out oil and wreckage on the water – all that was left of *U-629* (Bugs).

The elated aircrew resumed their patrol. They were still in the fight, for the Liberator's bomb bay still held six depth-charges and a homing torpedo. Jokingly, Moore commented over the intercom: 'Now let's get another one.' And they did. Ten minutes later the radar operator reported another contact, six miles away. The second attack was almost a replica of the first – again the adroit positioning of the U-boat up-moon, the radar silence during the approach and the straddle with six depth-charges. *U-373*'s bows rose slowly out of the water until they were almost vertical, then she slid backwards out of sight. Later her commander, *Oberleutnant* von Lehsten, and forty-three of the crew were rescued.

Moore's achievement – two U-boats sunk in less than half an hour – was a unique feat for an airman in either World War. He and his crew had been lucky to fall upon the non-*Schnorkel* boats of the Brest Flotilla streaming towards the invasion area. Yet they had exploited the opportunity to the utmost, and delivered attacks that combined skill with cunning. In neither attack had Moore thought it necessary to use his Leigh Light, or his homing torpedo. For this action Moore would receive the Distinguished Service Order.

Now only four U-boats were left out of the eight lacking the *Schnorkel* device that had set out from Brest on the evening of 6 June. The group's misfortunes were not yet over, for on the morning of the 8th *Oberleutnant* Sachse in *U-413* was caught by a Halifax of 502 Squadron and fought a pitched battle. The boat's gunners shot the plane's port-inner motor to pieces and it limped home. But in return the Halifax's depth-charges damaged the U-boat seriously enough to force her to return to her base also.

In the days that followed, the remaining three Brest boats were picked off one by one. On 9 June Sergeant Cheslin, flying a Liberator of No. 120 Squadron to the west of Brest – far from that unit's usual mid-Atlantic hunting grounds – caught and sank *U-740* (Stark). On the following day four Mosquitoes of No. 248 Squadron, two of them fitted with the 6-pounder gun, scored hits on *U-821* (Knackfuss); a Liberator of No. 206 Squadron finished her off with depth-charges.

Seven out of the original eight boats from Brest without *Schnorkels* had now been sunk or forced to return to base with damage; only *U-441* was able to continue with her attempt to get through to the invasion area. (Since her unfortunate experience as a 'submarine-aircraft-trap', *U-441* had reconverted into a commerce raider. Her commander in June 1944, *Kapitänleutnant* Klaus Hartmann, should not be confused with her commander at the time of the 'aircraft-trap' battle, *Kapitänleutnant* Götz von Hartmann.)

By now the German Navy had lost a total of six U-boats sunk by the patrolling aircraft, and a further six were limping home with damage; all except one of those boats lacked a *Schnorkel*. More to the point, despite these painful losses, no U-boat had yet been able to penetrate into the Channel even as far as the Channel Islands. On 12 June Admiral Krancke was forced to admit defeat. He noted in his War Diary:

> All submarines operating without the *Schnorkel* in the Bay of Biscay have been ordered to return to their bases, as the enemy air attacks are causing too many losses and too much damage. Only if an enemy landing seems imminent on the Biscay coast are the boats to operate. They will remain under shelter in a state of readiness . . .

The twenty-two surviving U-boats without *Schnorkels* now tried to extricate themselves from the grip of the air patrols. Five more suffered damage in the process, but only one was sunk.

The unlucky boat was *U-441*. During the twelve days up to the night of 18 June, *Kapitänleutnant* Klaus Hartmann had avoided attack from the air. Now he was on the final leg of his return journey; only some fifty miles separated the boat from the safety of the concrete pens at Brest. By rights he should have made it, for the aircraft responsible for covering that segment of the patrol area, a Leigh Light Wellington of No. 304 (Polish) Squadron, had suffered a radar failure. Yet Flight Lieutenant Antoniewicz continued his patrol without the device. Then, in the moonlight, he suddenly caught sight of a U-boat to his starboard in the act of surfacing. Antoniewicz swung the aircraft round and attacked, letting go his six 250 pound depth-charges in one stick. The weapons detonated on either side of *U-441*'s conning tower and split open her hull, then she disappeared in a wall of foaming water. The airmen had settled their score with the one-time 'submarine-aircraft-trap'.

By midnight on 23 June, less than three weeks after the invasion began, aircraft had sunk nine U-boats and damaged eleven more. As one Coastal Command officer noted at the time:

It is a fantastic harvest when one thinks of the old days of fruit-less search. The effect on the aircrews is good to see. The spirit on the station is amazing; barely a grumble. And the ground crews, who do so much without a glimmer of lime-light, are as pleased as those who fly. The smell of victory is very stimulating.

There still remained the *Schnorkel*-fitted boats, however. Six of these had crept slowly into the English Channel, though two more had been less successful and put into St Peter Port, Guernsey, with exhausted batteries.

On their way through the area patrolled by surface ships, the *Schnorkel* boats sank two Royal Navy frigates. Then the defenders reacted and sank one of the German boats. Not until the 15 June, nine days after the opening of the invasion, did *Oberleutnant* Stuckmann in *U-621* succeed in reaching the main shipping route to the Normandy bridgehead. He torpedoed and sank a tank-landing ship, and made unsuccessful attacks on two American battleships. But then Allied warships drove him away. Another fortnight elapsed before another U-boat reached these rich if hazardous hunting grounds.

The ability of the *Schnorkel* boats to run indefinitely on their diesel motors made them much safer from attack from the air, though they were not wholly immune. All they now exposed above the surface was the top three or four feet of the air pipe, capped by the float valve assembly, three feet long and one foot wide. With the naked eye it was almost impossible to see the *Schnorkel* head at ranges greater than about one mile. But if the sea was calm and the U-boat was moving at speed, the *Schnorkel* wake might be seen as much as five miles away. And sometimes the exhaust fumes condensed, to produce a smoke trail that could on occasions be seen at distances up to seven miles. Such detection ranges were of course possible only under ideal conditions. If the wind speed exceeded 14 knots, 'white horses' appeared and the search problem could be likened to that of a golfer searching for a ball in a limitless field of daisies.

Yet more important was the emasculating effect of the *Schnorkel* on a radar search. Even under ideal conditions, the best radar sets available in 1944 could not detect the head at distances much above four miles. And even if the radar operator was skilful enough to recognise the small echo signal from the *Schnorkel*, almost invariably the latter disappeared in the general sea clutter before the aircraft came within visual range. If the seas were rough, a radar search for a *Schnorkel* was a futile operation.

The first air attack on a *Schnorkel*-ing U-boat took place on 18 June. Lieutenant Commander J. Munson was flying a Liberator of US Navy Squadron VP-110 over the western end of the English Channel, when one of the crew sighted first the 'smoke' trail and then the *Schnorkel* head of *U-275* (Bork). The subsequent depth-charge attack caused only minor damage, however.

On 11 July Flight Lieutenant I. Walters, flying a Sunderland of No. 201 Squadron, sighted the *Schnorkel* head of *U-1222* (Bielfeld). In their haste to dive to safety, the U-boat's crew pushed down the bows of their craft too far. Her stem rose out of the water with propellers turning, giving the Sunderland crew an unexpectedly large and almost stationary target. Their depth-charges were both accurate and destructive.

While the great aircraft–submarine battle ran its course in the English Channel, an almost parallel action commenced to the north of the British Isles. There, Coastal Command had the task of blocking the U-boats heading for the invasion area from bases in Norway and Germany. During June the northern air patrols sank five U-boats and damaged four more.

One of the most notable actions there took place on 24 June, when a Canso flying-boat of the Canadian No. 162 Squadron caught *U-1225* on the surface (the Canso an amphibious version of the Catalina flying-boat, built under licence in Canada). As the aircraft captain, Flight Lieutenant David Hornell, closed in to attack, *Oberleutnant* Sauerberg's gunners opened up a witheringly accurate fire. Explosive shells tore large holes in the plane's star-board wing and set fire to the engine. The flying-boat became difficult to control, but undeterred by the fierce reception, Hornell took the Canso low over the U-boat and released his depth-charges. The explosions bracketed the submarine and she sank soon afterwards. Hornell pulled his aircraft up and gained a little altitude, but the flying-boat was in a sorry condition. The fire quickly spread from the starboard engine, then the mounting burned through and the motor fell into the sea. Hornell ditched the blazing Canso in the heavy swell, and the leaking flying-boat quickly settled in the icy waters. Before rescuers arrived twenty-one hours later, two of the crew had succumbed to exposure; Hornell himself died shortly afterwards, exhausted beyond recovery. For his determined attack on the U-boat, the Canadian captain afterwards received the posthumous award of the Victoria Cross.

During July the northern air patrols sank four U-boats and damaged six more. And on the 17th there was another noteworthy action. On that day Flying Officer John Cruickshank was flying a Catalina of No. 210 Squadron on patrol far to the north of Scotland and beyond the Arctic Circle. Through the patchy mist one of the crew observed what he thought was a ship, but as soon became clear, it was actually a submarine, *U-347*. As Cruickshank ran in to attack, *Oberleutnant* de Bhur's gunners kept up a steady if inaccurate fire. The flying-boat passed over the submarine but the depth-charges refused to leave their racks: there was a hang-up.

The Catalina had not been hit, however, so Cruickshank ran in for a second attempt. Then in the words of Flight Sergeant J. Appleton, one of the plane's gunners:

> We made a perfect run in at low level, but when we were almost on top of the U-boat a shell burst in the aircraft. Everything seemed to happen in a flash. Our navigator was killed and the captain seriously wounded. I saw the stuff exploding in the aircraft; the windscreen in front of the second pilot was shattered to smithereens and fire broke out inside the aircraft. I received lumps of shrapnel in my head and hands, Harbison [the nose gunner] was wounded in both legs.

Only much later did the extent of Cruickshank's injuries become known: he had been wounded in seventy-two separate places, including twice seriously in the lungs and ten times in the lower limbs. But he did not falter. He brought the Catalina over the submarine and this time the release gear worked perfectly. The stick of depth-charges fell across the boat, which heeled over and sank.

Yet those on board the Catalina had their own problems. After pulling the aircraft up, Cruickshank collapsed and the second pilot took the controls. Appleton extinguished a small fire that had broken out, then, when the smoke cleared, he helped carry the injured captain to one of the bunks in the rear fuselage. After that, the crew busied themselves trying to stop the holes in the flying-boat's hull, using canvas cut from the engine covers. Throughout the five-hour flight to Sullom Voe in the Shetland Islands, Cruickshank alternated between unconsciousness and periods of intense pain. Yet he refused a morphine injection, lest it dull his senses. When the Catalina arrived at her base Cruickshank insisted on being carried back to the cockpit, and he took the controls for the landing. Once she was on the water the flying-boat began to sink. So the co-pilot took control, reopened the throttles and taxied the aircraft towards the beach and ran her aground. When the aircraft came to rest a doctor clambered on board and gave Cruickshank a blood transfusion, which saved his life. Afterwards the gallant pilot received the Victoria Cross, the only airman to receive the award for attacking a submarine and surviving the action.

By the end of August 1944, Allied ground forces had taken almost the whole of France. One by one the German bases along the Bay of Biscay had been either captured or isolated. The U-boat tide of June and July, into the Bay of Biscay, was now reversed as the survivors streamed round the west of Ireland and then back to Norway or Germany.

No. 18 Group of Coastal Command, with its headquarters near Edinburgh, was responsible for patrolling the northern transit area. Jeaff Greswell, now a Wing Commander and Group Anti-U-Boat Operations Officer, later recalled:

> The big concentration of aircraft in the south for the invasion was gradually transferred north to No. 18 Group, after the Biscay ports had been overrun or cut-off. We thought we would have a field day among the U-boats transferring to the Norwegian bases. But it didn't happen: almost every boat leaving the Biscay ports now had a *Schnorkel*, and for the most part they escaped detection from the air.

In this vast area of wind-swept ocean, a U-boat could run on *Schnorkel* with little risk of air attack.

Probing the limits of their new-found immunity from detection from the air, the *Schnorkel* boats now began to reappear in unexpected places. In the shallow seas round the British Isles submarine hunting was difficult for warships, and the air patrols were almost ineffective. So, for the first time in almost four years, ships plying round the coast of Britain again became targets for U-boat attack.

The first to test the new waters, towards the end of August, was *Kapitänleutnant* Baron von Matuschka in *U-482*. Handling his boat skilfully but with caution, he made the utmost use of the *Schnorkel*: during a patrol covering more than 2,700 sea miles he spent only about 250 of them on the surface. Unchecked by the escorting ships or aircraft, he sank five ships running in convoy before departing, unseen, for his base in Norway. Later, other U-boat commanders tried to emulate von Matuschka's success. But by then the convoy escorts were stronger and more alert, and few achieved much.

During the last four months of 1944 U-boats sank fourteen ships in the waters close to the British Isles. Considering that more than twelve thousand merchant vessels sailed through the area during that time, the German figure is hardly impressive. But U-boat losses were low also – seven boats sunk, only one of them by an aircraft. And the boats continued to tie down huge numbers of Allied warships and aircraft. Both sides knew the period of stalemate would not last long. Just how long it did last depended on the production and working-up programmes for the formidable new German Type XXI and Type XXIII U-boats.

Until June 1943 the Allied strategic bomber attacks on U-boat bases and building yards had been a costly failure. But just as the strength and efficiency of the anti-submarine forces had improved markedly in effectiveness during 1943, so had the bomber fleets. Moreover, by the summer of 1944 Allied Intelligence officers were aware of the grave threat posed by the new U-boat construction programme. Aerial photographs had revealed hundreds of the drum-shaped Type XXI and Type XXIII sections in transit to the assembly yards on the coast. Nor was the importance of the German canal system to the programmes lost on the onlookers. For U-boat production, the most important waterways were the Dortmund–Ems Canal, linking the Ruhr industrial area with the Ems River, and the Mittelland Canal linking the Ems and Berlin via the River Elbe. In the autumn of 1944 both waterways came under repeated air attack. To RAF Bomber Command the canal-breaching operations formed part of its systematic offensive against the German communications system.

The first attack in the new series on the Dortmund–Ems Canal was on the night of 23 September 1944, when heavy bombers wrecked the aqueduct carrying the canal over the Glane River near Münster. A six-mile section of the canal drained through the breach, leaving many barges high and dry and stranding scores of others on either side of the aqueduct. After frantic repairs the canal reopened early in November; and the bombers returned, to wreck the aqueduct again. By the beginning of January 1945 the process had been repeated twice more. The Mittelland Canal suffered a similar pummelling.

To Otto Merker, wrestling with the intractable problems of meeting the ambitious production schedules for the new U-boats, the raids were like battering rams to judder his already shaky citadel. They made nonsense of his production plans, and in January 1945 he lamented to armaments minister Albert Speer:

> The transport situation in general is catastrophically bad. The large U-boat sub-assemblies can be transported only by waterway. Shipbuilding has therefore been especially hard hit by the various stoppages of canal navigation, and must change over to rail transportation.

Before they could be moved by rail, however, the sub-assemblies had to be broken down into smaller pieces, then reassembled at the assembly yards. It was a counsel of desperation, for it nullified the advantages of prefabrication. But what else could Merker do?

In the end the difficulty of moving the sub-assemblies to the shipyards was not the most serious bottleneck afflicting the Type XXI U-boat programme. With its greatly increased battery capacity, the new boat needed huge numbers of electrical accumulators. Four factories produced these, and all except one, the smallest, had been forced either to curtail or else reduce production as a result of bombing attacks. In addition, the strategic bombers mounted repeated raids on the U-boat assembly yards.

In spite of the difficulties besetting the U-boat production programmes, and in spite of serious delays in deliveries, during the final months of 1944 the new U-boat types became available in large numbers. By the end of the year ninety Type XXI U-boats had been launched, of which sixty had been delivered to the Navy; for the Type XXIII the figures were thirty-one and twenty-three respectively. Yet even when the new U-boats entered service, the Allied strategic bombers could still exert pressure. It seemed they came up with a further problem to meet each new German solution. The crews for the new boats had to be trained and the craft worked up for action. That took place in the Baltic, and RAF Bomber Command directed its main minelaying effort to those waters.

To the bomber crews these operations were known as 'gardening', with the various dropping areas code-named after trees, vegetables and flowers. For example, the area off Danzig was Privet, that off Gdynia was Spinach and that off Swinemünde was Geranium. The air-dropped mines planted in the Baltic in 1944 were as far removed from the 'round thing with horns' image, as the homing torpedo was removed from the depth-charge. The former were cylindrical in shape, and once in the water they sank to the seabed and remained there. Resting on the bottom they were difficult to locate, and impossible to drag mechanically. The magnetic field from a ship passing overhead, or the pressure waves from its screws, would activate the mine. That the charge exploded some distance from the vessel was not a disadvantage. The shock waves struck the ship from underneath and often lifted it high out of the water, breaking its back in the process.

To exacerbate the difficulties of sweeping, mine experts at the Royal Navy shore establishment of HMS *Vernon* had perfected several subtle forms of knavery. Some mines carried timers, to bring them to life only after several days of lying dormant in the water. Those timers could also render the mines harmless after a set period – an important point if Allied ships or submarines might need to use those waters later. They also carried electrical circuitry to trigger the mine after the mechanism had been activated a certain number of times. Thus a mine that had been passed safely on, say, six occasions would detonate on the seventh.

During 1944 strategic bombers planted more than seven thousand mines in the Baltic, most of them in the U-boat training areas and round their bases. During that year these mines destroyed several German ships but only three U-boats: *U-854* in February, *U-803* in April and the Type XXI boat *U-2542* in December, all off Swinemünde. The most important effect of such a mining campaign, however, was the general vexation it caused. The German Navy was able to hold down losses only by strict adherence to the frequently swept channels. The working-up areas for U-boats were often closed, and when they were open there were invariably restrictions on their use. The net result was serious delay in the working-up programmes of the new U-boats.

To compound the German Navy's difficulties, Coastal Command joined in the general harassment in the Baltic training areas. With the advance of the Red Army in the East, and the mining and the seasonal icing-up of some parts of the Baltic, by the end of January 1945 there were few stretches of water suitable for U-boat training. One of the last remaining areas was situated to the north-east of the Danish island of Bornholm. It was there that Sir Sholto Douglas decided to launch night operations with his long-range anti-submarine aircraft, under the code-name 'Chilli'. It was a daring venture, for even at this late stage of the war the area was heavily defended.

The first Chilli operation took place on the night of 3 February, when thirteen Leigh Light Liberators of Nos 206 and 547 Squadrons, flying in two waves, crossed over the Jutland Peninsula at low level and swept into the Baltic. The aircraft of the first wave combed the U-boat training area flying on parallel tracks, followed ten minutes later by those of the second wave. The Liberators attacked four U-boats and two surface craft, but inflicted no serious material damage; all the aircraft returned, though one had flak damage. The operation made it clear that there was no area where the trainee U-boat crews could consider themselves safe.

The second Chilli operation, on 23 March, was an almost exactly similar incursion by sixteen Liberators. There were seven attacks on U-boats and six on surface vessels, but no loss to either side. The third and final Chilli operation took place three nights later, again with sixteen aircraft. There were fifteen attacks on surface vessels and five on U-boats, which resulted in damage to two small auxiliary ships. Once again, all of the aircraft returned safely.

The cumulative effect of the Allied champing at each stage of the production and preparation for service of the new U-boats was to impose severe delays. Not until the end of January 1945 was the first of the small Type XXIII boats ready for action. On the 29th *Oberleutnant* Hass set out from Bergen in *U-2334* to join the U-boats operating off the British Isles. On 18 February he torpedoed and sank a steamer off Sunderland. Then, both his torpedo tubes empty, he had to return to base.

During the two and a half months the war had still to run, five other Type XXIII boats went into action. Between them they sank six ships, without loss to themselves. Although minor, that success was the more important since it came at a time when the British inshore defences had taken the measure of the older U-boats. Once a submarine delivered an attack and revealed its approximate position, massive air and sea forces swamped the area and usually exacted retribution. From the beginning of 1945 until the end of the war in May, more than thirty U-boats met their end in the waters round Britain. The relative invulnerability of the small Type XXIII boats, however, was a clear pointer to what they and the more powerful Type XXI submarines could do when they became operational in large numbers.

In the early part of 1945 a relatively ineffectual, though still noteworthy, part of the German anti-shipping campaign concerned the use of midget submarines. In the only large-scale use of this weapon ever, the German Navy operated in the shallow waters off the coasts of Holland and Belgium. Three types of midget were involved: *Seehund*, *Molch* and *Biber*. The two-man *Seehund* weighed fifteen tons; it was powered by diesel and electric motors in conventional fashion and had a range of some three hundred sea miles. Next in order of size was the one-man *Molch*, weighing ten tons; it was powered by a single electric motor, and its small battery capacity limited its range to some fifty sea miles. Smallest of all was the one-man *Biber*; weighing little over six tons and powered by both diesel and electric motors; it had a maximum range of just over one hundred sea miles. All three boats could carry two torpedoes mounted externally on the underside of the hull; alternatively, the *Molch* and *Biber* could each carry a couple of mines.

None of the midget boats carried a *Schnorkel*, so the *Seehund* and *Biber* had to surface to recharge their batteries; the batteries of *Molch* could not be recharged at sea.

The *Biber* was so small that it could be carried in a large aircraft. In one German Navy plan that was never implemented, a *Biber* was to be used to attack a ship in the Suez Canal. A six-engined Blohm & Voss 222 flying-boat carrying the midget submarine was to alight on one of the lakes along the canal. The aircraft's crew would lower the craft into the water, then take off and return to base. The *Biber* operator was then to take his boat into the main channel, and block it by sinking the next large ship that came along. The operator would then scuttle his craft and make his own arrangements to get home.

The first large-scale action using the midget submarines began on New Year's Day 1945, when eighteen *Seehund* craft set out from Ijmuiden to attack Allied shipping passing to and from the port of Antwerp. It ended in catastrophe. British surface escorts accounted for two of the boats, but stormy weather and the inexperience of the crews accounted for fourteen more. Only two boats returned to base, having sunk just one armed trawler.

During the months that followed, the German midget submarine crews gained in experience, and it became clear that unless they were checked they might inflict uncomfortable losses. To meet this new threat No. 16 Group of Coastal Command began flying special patrols, designed to intercept the small submarines as they passed down the coast of Holland. It was while engaged on one of these that the crew of an Albacore of No. 119 Squadron of the RAF made the first aerial sighting and attack on a midget, on 23 January; the U-boat survived the subsequent attack with six depth-charges, however. Not until 11 March was the first of these craft sunk from the air, when a Swordfish of No. 119 Squadron depth-charged a *Seehund*.

To make life difficult for *Seehund* boats attempting to reach the cross-channel convoys, No. 16 Group began operating special patrols of Beaufighters over the areas where the boats were likely to surface to recharge their batteries; the midgets were relatively thin-skinned craft, and vulnerable to cannon fire. Even the single-engined Spitfire fighters of No. 12 Group of Fighter Command joined in the hunt; they carried the battle into the waters close to the German bases in Holland.

As the extent of the midget submarine operations increased, so did the variety of aircraft and weapons used against them: Barracudas, Albacores, Swordfish and Leigh Light Wellingtons using depth-charges; Beaufighters with cannon and bombs; Spitfires with 20 mm cannon and Mosquitoes with 6-pounder guns.

From German Navy records we know that between the beginning of January 1945 and the end of the war midget submarines made a total of 244 operational sorties into the area at the southern end of the North Sea. From Allied records we know that their mines and torpedoes sank sixteen ships totalling some 19,000 tons, and damaged a further five. One hundred and five midget boats failed to return from these operations. Surface warships accounted for about fifty of these, aircraft for sixteen sunk and ten possibly sunk, and the remainder fell to other or unknown causes. In terms of shipping sunk, the German midget submarine offensive did not justify the effort put into it. On the other hand, Allied losses were held down only by mounting a large-scale aerial patrol and naval escort effort.

The Type XXIII U-boats and the midget submarines were interesting diversions, but it was the conventional U-boats, making judicious use of the *Schnorkel*, that constituted the main threat to Allied shipping – and the main target for Allied anti-submarine aircraft. During 1944 the operational research teams had devoted much effort to the problem of detecting the elusive *Schnorkel* head. Towards the end of the year a 3-centimetre-wavelength radar, the American-built APS-15 (ASV Mark X in British service), entered service with Coastal Command. With its improved definition the new radar had a definite edge over the earlier sets for *Schnorkel* detection, though if the sea was rough the old problems remained. The two underwater sensing devices, the magnetic airborne detector and the sonobuoy, were both tested as methods for detecting submarines moving at *Schnorkel* depth. But both devices had such a short range that they were useless for general area search. Outside a confined sea area like the Straits of Gibraltar, the magnetic detector could achieve little unless the U-boat had previously been found by another means. The same could be said of the sonobuoy, which was, moreover, much affected by wave noises, which rendered it unusable in sea states above Force 4 – the norm in the north Atlantic. So, in the absence of anything better, visual and radar search continued to be the primary methods for *Schnorkel* detection.

Once a U-boat's approximate position was known, the exact location and attack phases of the action could begin. Making the fullest possible use of the inadequate equipment available, the operational research and tactical development teams put together a procedure for attacking submerged U-boats using sonobuoys and homing torpedoes. For its success the method demanded a rare coincidence of skill and luck. Yet by this stage of the war the Allied anti-submarine effort was vast, and from time to time a crew was able to beat the odds.

The first successful attack to bring together 3 cm radar, sonobuoys and a homing torpedo to defeat a U-boat running at *Schnorkel* depth was on 20 March 1945. Flight Lieutenant N. Smith and his crew had been patrolling off the Orkney Isles in a Liberator of No. 86 Squadron when the radar operator reported a suspicious contact three miles away. Smith closed on the object, but it merged into the sea returns on the radar screen at a range of half a mile. By then it was almost dark, and since the aircraft did not carry a searchlight or flares, its lookouts saw nothing. Two further attempts to sight the mystery object drew similarly nega-tive results. The object might, of course, have been a piece of flotsam, but the crew's suspicions were now aroused. Meticulously they laid out a pattern of sonobuoys and flame floats: one buoy and a flame float at each corner of a square with sides three miles long, and one further buoy accompanied by a flame float in the middle of the pattern. This painstaking course brought its reward as the first sonobuoy came on the air: the operator caught the un-mistakable swishing sound of a propeller thrashing water at

114 rpm. With no large object on the surface visible on radar, there could be no doubt that this was a U-boat. Tuning his receiver to each sonobuoy in turn, the operator narrowed the U-boat's position to within one part of the pattern.

While he was thus reducing the 'area of uncertainty' surrounding the prey, the radar operator caught a further brief glimpse of an echo from the *Schnorkel* head. Smith then pulled the Liberator round to attack. With no further sign of the target on radar, and only a vague idea of its position from the sonobuoys, the crew guided him along the final radar bearing to the target. Smith released a pair of 'Mark 24 Mine' homing torpedoes on a count-down from a stopwatch, then circled the pattern of lights bobbing on the surface. Beneath him, the unsuspecting U-boat continued purposefully towards its operating area. The sonobuoy operator heard engine noises for the next six minutes, then a long reverber-ating sound followed by sea noises. In the darkness there was nothing to be seen, it was slim evidence on which to claim a 'kill'. Yet examination of German Navy records after the war made it clear that *U-905* (Schwarting) had disappeared without trace in that area at about that time.

The six-minute run of Smith's homing torpedoes had seemed like an age. But two days later a Liberator of No. 120 Squadron located *U-296* (Rasch) with sonobuoys; its 'Mark 24 Mines' ran for thirteen minutes before they finally found their mark. There was a further remarkable homing torpedo attack on 25 April, when a US Navy Liberator of VP-103 sighted the *Schnorkel* of *U-1107* (Parduhn) and planted their weapons just eighty yards away from the head (a figure confirmed by attack photographs). Yet the homing torpedoes ran for three minutes before they exploded against the boat – nine times as long as they should have needed to cover that short distance. The most likely explanation is that the torpedoes lost contact with their target, entered their circular searching patterns, re-acquired the U-boat and then homed onto her.

In each of those three successes luck, skill and near-ideal con-ditions had all played a major role in the sinkings. The tactics for engaging boats cruising in open water on *Schnorkel* were of only marginal effectiveness, and despite a huge patrol effort they scored few 'kills'.

As the Red Army advanced westwards into Germany during the spring of 1945, the German Navy had to abandon its bases one by

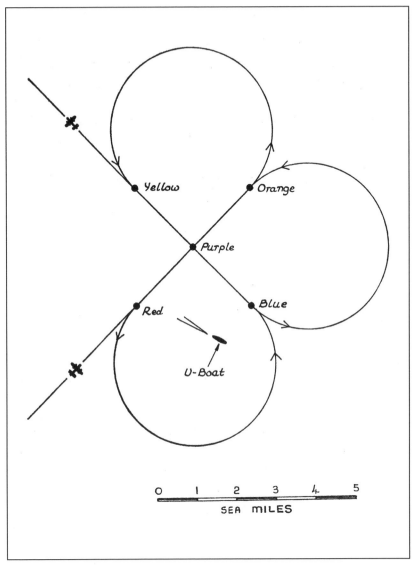

Laying a sonobuoy pattern. Each buoy carries a different colour coding, radiates on a different frequency and is released with a smoke marker by day or a flame marker by night. The aircraft releases a 'Purple' buoy nearest to the suspected position of the U-boat, and then, two miles later, an 'Orange' buoy. The pilot flies a precise turn to port, crosses the marker at the 'Purple' buoy and, two miles later, releases a 'Blue' buoy. This process is repeated for the 'Red' and then the 'Yellow' buoy. The entire pattern takes about thirteen minutes to lay, during which time a U-boat moving at 4 knots would cover about a mile. If everything went according to plan, in this example, and the submarine was at the position marked, its noises would be received loudest from the 'Blue' buoy.

one along the Baltic shore. Forced out of what had been their
private lake, the U-boats working up for action – more than seventy
of them – began streaming through the Kattegat on their way to new
bases in Norway. The waters separating Denmark and Sweden are
narrow and shallow, however, and Allied mines compounded the
difficulties of making an underwater passage. As a result the
U-boats were forced to pass through the narrows on the surface.
Moreover the *Luftwaffe*, which should at least have been guarding
the skies so close to its homeland, was nowhere to be seen.

The hard-hitting strike squadrons of Coastal Command were
trained and equipped to fight pitched battles against convoys of
heavily armed surface ships. So far as they were concerned, a U-boat
on the surface was like a poorly armed surface vessel, to be disposed
of accordingly. The exodus of the U-boats provided an unprecedented opportunity, and the Royal Air Force exploited it to the full.
On the afternoon of 9 April a rampaging force of thirty-three
Mosquitoes of the Banff Strike Wing came upon *U-804* (Meyer) and
U-1065 (Panitz), as they were making their way through the
Kattegat. On the order of Squadron Leader Gunnis, the formation
leader, twenty-two aircraft peeled out of the sky and descended like
wasps on the helpless and exposed prey. Each aircraft carried eight
60 pound rockets, and ten planes launched their salvoes at the
leading U-boat. More than sixteen rockets scored hits, and the boat
exploded violently. The second U-boat, struck by at least ten
rockets, also blew up. Some Mosquitoes with rockets left then found
U-843 (Herwartz) and she suffered a similar fate.

The difficulties facing the U-boat crews were well described in
the log of *U-2613* (Topp), one of the new Type XXI boats that
made the dangerous passage early in May:

> Ran through the Great Belt under escort. Only a narrow
> channel cleared of mines. No chance to dive, no room to
> evade. We were the last boat to get through the Belt
> unharmed. On the following day Wächter's boat [*U-2503*]
> was hit . . .

Since there was no air opposition of any sort, the heavy four-
engined aircraft of Coastal Command could also take part in the
battle. Finally, attesting to the fact that anyone could join in,
single-engined Typhoon fighter-bombers operating from newly
captured airfields in Germany sank at least eight U-boats with their
rockets.

Faced with this overwhelmingly powerful attack, the U-boats fell like ninepins. Between 9 April and the end of the war, less than a month later, no fewer than twenty-six boats were sunk by aircraft operating off the south and west coasts of Sweden. That was the same number as had been destroyed during the climactic phase of the battle in the Bay of Biscay, two years earlier. Yet, in spite of the success of the air operations off the coast of Sweden, there is little for the student of anti-submarine warfare to learn from them. The circumstances that gave rise to this 'happy time' were unique and are unlikely ever to be repeated.

Coastal Command's final attack on a U-boat took place in open water off the Shetland Islands, on 7 May. Flight Lieutenant K. Murray, piloting a Catalina of No. 210 Squadron, depth-charged the swirl left by a hastily retracted *Schnorkel* head. The crew then laid out a sonobuoy pattern, which picked up the sounds of a U-boat stopped in the water. After that came intermittent engine and machinery noises, which made it clear that the boat was in trouble. It was *U-320* (Emmrich), which later radioed that she had suffered serious damage. On 9 May, the first day of peace in the west, she foundered with all hands.

Meanwhile, what had become of the Type XXI boats, Adolf Hitler's last 'secret weapon' and the most formidable of all the U-boat types? On 30 April *Korvettenkapitän* Adalbert Schnee nosed *U-2511* out of the harbour at Bergen, for the first operational cruise by one of these boats. During his submerged passage through the North Sea, Schnee encountered a Royal Navy submarine-hunting group. But by retracting the *Schnorkel* and increasing speed to 16 knots, he easily evaded the warships. At last the German submarine arm had the weapon it needed, to cleave apart the sea links between Britain and her Allies. But it was too late.

At midnight on 8 May under the orders of *Grossadmiral* Dönitz, Hitler's successor as leader of the Third Reich, the German armed forces laid down their arms. The surrender terms detailed how the U-boats at sea were now to act. They were to proceed to designated surrender ports on the surface, displaying a large black or blue flag. In the days that followed, Coastal Command aircraft kept a close watch on the boats complying with this order. For many of the crews, it was the first chance to take a good look at the foe they had hunted and harassed for so long and with such success.

So ended the hardest-fought anti-submarine campaign in history. The U-boats had sunk more than two thousand five hundred

Allied merchant ships, totalling about fourteen million tons. Out of a total of 1,162 submarines – excluding midget boats – commissioned into the German Navy, 727 were destroyed by enemy action. Of that total, 288 were sunk in open water by aircraft operating alone (two-thirds of them by RAF Coastal Command); forty-seven were accounted for by aircraft and ships working together; and a further eighty were destroyed during strategic bombing attacks on harbours or after detonating air-dropped mines. The comparatively small and ineffective Italian submarine arm lost a total of seventy-five submarines in action, fourteen of them to air attack.

Throughout the conflict, even during those periods when the U-boats were no longer able to inflict serious losses, they tied down immense numbers of Allied aircraft and warships supported by a major industrial effort.

Grossadmiral Dönitz had shown an almost parental devotion to his U-boats and his crews, and his men repaid him with their unswerving loyalty. Of some forty thousand German sailors who set out against the enemy in U-boats during World War II, no fewer than twenty-eight thousand were killed in action and some five thousand were taken prisoner. As a proportion of a large and highly trained force engaged in a protracted campaign, that loss can have few equals in the history of warfare. To the end the U-boat crews continued fight doggedly on in the face of overwhelming odds – a fact that speaks highly for the quality of *Grossadmiral* Dönitz's leadership and the *esprit de corps* within his force.

Immediately after the end of the war, Allied Naval Intelligence officers swarmed over examples of the German Type XXI submarine, endeavouring to learn the truth of the 'wonder U-boat' they had previously seen only on aerial photographs. Was it really as potent a weapon as loquacious prisoners had said? It was. And it became clear how narrowly the Allied merchant fleets had avoided the scourge intended for them. The scale of production planned for the Type XXI boat was such that had it been realised even partially on time, and the U-boat been deployed in large numbers, it could have overrun the Allied convoy escorts and massacred the merchant ships.

That the Type XXI submarine never launched a torpedo in anger was due, to a large extent, to the efforts of the Allied strategic bomber forces. Up to the summer of 1943 the bomber offensive had been painfully ineffective in reducing the number of U-boats built. But after that date it achieved some brilliant successes. The bombers, with their attacks on component factories and assembly yards, greatly increased the difficulties of producing the new submarines. They also wrecked the transport system that should have brought the completed sections of the boats together. And finally, they imposed severe delays on the working-up of boats already in commission, with imaginative airborne mining operations in the Baltic exercise areas. It is impossible to put a figure to the cumulative effect of these delays, but undoubtedly it was substantial. At the beginning of 1945 the German Navy had twenty Type XXI boats that had been in commission for three months or longer, and fifty-one that had been in commission for less than three months. Without the hindrance from the mining operations, at least ten of the new submarines might have been in action before the end of January, and perhaps forty by May 1945. It can, of course, be argued that by the beginning of 1945 events had reached a point where even a few score Type XXI boats could have done little to delay the end of the Third Reich. Yet, had it been fought, the second great battle in mid-Atlantic would have been a horrifying experience for the Allied merchant sailors.

CHAPTER 11

Battles Elsewhere

December 1941 to August 1945

The atomic bomb was the funeral pyre of an enemy who had been drowned.

Theodore Roscoe

To complete the description of aerial anti-submarine methods during World War II, we need to shift our attention to the Pacific theatre. In his comprehensive and detailed fourteen-volume official history of the US Navy in World War II, Professor Samuel Morison wrote:

> Readers of this History may wonder why so little has been said about anti-submarine operations of the United States Navy in the Pacific. The principal reason is that we have little to tell. Japanese submarines were always far less numerous and much less enterprising than the German U-boats. According to pre-war doctrine, they were used mainly to attack warships or as scouts for the fleet, not to attack convoys or merchant vessels . . .

US Navy aircraft had begun hunting Japanese submarines immediately after the attack on Pearl Harbor in December 1941. But, as had been the case with their British counterparts in the autumn of 1939, the aircrews were eager rather than able. One week into the war Vice-Admiral William Halsey, commanding the task group built round the aircraft-carrier USS *Enterprise*, was moved to tell his men: 'If all the torpedo wakes reported are factual, Japanese submarines will soon have to return to base to reload and we will have nothing to fear. In addition, we are wasting too many depth-charges on neutral fish.'

Yet during this time there had been one success. Shortly before dawn on 10 December Lieutenant Edward Anderson, piloting a

Dauntless aircraft from *Enterprise*, sighted a real submarine on the surface some 200 miles to the north of Hawaii. Anderson dive-bombed the Japanese submarine *I-170*, and damaged her to such an extent that she could no longer submerge. Later that day another Dauntless from *Enterprise* relocated the boat and finished her off.

During the years that followed the US anti-submarine effort in the Pacific improved greatly, as did its equipment. But Japanese boats avoided convoys and other intensively patrolled areas, so only rarely did the aircraft engaged in hunting them make contact. Between January 1942 and the end of 1944 aircraft sank only two Japanese boats in the Pacific, and co-operated with surface ships to sink three or four more.

In November 1944 the Japanese Navy introduced into service the so-called *Kaiten* torpedo, similar to the Italian SLC manned torpedo: a small manned craft, it was carried to the scene of oper-ations in containers attached to the deck of a submarine. But in its method of operation the *Kaiten* differed from its Italian counter-part in one important, if characteristically Japanese, respect: the crewman was to ram his craft into the target, and perish when the warhead exploded. Freed of the need to make any compromise for safety or habitability when designing the craft, the Japanese Navy produced a boat with a truly formidable underwater per-formance: top speed approximately 40 knots; cruising speed 30 knots for 23 sea miles, or 12 knots for 78 sea miles.

During its gruesome initial operation, in November 1944, three submarines, each laden with four *Kaiten*, set out to attack the US Navy anchorage at Ulithi in the Carolines. To carry the manned torpedoes to within range of a worthwhile concentration of ship-ping, Japanese submarines had to run the gauntlet of the air and sea patrols. They suffered accordingly. One submarine was sunk by US destroyers on the way to Ulithi. Another boat was able to release only one of her *Kaiten* and returned with the other three still in their containers. The third boat released all four manned torpedoes. Thus five *Kaiten* were launched, but in the darkness three became lost. Only two craft entered the anchorage. One *Kaiten* hit the large fleet oiler *Mississinewa* laden with aviation fuel, and she blew up. The remaining craft was sunk by destroyers.

Subsequent *Kaiten* operations achieved little. During the Iwo Jima campaign in February 1945, three *Kaiten*-laden submarines set out for the landing area. One fell foul of a destroyer on the way out and was sunk. A second, *I-368*, fell to attack by aircraft from the escort carrier *Anzio*. The third came under continual harassment, and her crew had to abandon the attempt to reach the concentration of shipping. No *Kaiten* was launched.

During the Okinawa campaign in April 1945, the *Kaiten* force tried again; and again it had no success. On the 18th, aircraft from the escort carrier *Bataan*, assisted by destroyers, caught the 'mother' boat *I-56* on the surface and sank her. And, on 30 May, aircraft from the *Anzio* disposed of the similarly fitted *I-361*.

In addition to the above, US Navy aircraft in the Pacific sank three Japanese boats during 1945; they shared a fourth with surface craft, and destroyed a fifth during an attack on its base. Unlike their German counterparts, the Japanese submarine crews made no attempt to fight back against attacking aircraft. Nor was there any repetition of the seesaw technical battle we have followed in the Atlantic. There is little of outstanding interest in the Japanese submarine force for the student of anti-submarine warfare.

So much for the Allied aerial anti-submarine measures during World War II. What of those of the Axis powers? Those by the Germans were unimpressive, and their few actions have already received the cover they deserve. The Italian Naval Air Arm devoted a somewhat greater, though still limited, effort to countering British submarines operating against its shipping in the Mediterranean. Its aircraft failed to sink any boats, though they drove several away from their prey.

Japan alone could not afford to ignore the threat, for she was almost entirely dependent upon raw materials brought in by sea. She was self-supporting in scarcely any major commodity needed to fight a war: she produced no cotton, wool, rubber or Bauxite (aluminium ore), and she had no indigenous oil. She produced only a quarter of the iron ore she used, one-third of the wood pulp and half the industrial salt. During the initial victorious campaign in the Pacific and south-east Asia the Japanese armed forces captured no significant industrial area. So, with the exception of the oil from the Dutch East Indies that could be refined on the spot, almost all the raw materials from the newly captured areas had to be transported to the home islands for processing. That placed a severe strain on the Japanese merchant marine, which had been scarcely large enough for the task even at the beginning of the war.

At the start of the war in the Pacific the US and Dutch Navies had a total of sixty-two submarines available for operations.

During the initial Allied retreat this force was engaged mainly in defensive operations. Then the battlefront stabilised and these submarines, aided by a few Royal Navy boats in the Indian Ocean, took an increasing toll of Japanese merchant shipping.

In spite of the importance of the merchant fleet to the nation, the Japanese Navy was dilatory in introducing the convoy system. Not until January 1944 did it come into general use. For that negligence the Japanese merchant marine paid a heavy price: during the first two years of war it lost three million tons, about half its pre-war total. Even with the addition of 1,800,000 tons of new construction, and captured and salvaged ships, the fleet was reduced by a quarter. Two-thirds of the losses were due to submarine attack.

In November 1943, in a tardy attempt to lessen the increasingly dangerous rate of loss, the Japanese Navy unified its anti-submarine effort with the formation of Admiral Koshiro Oikawa's General Escort Command. The idea was good but execution was poor. Oikawa took control of four very small escort carriers, numerous worn-out destroyers and improvised escorts, and three Air Groups with a total establishment of 450 aircraft. However, there were grave deficiencies in the quantity and quality of both the Command's men and equipment.

Of the Axis powers, the Japanese Navy was the only service to make a sustained effort to develop a large and specialised force of anti-submarine aircraft. The main types of aircraft assigned to the anti-submarine role were the twin-engined Mitsubishi G3M (Allied name Nell), early versions of the twin-engined Mitsubishi G4M (Betty), and the single-engined carrier-based Nakajima B5N (Kate); all three types were obsolescent. Yet surprisingly, in view of its general apathy to anti-submarine work, the Japanese Navy was the only armed service to field a purpose-designed aircraft for that role during World War II. This was the Kyushu Q1W (Lorna), a small and simple twin-engined machine weighing five tons fully loaded. Carrying 1,000 pounds of depth-charges, it had a maximum speed of about 200 mph and a range of 800 miles. The Kyushu company had built 153 of them.

Compared with those of the Western Allies, the Japanese airborne systems for submarine detection were crude and inefficient. Not until mid-1943 did an airborne radar become available in quantity: the Navy Air Mark VI, based on a captured British ASV Mark II. In addition there was the *Jikitanchiki* magnetic airborne detector, an equipment similar in performance

to the American device but owing nothing to it. Lacking any equivalent to the Leigh Light or the high-intensity flares used by the
Allies, Japanese aircraft rarely pressed home attacks at night. The
main anti-submarine weapons were simple depth-charges, and
small bombs. There were no retro-bombs for use with the magnetic
detector, nor were there homing torpedoes or air-launched
rockets.

To exploit the Japanese weakness at night, US Navy submarines
carried an efficient surface-search radar, and during the latter part
of the war they made most of their torpedo attacks during the hours
of darkness. US boats carried air-search radar and also radar-
warning receivers. Emulating the German boats in the Atlantic, the
US Navy employed the 'Wolf Pack' tactic against Japanese convoys.

An insight into the way Japanese anti-submarine aircraft
operated is to be found in the records of the General Escort
Command, dated 27 August 1944:

> A magnetic detector aircraft of the Manila detachment of the
> 901st Air Group found a submarine at 09.16 on the 27th at
> 16° 28' N, 119° 44' E. Bombed with two 250 kg bombs, result
> unknown. Then at 09.35 another magnetic detector aircraft
> found a submarine near the previous position, and co-
> operated with seven medium bombers, some floatplanes of
> the 944th Air Group and some Army planes to bomb it. The
> following day an aircraft observed an oil slick 10 km long and
> 4 km wide in the same area, and so confirmed [sic] that the
> submarine had been destroyed.

While an oil slick is a pointer to the destruction of a submarine, by
itself it did not constitute proof of a kill. So readers will not be
surprised to learn that there was no US Navy record of a boat
having been lost on that date.

In general, co-operation between Japanese Navy ships and
aircraft was poor. Rear Admiral M. Matsuyama, a member of the
General Escort Command, lamented:

> The escorts were hardly ever able to produce results, when
> sent by the convoy commander to exploit contacts made by
> magnetic detector aircraft.

One of the few occasions when the system worked reasonably well
was on 14 November 1944, following an attack by the submarine

Halibut on a convoy off the southern end of Formosa. A *Jikitanchiki* aircraft located her and dropped markers, then two surface escorts counter-attacked with such vigour that the damaged *Halibut* was lucky to escape.

Nor could the General Escort Command carry out its sub-marine-hunting operations with impunity. During the summer and autumn of 1944 US Navy submarines sank three out of the four escort carriers assigned to hunt them. Also during 1944, the US Navy began sending powerful carrier task groups into the China Sea and against the harbours through which many of the convoys passed. The air strikes inflicted severe losses among merchant ships, their escorts and the anti-submarine aircraft units.

In the face of ever-stronger attacks by the US submarine arm, the Japanese anti-submarine forces could do little to stave off disaster. During 1944 merchant shipping losses to all causes amounted to 3,900,000 tons, more than the previous two years put together; when that year ended, only 2,800,000 tons of shipping remained.

Japanese convoys passing through the China Sea in 1945 had a terrible time. For example, on the last day of December 1944 a convoy of seven tankers and seven cargo ships set out from Japan. Its destination was Sumatra (in what is now Indonesia), passing via Formosa, Saigon and Singapore, and the escort comprised eight warships. As the convoy neared Formosa, US submarines sank four ships; and while the convoy was in harbour there, bombers sank four more. Soon after the convoy left Formosa one of the escorts suffered a mechanical breakdown and had to turn back. Then came news that a US Navy carrier task force was rampaging through the area, so the convoy made a hasty dash for Hong Kong. US carrier-based planes attacked ships at the anchorage and the convoy lost two more cargo ships and two tankers sunk, and three escorts and one cargo ship were seriously damaged. The remnant of the convoy, comprising just one tanker and four escorts, came under submarine attack off Malaya; one escort suffered damage and had to drop out. The convoy finally reached Singapore, its penultimate point of call, on 24 January after twenty-five days in transit. As the tanker *Sarawak Maru*, the sole surviving merchant ship, was passing through the channel into the harbour, she detonated an air-dropped mine. The vessel suffered serious damage and had to be beached.

Convoys moving in the opposite direction fared no better. During January Convoy HI 86 on passage from Singapore to Japan with ten merchant ships and two escorts was completely destroyed. A similar fate overtook a Saigon-to-Formosa convoy that month, when repeated air and submarine attacks sank all five escorts and sank or drove ashore all the merchant ships.

Between 24 January and 26 March 1945 thirteen convoys attempted the hazardous journey from Singapore to Japan, comprising 53 cargo ships and tankers totalling 210,000 tons; few of them reached their destination. From the final two convoys, 88I, which set out with six merchantmen on 12 March, and 88J, which set out with seven on the 21st, all thirteen merchant ships were sunk during a series of air and submarine attacks. Those losses are all the more remarkable if one considers that during this two-month period the US Navy had on average only eighteen submarines on patrol in the China Seas between Singapore and Japan.

In a report to the Japanese War Cabinet at the end of 1944, the Mobilisation Bureau stated:

> The preservation of communications between the southern occupied territories and Japan is absolutely necessary for the maintenance of supplies to the nation. It is recognised that if the resources of the south, especially petroleum, are abandoned, as time passes we shall gradually lose our ability to resist attack . . .

In March 1945 the Japanese Navy was forced to abandon the dangerous convoy route from Singapore to Japan. Denied the supplies from the Dutch East Indies, the usable oil production fell to about one-sixth of the national requirement.

The effect of the near-complete maritime blockade, as one by one the Japanese convoy routes had to be closed down, pervaded almost every aspect of the nation's life. It strangled war production and deprived her ships and aircraft of fuel. For the final few months there was virtually no leather for shoes or fabrics for clothing. Food supplies were greatly reduced, and the civilian food ration fell to about sixteen per cent below the minimum calorific requirement.

There is little that is remarkable in the air attacks on individual US submarines in the Pacific, for the reader who has followed the cut and thrust of the Atlantic battle. The last US submarine sunk was on 6 August 1945, the same day as the atomic bomb was dropped on the city of Hiroshima. Off the coast of Bali, a Japanese Army aircraft caught USS *Bullhead* (Holt) on the surface. The pilot attacked and claimed two direct bomb hits on the boat, which sank from view; soon afterwards a large oil slick spread across the water. *Bullhead* was lost with all hands.

The atomic bombs dropped on Hiroshima and Nagasaki brought the Pacific war to an abrupt halt in August 1945. By then US submarines had played a major part in the destruction of the Japanese sea power. These boats had sunk 1,150 merchant ships of 500 tons or more, and at the end of the conflict the Japanese merchant fleet possessed only one-eighth of the tonnage it had had at the beginning. US submarines also sank more than two hundred Japanese warships, including a battleship and nine aircraft-carriers.

The US submarine force suffered serious casualties in its war of attrition against the Japanese Navy, however. Fifty-two of the 288 American boats employed on operations were lost, an estimated forty-one of them to enemy action in the Pacific. Of those forty-one, seven are believed to have been lost to air attack, including one that was in harbour at the time. For the most part the US Navy boats lost had been sighted visually, and attacked on the surface.

Had it not been for the massive resources devoted to containing the U-boat menace in the Atlantic, the British people might well have suffered a fate similar to that which befell the Japanese.

During the six years of World War II, the anti-submarine aircraft had evolved from a short-range, short-sighted, poorly armed daytime nuisance into a proved killer, holding dominion by day and by night over the surface of the sea – and woe betide any submarine skipper who dared dispute that fact.

Yet the submarine also evolved during the conflict. At the end of it, the latest German Type XXI boats could operate effectively without having ever to surface fully. Cruising on *Schnorkel* in open and wind-tossed seas, they would have been almost immune to detection from the air. After the war, Coastal Command tested its equipment against a Type XXI U-boat running below the surface with the breathing tube extended. Even with the best radars available in 1945, the air search was only about six per cent efficient. That is to say, for every six *Schnorkel* heads that were detected, ninety-four had for a time been within radar range but had passed unnoticed. Moreover, if its batteries were fully charged, the Type XXI submarine could cruise completely submerged for almost 300 miles – about three times as far as the earlier boats, and sufficient to outflank any but the most overwhelming aerial blockade.

By the spring of 1945 the wheel had turned full circle. Having evolved from a blunt and ineffectual weapon into a deadly killer of submarines, at the end of the war the anti-submarine aircraft was – for want of an adequate method of detecting submerged boats at a reasonable range – almost back where it had started. The German Type XXI submarine, with its *Schnorkel*, greatly enlarged battery capacity and high underwater speed and endurance, emerged from World War II technically, if not militarily, triumphant.

Bibliography

Author not stated (1965) *Arbeitsgemeinschaft Rotterdam*. Munich: Deutsche Gesellschaft fur Ortung und Navigation EV.

Bolitho, Hector (1948) *Task for Coastal Command*. London: Hutchinson.

Brassey's Naval Annual 1948. London: Brassey.

Fock, H. (1968) *Marinekleinkampfmittel*. Munich: J.F. Lehmanns Verlag.

Francillon, René (1979) *Japanese Aircraft of the Pacific War*. London: Putnam.

Gambel, C.F. (1928) *The Story of the North Sea Air Station*. London: Oxford University Press.

Gayer, M. (1931) *Die deutschen U-Boote in ihrer Kriegsführung 1914–18*. Berlin.

Heslet, Vice-Admiral Sir Arthur (1975) *The Electron and Sea Power*. London: Peter Davis.

—— (1969) *The Submarine and Sea Power*. London: Peter Davis.

Hinsley, F. (1979–90) *British Intelligence in the Second World War* (5 vols). London: HMSO.

Jones, H. and Raleigh, W. (1922–37) *The War in the Air* (6 vols). Oxford: Clarendon Press.

Kahn, David (1968) *The Code Breakers*. London: Weidenfeld and Nicolson.

Kruska, E. and Rössler, E. (1969) *Walter-U-Boote*. Munich: J.F. Lehmanns Verlag.

Morison, Samuel (1948–62) *The History of United States Naval Operations in World War II* (15 vols). London: Oxford University Press.

Neumann, Georg (1921) *The German Air Force in the Great War*. London: Hodder and Stoughton.

O'Neill, Richard (1981) *Suicide Squads*. London: Salamander Books Ltd.

'PIX' (1919) *The Spider Web*. London and Edinburgh: William Blackwood and Sons.

Poolman, Kenneth (1972) *Escort Carrier, 1941–1945*. London: Ian Allan.

Robinson, Douglas (1962) *The Zeppelin in Combat*. London: Foulis.

Rohwer, J. and Hummelchen, J. (1974) *Chronology of the War at Sea 1939–1945* (2 vols). London: Ian Allan.

Rohwer, J. and Jäckel, E. (1979) *Die Funkaufklarung und ihre Rolle im Zweiten Weltkrieg*. Stuttgart: Motorbuch Verlag.

Roskill, Captain S. (1954–61) *The War at Sea* (3 vols). London: HMSO.

Rössler, E. (1967) *U-Boottyp XXI*. Munich: J.F. Lehmanns Verlag.

Rössler, E. (1967) *U-Boottyp XXIII*. Munich: J.F. Lehmanns Verlag.

Saunders, Hilary St George (1944) *Per Ardua*. London: Oxford University Press.

Saunders, Hilary St George and Richards, Denis (1954) *The Royal Air Force 1939–45* (3 vols). London: HMSO.

Snowden Gamble, C. (1966) *The Story of the North Sea Air Station*. London: Neville Spearman Ltd.

Swanborough, Gordon and Bowers, Peter (1968) *United States Navy Aircraft since 1911*. London: Putnam.

Thetford, Owen (1954) *Aircraft of the 1914–1918 War*. Harleyford: Harleyford Publications.

Trenkle, Fritz (1965) *Deutsche Ortungs- und Navigationsanlagen*. Munich: Deutsche Gesellschaft fur Ortung und Navigation EV.

Watson-Watt, Sir Robert (1957) *Three Steps to Victory*. London: Odhams Press.

Werner, Herbert (1969) *Iron Coffins*. London: Arthur Barker Ltd.

Official Monographs and Publications

Air Historical Branch Monograph (1951) 'Royal Air Force Armament History' (2 vols). London: AHB.

Air Historical Branch Monograph (1950) 'Royal Air Force in the Maritime War'. London: AHB.

Air Historical Branch Monograph (1954) 'Signals, Volume VI, Radio in Maritime Warfare'. London: AHB.

Naval Staff History Monograph (1954–6) 'The Development of British Naval Aviation, 1919–1945' (2 vols). London: NHB.

Naval Staff History Monograph (1949) 'The U-boat War in the Atlantic' (2 vols), NHB, London.

Royal Air Force Official Journal (1942–5) 'Coastal Command Review'.

US Official (1945–7) 'United States Strategic Bombing Survey', various reports.

Unpublished Papers

Bulloch, T., private papers.

Elmhirst, Air Marshal Sir Thomas, papers held at the Churchill College Library, Cambridge.

Greswell, Air Commodore J., private papers.

Leigh, Humphrey de Verde, private papers.

Williamson, Hugh, 1912 paper on anti-submarine aircraft held at Churchill College Library, Cambridge.

Index